Work, Health, and Income among the Elderly

Studies in Social Economics

SELECTED TITLES

STUDIES IN SOCIAL ECONOMICS

Gary Burtless, Editor

Work, Health, and Income among the Elderly

THE BROOKINGS INSTITUTION
Washington, D.C.

Copyright © 1987 by
THE BROOKINGS INSTITUTION
1775 Massachusetts Avenue, N.W., Washington, D.C. 20036

Library of Congress Cataloging-in-Publication data

Work, health, and income among the elderly.

(Studies in social economics)
Includes bibliographies and index.
1. Aged—Employment—United States. 2. Age and
employment—United States. 3. Aged—Health and hygiene—
United States. 4. Social security—United States.
I. Burtless, Gary T., 1950–   . II. Series.
HD6280.W68 1987   331.3'98   86-26892
ISBN 0-8157-1176-0

9 8 7 6 5 4 3 2 1

THE BROOKINGS INSTITUTION is an independent organization devoted to nonpartisan research, education, and publication in economics, government, foreign policy, and the social sciences generally. Its principal purposes are to aid in the development of sound public policies and to promote public understanding of issues of national importance.

The Institution was founded on December 8, 1927, to merge the activities of the Institute for Government Research, founded in 1916, the Institute of Economics, founded in 1922, and the Robert Brookings Graduate School of Economics and Government, founded in 1924.

The Board of Trustees is responsible for the general administration of the Institution, while the immediate direction of the policies, program, and staff is vested in the President, assisted by an advisory committee of the officers and staff. The by-laws of the Institution state: "It is the function of the Trustees to make possible the conduct of scientific research, and publication, under the most favorable conditions, and to safeguard the independence of the research staff in the pursuit of their studies and in the publication of the results of such studies. It is not a part of their function to determine, control, or influence the conduct of particular investigations or the conclusions reached."

The President bears final responsibility for the decision to publish a manuscript as a Brookings book. In reaching his judgment on the competence, accuracy, and objectivity of each study, the President is advised by the director of the appropriate research program and weighs the views of a panel of expert outside readers who report to him in confidence on the quality of the work. Publication of a work signifies that it is deemed a competent treatment worthy of public consideration but does not imply endorsement of conclusions or recommendations.

The Institution maintains its position of neutrality on issues of public policy in order to safeguard the intellectual freedom of the staff. Hence interpretations or conclusions in Brookings publications should be understood to be solely those of the authors and should not be attributed to the Institution, to its trustees, officers, or other staff members, or to the organizations that support its research.

Foreword

Living conditions among America's elderly have improved dramatically in this century. Death rates have fallen and continue to fall at a rapid pace. Real income has risen because of increases in the availability and level of social security and private pension benefits. Health insurance under the medicare and medicaid programs has made expensive medical care affordable for most older Americans. And poverty among the elderly has dropped sharply in the past quarter century, especially in comparison with poverty among the nonaged population.

In spite of these gains, the problems of the elderly and programs to aid them continue to attract wide public attention. Some aged Americans live in deprived or squalid circumstances over which they exercise little control. In more recent years the public and private programs intended to help the elderly have run into financing difficulties as the rising costs of pensions and medical care threaten to outpace the growth in resources used to pay for them. In an effort to trim government spending, social security retirement benefits were twice cut back in the past decade and medicare reimbursement procedures have been drastically overhauled. Some observers fear that these reforms threaten the improvements in income and health that the aged have enjoyed in recent decades.

The papers in this volume examine a range of issues affecting the current and future living conditions of the elderly. A topic of central interest is the health of the elderly and the implications of declining mortality rates for the future health and work capacity of older Americans. Improvements in medical technology and public health have resulted in marked gains in longevity, especially at older ages. Do these gains imply that the United States faces sharply higher outlays on programs that aid the elderly? Do they suggest that Americans retain their ability to work at even higher ages? A related topic is the effect of social security and pensions on living standards and work incentives among the elderly. Are benefits high enough to keep older workers from suffering deprivation when they are forced to retire? Are they so high that they encourage premature retirement? In addressing such questions, the authors of these papers provide important original contributions.

The research reported in this volume was supported by a grant to the Brookings Institution from the U.S. Department of Health and Human Services. The volume is the third in a series supported by this grant. The earlier volumes were *Economic Effects of Social Security,* by Henry J. Aaron, and *Retirement and Economic Behavior,* edited by Henry J. Aaron and Gary Burtless. The papers in this volume were presented at a conference held at Brookings on May 2, 1985. The introduction contains a nontechnical summary of each paper and its main conclusions.

Gary Burtless is a senior fellow in the Brookings Economic Studies program. Alice M. Rivlin, director of that program, played an invaluable role in organizing the conference at which the papers in this volume were presented. Thomas A. Gustafson, Anthony J. Pellechio, and Daniel H. Weinberg, at the Department of Health and Human Services, assisted with the selection of topics and participants for the conference.

Caroline Lalire, James McEuen, and Nancy D. Davidson edited the manuscript; Almaz S. Zelleke, Nathaniel Levy, and Barbara Koremenos verified its factual content; and Florence Robinson prepared the index. Kathleen Elliot Yinug assisted at the conference, and Kathleen M. Bucholz assisted in the preparation of the manuscript.

The views expressed here are those of the authors and discussants and should not be ascribed to the Department of Health and Human Services, or to the trustees, officers, or other staff members of the Brookings Institution.

BRUCE K. MAC LAURY
President

November 1986
Washington, D.C.

Contents

Tables

Figures

**Work, Health, and Income
among the Elderly**

Gary Burtless

Introduction and Summary

The problems of the aged have attracted growing attention over the past decade for two reasons. First, the cost of programs that help the elderly has risen sharply. Outlays on social security, medicare, and medicaid constitute a rising share of federal government expenditures. In an era of limits on government growth, the administration and Congress have been forced to tackle the politically difficult issue of reducing the rise in outlays. In 1983 Congress for the first time permitted the taxation of social security benefits and also raised the normal retirement age under social security from 65 to 67, though the full effect of the second reform will not be felt until the next century. The system of reimbursing bills for hospital care under medicare was changed in 1984. Again, the purpose of the reform was to limit growth in outlays. The debate over these reforms has forced Americans to think carefully about the income and health needs of the elderly and about the most efficient way to meet them.

Second, the public has gradually become aware of the enormous *future* costs of programs for the aged. Even if social insurance and public assistance programs become no more generous than they are now, they will be far more burdensome in the next century, when the baby boom generation begins to retire. Because of the decline in births and in the growth of productivity, the cost of programs for the aged will represent an increased claim on national output, even under favorable assumptions about economic performance. To the drumbeat of bad demographic and economic news, young Americans have become pessimistic about their own chances of ever drawing social security benefits. Even though fears about the solvency of social security and medicare are often wildly exaggerated, the new climate of public opinion has encouraged economists and other policy analysts to consider fundamental reforms in these programs. One suggested reform, for example, is to privatize social security retirement benefits for younger workers.

1

The papers in this volume discuss fundamental questions that are relevant to the debate over reforms in public programs for the aged. How healthy are the elderly? Have increases in longevity been associated with improvement or deterioration in average health? Have longer life spans placed a growing burden on the nation's hospitals and doctors? Are the elderly more capable of working? Or are more of them ill, disabled, and otherwise incapacitated? What kinds of retirees will be most affected by raising the normal retirement age? How will a change in social security benefits affect the work habits of the elderly?

The answers to these questions are difficult to obtain because the data needed to address them are not routinely collected and may not be collected at all. Therefore analysts must be imaginative and resourceful in teasing answers out of data that do exist. The papers approach these questions in different ways. Some survey relevant economic theory and then try to make sense out of the recent historical statistics. Others focus on a specific source of information, such as the Retirement History Survey (RHS), and develop sophisticated econometric models to explain one or more of the important relationships in the data. None of the papers is intended to be a thorough synthesis of the existing literature on a particular topic. All represent original contributions at the frontier of knowledge. And in most cases they offer pointed suggestions for new data collection that would substantially improve current understanding of basic issues.

Declining Old-Age Mortality and the Health of the Aged

Mortality rates among the aged, particularly among men and women over 75, have declined dramatically in the past two decades. This trend has led to corresponding, substantial increases in longevity, notably for the very old, that may have important implications for future public policy. James M. Poterba and Lawrence H. Summers examine the reasons behind the rapid drop in mortality and consider its consequences for policy, especially health care policy. If mortality rates continue to drop at their current rate, the population over 65 will grow faster than previously expected. In particular, the very elderly—people over 85—will become a much larger fraction of all the elderly. Under a pessimistic view, this change could lead to sharply rising health and support outlays because the very elderly often require a great deal of medical and other help for daily sustenance. But an optimistic view is also possible. Mortality could be falling because of general improvements in the health of the aged. Under this interpretation, health outlays might be no higher—and might actually be lower—as a consequence of reduced mortality.

In the first substantive section of their paper, Poterba and Summers present some basic data showing the extent of the mortality decline in recent decades. The most dramatic gains have been registered by men and women past 65, especially those older than 75 or 80, leading to rapid extensions in the expected remaining life span of the oldest Americans. Though the cause of the gains is not clear, the authors point out that the decline in mortality accelerated after the introduction of medicare and medicaid in 1965.

Poterba and Summers compute the number of older people who remain alive solely because of recent reductions in mortality. These people are referred to as marginal survivors. In 1980 about 4 percent of men and 1½ percent of women aged 60 were marginal survivors when compared with men and women born twenty years earlier. That is, 4 percent of 60-year-old men in 1980 would not have been alive if they had faced the same life chances as men born twenty years before they were. The proportion of marginal survivors is much higher at more advanced ages. About 8 percent of men 80 years old and 22 percent of women of the same age were marginal survivors according to the definition described above. Thus a moderate fraction of men and a high fraction of women over 80 owe their existence to improvements in longevity that have occurred in the past two decades.

A natural question is whether the growing number of marginal survivors has any implications for the average health status of the elderly population. If the increases in longevity arise from fundamental improvements in health, such as better diet or control of cardiovascular disease, it is plausible that the health of the elderly has improved. But if medical science is most effective at keeping alive the very frail who would otherwise die, it seems likely that the surviving elderly are becoming less healthy on average.

Poterba and Summers examine this question by first setting out a mathematical model of frailty and survival under evolving medical conditions. They assume that frailty is an inborn trait that is distributed in an identical way within each age cohort. People who are more frail than average are more likely to die at any given age. But medical progress reduces the *average* death rate of each succeeding cohort. Under plausible assumptions about the underlying distribution of frailty, the authors show that mortality rates may have been affected by the changing frailty of the population. Under their assumptions, the reductions in mortality have kept some frail people alive, and the resulting increase in average frailty has in turn limited gains in mortality at more advanced ages. If average frailty at each age had remained unchanged, the gains in mortality would have been even greater. But when one corrects for the effects of rising frailty, the gains in longevity at older ages are indeed remarkable.

Poterba and Summers interpret this finding as an argument against the view that longevity is currently pushing up against some natural limiting age, such as 95 or 100. They also point out that the differences in frailty at advanced ages are now greater than they once were. A greater proportion of extremely frail people now survive to age 70 or 80. This finding implies that the health of the very elderly should be declining. An alternative theory has been advanced by Victor Fuchs.[1] He argues that health is better viewed in relation to the time remaining until death rather than in relation to the time since birth (which is measured by age). Health outlays, for example, tend to be concentrated in the last year or two before death. As improvements in longevity postpone the age of death, people of any given age will be further away from death, and hence healthier on average.

The conflict between these two views resolves into a disagreement over the relative effects of medical progress on mortality, on the one hand, and on morbidity, on the other. Under the first view, gains in mortality will be associated with greater average morbidity in the surviving population, with especially strong deterioration in the health of people at the highest ages. According to Fuchs's view, improvements in longevity will be associated with declines in morbidity at any particular age.

Poterba and Summers examine various data on morbidity and health outlays to help resolve the conflict. The rate of institutionalization of old people has fallen in recent years, suggesting that their health is improving. On the other hand, the amount of medicare expenditures per person for those 85 and over relative to the expenditures per person for 65-year-olds has hardly changed at all, which suggests that the relative health of 85-year-olds is unchanged. The authors interpret this as evidence that medical progress has improved the health of survivors by about enough to offset the expected decline in health arising from the growing number of marginal survivors. They draw the same conclusions from trends in days of

1. Victor R. Fuchs, "'Though Much Is Taken': Reflections on Aging, Health, and Medical Care," *Milbank Memorial Fund Quarterly,* vol. 62 (Spring 1984), pp. 143–66.

restricted activity and days of bedridden disability, which also show little trend over time.

The authors next turn to microeconomic evidence. Using data from the RHS, they estimate the relation between reported health limitations, on the one hand, and both age and time to death, on the other. They find that both age *and* years until death have a statistically significant and nontrivial effect on reported health limits. This finding suggests that health deteriorates with advances in age even if an older person is not especially near death, but that nearness to death has an effect on health that is independent of an older person's age. The authors infer from the finding that advances in longevity will reduce the age-specific rates of activity limitation among the elderly.

Poterba and Summers mention several policy implications of their study. They argue that the historical evidence is inconsistent with either a very optimistic or very pessimistic view of future health trends among the surviving elderly. Though more frail elderly have survived, medical progress has ensured that the age-specific health status of the elderly has remained roughly unchanged. The growth in the size of the elderly population is nonetheless worrisome. Even if the average health of the elderly is not declining, the health care costs of a much larger elderly population will be burdensome in the next century, especially in view of the rapid gains in longevity. The pressure of growing costs will stimulate a reconsideration of who is elderly and in need of public help. But Poterba and Summers warn against any arbitrary redefinition of the onset of old age. Because medical progress has succeeded in keeping the more frail elderly alive, at any given age health varies more widely than it once did. The authors suggest instead that society should consider greater flexibility in defining who is aged, perhaps linking that definition to measurable health status.

Aging and the Ability to Work

Work capacity declines as workers age. Although the great majority of men and women aged 50 are at work, only a comparatively small fraction remain employed when they reach age 70. Many retiring workers report that poor health was a contributing, or the decisive, cause of their retirement. If bad health is a cause of retirement, improvements in average health should contribute to a delay in normal retirement. It is not clear, however, that medical progress has tended to improve the average health of workers. As Poterba and Summers point out, some forms of progress have helped to keep alive very infirm people who would otherwise have died. These marginal survivors may be incapable of working. Instead of raising the work capacity of the older population, medical progress may actually be reducing it.

Martin Neil Baily examines this set of issues in his paper. He concentrates especially on the implications that trends in work capacity have for the optimal design of public retirement and disability programs. The paper begins with a formal economic model of retirement in response to the social security pension program. Baily starts by considering the optimal design of a simple forced-savings retirement program. Using straightforward assumptions, he is able to show that the optimal age at retirement rises with the expected life span and the population's ability to work. The government can use this optimal age to set the "normal" retirement age, that is, the age at which workers are first eligible to draw full public retirement benefits.

The optimality of a single normal retirement age is less clear when there are wide differences among workers in their ability to work. Baily considers a simple extension of his basic model in which some workers are in good health while others are suddenly struck with a work disability as they age. If the government allows only a single normal retirement age for the drawing of retirement benefits, the healthy workers would retire at an age that from a social perspective is too young; the disabled, in contrast, would retire at an age that is too old. At the normal retirement age, healthy workers would be offered a financial incentive to leave work which is too generous in view of their continued willingness and ability to participate actively in the labor market. Baily points out that the problem could be circumvented if the government permitted more than one retirement age— for example, a higher retirement age for workers in good health and a lower one for workers suffering a work disability.

The problem with this solution is that the information required to implement it may be unattainable. True states of health are not directly observable. Workers with a taste for leisure have an incentive to describe themselves as disabled in order to qualify for generous retirement benefits at an early age. Workers who are truly disabled may be denied benefits if they are erroneously classified as nondisabled. Depending on its ability to distinguish between the truly disabled and the nondisabled, society can be more or less generous in its treatment of workers who suffer a decline in work capacity. If the test is imperfect and many nondisabled workers apply for benefits, the allowable retirement age for the disabled might not be much below that for the nondisabled. If the test is accurate, greater generosity is possible. But as Baily points out, even with an accurate disability test a problem of moral hazard would remain. The health status of workers is to some degree under their own control. Smoking, exercise, and diet can affect a worker's capacity to hold a job. If early disability benefits encourage workers to be less zealous in protecting their own health, the adverse side effects of generous benefits might be costly.

Baily considers the historical statistics on mortality in light of his model of optimal retirement and pensions. Since the inception of social security in the mid-1930s, mortality has clearly fallen and longevity has increased. The proportion of workers surviving to 65 has risen, and the remaining life span of new retirees has increased. If 65 was the optimal retirement age when social security was introduced, the optimal age ought to have risen since then.

The author next examines population statistics on average health status. The evidence here is mixed. The most important source of longitudinal information on health status is the Health Interview Survey, which shows a rising frequency of work incapacity over time. Among men and women aged 45 to 65, the rise in reported disability was especially pronounced in the late 1960s, when the questionnaire was modified. This coincidence causes Baily to be somewhat suspicious of the data, but he concludes that self-reported health status probably has deteriorated over the past two decades. The trend in social security disability claims partly mirrors the trend in self-reported health. From 1960 to 1977 the number of claims per thousand insured workers rose rapidly, though the frequency of claims has fallen in more recent years. Baily argues, however, that the frequency of disability claims is not a reliable indicator of average health status. The frequency of claims probably rose as workers became more familiar with the program. The rate of claims has also proved to be sensitive to the Social Security Administration's leniency in defining disability.

Baily also explores the possibility that medical science has kept alive a growing number of disabled workers who would otherwise have died. In their paper Poterba and Summers argue that this factor is extremely significant for the very old—those over 80 or 85. But Baily finds it to be unimportant for people under 65. Even if every marginal survivor between 45 and 64 were disabled, the disability rate of this age group would have risen by only 1.25 percentage points between 1960 and 1980. The disability rate for people 65 to 69 years would have risen by only 2.83 percentage points. These modest changes are too small to account for the rises in self-reported work limitations and disability insurance claims.

Besides health and mortality patterns, Baily also considers the effects of other factors on trends in retirement. For example, he examines the changing nature and health requirements of U.S. employment. Not surprisingly, he finds that today a smaller fraction of jobs require strenuous physical effort. Jobs needing little physical effort or only light effort have become more common. If 60-year-old workers are in the same physical condition today that they were in twenty years ago, they should be able to meet the physical demands of a higher proportion of today's jobs. The optimal retirement age should rise in response to easier physical work requirements.

The conflicting evidence about health trends among older workers is not easy to interpret. Baily suggests that the true health of older workers has probably improved, but that other factors are causing self-reported work limitations and disability to rise. The disability insurance program offers sizable incentives for workers with limited disabilities to report more severe ones. Workers who are thinking of applying for such benefits will often report a disability to an interviewer. Moreover, poor health provides a socially acceptable explanation for failure to work full-time. With this interpretation in mind, Baily argues that the normal retirement age for nondisabled workers ought to be raised. Because life expectancy has risen and average work capacity has improved (or got no worse), a clear argument exists for later retirement. When the normal retirement age is raised, however, the needs of truly disabled workers must be borne in mind. An effective early retirement program is needed for disabled workers. If only limited insurance protection is available to them, their welfare can be seriously harmed by the delay in full benefits that will be the result of raising the normal retirement age.

Occupational Effects on Health and Work Capacity

The paper by Gary Burtless provides an econometric treatment of the relation between occupation and poor health, on the one hand, and poor health and early retirement, on the other. Burtless begins his paper by observing that poor health is apparently a critical determinant in the timing of retirement. In the ten years between 1969 and 1979, about a quarter of the men participating in the RHS reported leaving a job because of poor health. Some analysts, however, are suspicious of self-reported work limitations that are attributed to bad health. These researchers have suggested that retirees merely justify their retirement by reference to poor health, but that the true reason for retirement is a preference for leisure and the availability of pension benefits to finance leisure consumption.

Even if it were true that trends in health have played no role in the trend toward early retirement, health differences among workers of the same age serve to explain many of the differences in their retirement ages. Workers in poor health retire earlier than workers in good health. The purpose of Burtless's paper is to identify and estimate the effect of factors contributing to health impairment and work limitations in men between the ages of 58 and 73. Of particular interest is the association between a worker's industrial and occupational attachment and his health and work status as he enters old age. If certain industries and occupations cause bad health and early retirement, there may be a justification for policies to permit earlier public pensions in particularly hazardous lines of work.

Burtless's analysis begins with a survey of the RHS data on poor health and early retirement. He uses four different measures of health limitations—three of them based on self-reports by the respondents and the fourth related to the respondent's mortality during the ten years covered by the survey. One of the self-reported measures is closely related to the respondent's current work status: "How much does health limit your ability to work?" The response to this question might be colored by a respondent's desire to justify early retirement or low weekly hours of work. The mortality measure, by contrast, is objective, though probably a crude indicator of a worker's health capacity. Under all four measures of health status, the raw data show a strong relation between a worker's industry and occupation and his measured health in old age. The strongest correlation, however, is between industry or occupation and specifically work-related health measures. The connection is less powerful for measures, such as subsequent mortality, that are less directly related to work capacity.

Burtless then proposes a formal statistical model of health capacity. The model takes account of many factors affecting health status besides industry and occupation. It is somewhat complicated for several reasons. First, the health status variables are categorical rather than continuous, which rules out simple multivariate models, such as ordinary least-squares models. Second, the available data are derived from six interviews covering a ten-year period. Because a respondent's health status is correlated across interviews, Burtless cannot treat observations from successive interviews as statistically independent. He proposes a multiperiod ordered-probit model to circumvent these two statistical problems.

The results from this model confirm the importance of industry and occupation for self-reported health. Several of the industrial and occupational categories have a consistent and usually significant effect on the three self-reported measures of health impairment. Health limitations are especially common in mining and construction and much less frequent in professional industries and personal services. Managers, professionals, and clerical and sales personnel report better than average health; operatives and laborers report more work limitations than average. The differences between the most healthful and least healthful industries and occupations are wide. For example, Burtless reports that a 62-year-old miner is 50 percent more likely to suffer a work limitation than an average worker is, whereas a 62-year-old professional worker is one-third less likely to face a work limitation. Among other variables that influence reported health, the effects of age, educational attainment, and preretirement wage rate are especially strong. Men who are older, less well educated, and more poorly paid report health significantly worse than average.

The effects of industrial and occupational attachment on early mortality are far smaller than its effects on self-reported health. This finding indicates that objective health measures are much less affected by industry and occupation than more subjective measures are. However, self-reports of work limitations convey two kinds of information. First, they tell something about the worker's (subjective) health. Second, they tell something about the perceived health requirements of the worker's customary job. Objective measures of health provide information only about the former. For that reason it is easy to see that industrial and occupational attachment will have a greater effect on perceived work limitations than it will on objectively measured health.

Burtless concludes by estimating the effects of health and other variables on employment status in old age. As expected, the effect of a self-reported health limitation is quite large. The average probability of working full-time for a 62-year-old man with no reported health limitation is 82 percent. For a 62-year-old with a health limitation, the probability is only 63 percent—nearly a quarter less. The worker with a health limitation is also more likely to work part-time. In a sensitivity test of these results, the author restricts his sample to men who were actually at work in 1969. Instead of using a contemporaneous self-report of health to explain current work status, he uses the health index from a previous interview. Despite these changes, he estimates that health limitations have a very significant effect on employment status.

Even when the effects of self-reported health are taken into account, Burtless finds that industrial and occupational attachment has a large and statistically significant influence on work patterns in old age. That is, after controlling for the effects of health, he finds that workers in industries and occupations associated with generally poor health leave employment at younger ages. Some of these differences in work patterns are undoubtedly attributable to distinctive provisions for early retirement in different lines of work. But Burtless argues that this is only part of the explanation. In addition, differing health requirements across industries and occupations cause different retirement patterns for men with the *same* reported health status.

Burtless interprets his results to show that both health status and industrial and occupational attachment figure prominently in the timing of retirement. Workers employed in the most healthful and least physically demanding industries and occupations are far less likely to report a work disability, and more likely to continue working to age 65, than workers in the least healthful and most demanding industries and occupations. The author argues that these systematic differences are likely to remain important. Unless special provision is made for the least healthy workers and for workers in the most physically demanding industries, the rise in the social security retirement age from 65 to 67 can seriously harm the retirement incomes of some older workers.

Involuntary Early Retirement and Consumption

Jerry A. Hausman and Lynn Paquette consider the effects of poor health and early job loss from another perspective. Rather than examine the influence of health on the age at retirement, they consider the amount of hardship caused by forced early retirement. They specifically estimate the reduction in food consumption that occurs in families in which the breadwinner is forced to retire early.

One important aspect of this research is the light it sheds on the degree of compulsion involved in involuntary early retirement. As mentioned earlier, some analysts are skeptical that workers who report forced early retirement are genuinely compelled to retire because of poor health or involuntary job loss. Instead, these analysts interpret most early retirement to be a rational economic response to generous retirement benefits such as severance pay, disability insurance, or public and private pensions. But if the drop in food consumption after early retirement is large, it is doubtful that workers have chosen early retirement voluntarily.

Hausman and Paquette base their research on the RHS. They distinguish between voluntary and involuntary retirement in their sample in a straightforward way. Workers are considered as involuntarily retired if they were discharged from their job or forced to leave work because of poor health or an employer-initiated layoff. Food consumption is measured by expenditure on food consumed both within and outside the home.

Under their definitions the authors find that 37 percent of the retirements in their sample were involuntary. Involuntary retirement is much more common for men leaving work at younger ages, say 62 or under. For example, slightly more than 60 percent of retirements occurring between ages 56 and 59 are involuntary. Many of these early retirees must wait one or more years for retirement income to commence. A 60-year-old retiree, for instance, must wait two years for social security early retirement benefits to begin. If this retiree has no other source of retirement income, the two-year delay might be a severe hardship for him. Hausman and Paquette find that approximately 45 percent of men retiring between 55 and 61 must wait at least a year after retirement before retirement income begins. And an important fraction of early retirees accumulated almost no savings by the time of retirement. Early retirees who are forced to leave work involuntarily are disproportionately represented among those workers with low wealth. This fact suggests that their assets do not provide a comfortable cushion against unanticipated loss of earnings.

Hausman and Paquette measure the decline in food consumption at the point of retirement for all retirees, including both voluntary and involuntary job leavers. The decline is measured as a percentage of average preretirement consumption. They find that for men retiring before age 62, the percentage decline is substantially larger for involuntary than for voluntary retirees. They also calculate the percentage decline for men who retire after 62, when social security retirement benefits first become available. Here the difference between voluntary and involuntary retirees is somewhat smaller than it is for men leaving work before 62, though the difference is still sizable.

In the second part of their paper, the authors use more sophisticated statistical techniques to examine the decline in food consumption. Their results merely confirm or strengthen the conclusions drawn in the first part of the paper. When the authors statistically control for a variety of factors that affect changes in food consumption, they still find that the postretirement decline is much larger for involuntary than voluntary job leavers. Retirement leads to a decline in food expenditures of about 14 percent for voluntary retirees. For involuntary retirees who leave work before 62, retirement leads to an additional 9-percentage-point decline. And for early involuntary retirees with lower wealth than the median, retirement leads to yet a further 9-percentage-point decline. The decline in food expenditures is still larger for involuntary retirees under 62 whose preretirement earnings were in the top three-fourths of the earnings distribution. For men in the top half of the earnings distribution, involuntary retirement is associated with a 10-percentage-point decline in food consumption in addition to the possible 18-point decline already described. Some, though not all, of the drop in food consumption is reversed when involuntary retirees become eligible to begin drawing social security benefits.

The authors' results thus imply that involuntary early retirees suffer a 9- to 28-percentage-point decline in food consumption on top of the 14 percent decline that normally accompanies retirement. This finding suggests that involuntary retirement is associated with substantial welfare losses for early retirees. As noted by Edward Lazear in his comment, the authors' distinction between voluntary and involuntary retirements appears to be meaningful.

Hausman and Paquette conclude from their study that eligibility for social security early retirement benefits may be unnecessarily restrictive. They suggest that involuntary early retirees should be permitted to draw benefits before age 62. Workers are already permitted to make early withdrawals from some tax-preferred pension plans under specific hardship conditions. They should similarly be allowed to collect an actuarially reduced social security pension before turning 62 if they meet a test of hardship.

Lazear points out a problem with this proposal. He suggests that employers and workers could collude to make most early retirements appear "involuntary" under the definitions proposed by Hausman and Paquette. In the general discussion at the conference, Lawrence Summers mentioned a more fundamental issue in interpreting the authors' results. Noting that involuntary retirees had typically suffered severe financial reverses, Summers was uncertain whether their subsequent reductions in food consumption should be considered large or small. Though Hausman

learly consider the drops to be large, the reductions might
dest in view of the reported absence of wealth and retire-
or many early retirees. Whether large or small, the esti-
is in food consumption suggest that forced early retirement
reporting phenomenon. There is a genuine welfare loss
associated with involuntarily leaving a job in old age.

Time-Series Analysis of the Effect of Social Security on Labor Supply

Nearly all detailed analyses of the effect of social security on labor supply have been based on microeconomic methods. Economists have used microlevel information from such sources as the RHS and the National Longitudinal Survey to estimate individual responses to detailed incentives embedded in the social security formula. One problem with this type of evidence is that all workers is a cross-sectional survey confront the same social security system. It is almost impossible to estimate the effect of factors that are common for everyone in a sample. Cross-sectional analysis is nonetheless the basis for most of the current estimates of social security effects that are used in policymaking.

Robert Moffitt proposes and estimates an alternative type of model. He uses information about aggregate labor supply over the past three decades to estimate the effects of the changes in social security benefits and taxes in those years. This aggregate time-series analysis provides a check on the estimates of social security effects that have been obtained from cross-sectional studies.

The estimation problem for Moffitt is more formidable than may at first appear. The information available on aggregate labor supply and its determinants is not well suited to his requirements. To study the effect of social security on labor supply, one needs to distinguish among the program's effects at various stages of the life cycle. This distinction requires detailed information on workers' and retirees' earnings, hours of work, labor-force participation rates, wealth holdings, and social security entitlements and taxes by narrowly defined age groups. Since the available data do not remotely approach this ideal, Moffitt had to rely on somewhat imperfect information and to develop a model that circumvents the worst limitations of his data.

For example, the census data on earnings are not published (or even available) by age group. As a substitute, Moffitt uses information on social security–covered earnings published by the Social Security Administration. Data on hours of work by age group do not begin until 1955. After that year the data on hours worked are available only by broad age category, a limitation that necessitates a cumbersome modification in Moffitt's main estimating equation.

Despite the problems with the data, the importance of time-series analysis should be obvious. Most of the criticism of the effects of social security on retirement is based on the casual empirical observation that retirements have occurred earlier as social security benefits have become more generous. When labor-force participation rates are used as a rough indicator of retirement behavior, the decline in the average retirement age since World War II seems large. For men over 65, the labor-force participation rate fell by more than half, from 46 percent in 1950 to 20 percent in 1979. Real social security benefits were of course rising strongly over that period. For men aged 55 through 64, the participation rate fell from 87 percent to 73 percent over the same period. Strikingly, all this decline occurred after 1961, when early social security benefits were first extended to men between 62 and 65. Yet despite these large movements in aggregate labor supply at older ages, cross-sectional studies often show that social security has a relatively modest influence on retirement. The estimated effect, if applied to the national population, is usually too small to explain the drop in labor-force participation that has occurred. Moffitt applies a rigorous econometric model to the time-series evidence, the same evidence often used to "prove" that social security has had a dramatic effect.

The analysis in the paper depends critically on an accurate measurement of the amount and timing of surprises, or "shocks," in social security wealth. A person's social security wealth is simply the expected value of the difference between anticipated social security benefits and social security taxes. If a person is surprised by a sudden rise in future benefits compared with future taxes, he or she has received an unanticipated (and positive) shock in wealth. Moffitt shows that the later a shock occurs during a worker's lifetime, the larger will be his or her response per year of remaining life. The statistical problem is to derive an accurate measure of the aggregate wealth shocks that have occurred and to correlate their size and timing with changes in labor supply for particular cohorts of workers.

In computing wealth changes attributable to social security, Moffitt finds that positive shocks were much greater during the 1950s than they were in the late 1960s and early 1970s. This finding will come as a surprise to many students of social security who believe that the large increases in benefits enacted in 1969–72 were some of the most important positive shocks of the postwar period. But Moffitt argues that the trend growth in net social security wealth was actually much faster (and much faster than anticipated) in the 1950s than in the early 1970s. During the 1950s not only did benefits rise strongly but social security coverage was extended to many new groups of workers.

When Moffitt estimates the effect of the social security shocks on labor supply, he finds little to support the idea that they have substantially influenced total work effort. The timing of the social security shocks simply fails to correlate closely with movements in aggregate labor supply. Moffitt performs several sensitivity tests to examine the effect of changing his definition of shocks and of altering his basic model. His fundamental results do not appear especially sensitive to those changes. Thus a major finding of the analysis is that there is an important inconsistency between the cross-sectional studies for the 1970s and a time-series study covering the entire postwar period. The cross-sectional studies usually show that social security has had significant but comparatively small effects. They support the hypothesis that the effects of social security accelerated in the 1970s. Moffitt's findings imply that those effects are much smaller, and conceivably nil. Moreover, the accelerating fall in the labor-force participation of older workers in the 1970s cannot be explained by trends in social security wealth. Wealth rose much more sharply in the 1950s than it did later on. When he subjects casual empiricism to careful scrutiny, Moffitt finds the opposite of what is expected. Instead of confirming the hypothesis that the effects of social security are larger than estimated in the cross-sectional studies, the time-series evidence seems to imply that the effects are much smaller.

The Adequacy of Life Insurance among the Elderly

Despite a general reduction in poverty among the elderly, approximately a third of aged single women, many of them widows, have incomes below the poverty line. That many widows live in poverty while few elderly married women are poor suggests that many families fail to obtain enough life insurance. When an uninsured or underinsured husband dies, his widow is left without adequate protection against the loss of his income.

The paper by Alan J. Auerbach and Laurence J. Kotlikoff examines the adequacy of life insurance protection among married families represented in the RHS. The authors estimate insurance protection among married couples in the 1969 baseline survey, and specifically examine data on widows' resources from surveys after the death of a husband. They then describe an economic model in which the adequacy of insurance can be measured. They conclude their paper with some empirical estimates of the economic determinants of life insurance purchases.

The authors begin by presenting basic descriptive information about the extent and adequacy of life insurance protection in the RHS sample. The RHS questionnaire does not necessarily provide an ideal source of information about insurance protection. Respondents were not asked to distinguish between the face value of their policies and the cash value if the policies were redeemed. Though one can be reasonably confident that a $10,000 policy on the life of a husband would provide $10,000 to his wife in the event of his death, one does not know whether the policy represented an asset to the couple while the husband was alive. If the policy was term insurance, it would have no value as an asset; if it was whole-life insurance, it would be an asset of unknown value. The authors test the sensitivity of their results to alternative assumptions about the fraction of reported insurance that consists of whole-life policies.

Auerbach and Kotlikoff assess the adequacy of insurance in relation to the ability of a surviving spouse to maintain the standard of living that he or she enjoyed in marriage. The standard of living in marriage is measured as the sustained level of consumption that a spouse can afford on the basis of the married couple's assets and current and future income while both spouses are alive. When one of the spouses dies, certain sources of income may cease, but the cost of providing consumption to the deceased spouse ends as well. The standard of living as a widow or widower is computed as the level of consumption that the survivor can afford once the income and consumption requirements of the deceased spouse are absent. Life insurance obviously raises the resources available to the surviving spouse and is taken into account when the authors calculate the standard of living of a survivor.

Auerbach and Kotlikoff mention two complicating issues. First, it is unclear how much it costs to support a single person living alone compared with the cost of providing a couple with the same standard of living. If a surviving spouse needs nearly as much income to live on as the intact couple did, the spouse's insurance requirements are obviously high. The authors compute insurance requirements under alternative assumptions about the economies of scale in family consumption.

Second, there is more than one way to translate a person's assets into a smooth flow of income that ceases at his or her death. The usual mechanism for transforming assets into income is the purchase of an annuity. An annuity can be purchased for a fixed sum of money and provides a level payment (for example, $5,000 a year) until death. The cost of the annuity depends on the purchaser's remaining life expectancy. Because of adverse selection, high transaction costs, and other factors, annuities are frequently much more expensive to buy than they are worth from a strictly actuarial viewpoint. Auerbach and Kotlikoff argue, however, that surviving spouses do not really need to rely on the financial market to provide them with annuities. Instead, they can in effect rely on their extended families to provide actuarially fair annuities in exchange for a claim on assets remaining after their deaths. Although this technical issue might seem trivial, it is actually significant in determining the assets and insurance protection needed to maintain a level living standard.

From the authors' calculations it appears that a significant minority of older couples are inadequately insured, even when the insurance protection provided by social security survivor benefits is included. Insurance protection is especially poor for wives. Using assets and income information for 1969, the authors find that a quarter of the wives would suffer a drop in their standard of living of at least 25 percent if their spouses suddenly died. Seven percent would suffer at least a 30 percent decline in their standard of living. Among married women whose husbands actually died between 1969 and 1971, the measured drop in standard of living was even greater. More than a third of these women suffered a decline of at least 25 percent in their standard of living; 16 percent of new widows suffered a drop of at least 50 percent. Not surprisingly, the estimated and actual declines in the standards of living are much smaller for husbands who survive their wives. Only 2 percent of husbands could expect to suffer a 25 percent drop in their standard of living if their wives suddenly died.

Auerbach and Kotlikoff urge a reassessment of the relative size of survivor and retirement benefits in social security. Survivor benefits currently provide a substantial amount of insurance protection for wives, but the amount is too low for many whose standard of living depends on continuation of their husbands' earnings. The authors conclude by noting that the poverty of elderly widows could be reduced by a public program to encourage families to purchase more adequate private insurance.

James M. Poterba and Lawrence H. Summers

Public Policy Implications of Declining Old-Age Mortality

Recent years have witnessed dramatic improvements in the longevity of the elderly population. Life expectancy for women at age 65 increased by 3.3 years, a 22 percent change, between 1950 and 1980.[1] Age-specific death rates fell by 29 percent for white females over 85 and by 19 percent for white males over 85.[2] Continuation of these trends could have major implications for public policy toward the elderly. If mortality rates continue to drop, the elderly population will be substantially larger than if the rates remain constant at their current level. The number of very elderly, those over age 85, could rise especially rapidly.

This paper explores some policy implications of the dramatic longevity gains that have occurred and are likely to continue. We focus on the potential burden, through demand for medical care and other resources, that the elderly are likely to create. Different views on this issue are possible. A pessimistic outlook would hold that improvements in life expectancy are likely to be associated with large increases in the costs of supporting the elderly. The elderly will grow more numerous, particularly at very old ages where support costs are greatest. These costs may be

We are indebted to Benjamin Hermalin for outstanding research assistance and many extremely helpful conversations. We also greatly benefited from comments by Victor R. Fuchs. Martha Happel of the Health Care Financing Administration and Stanley Kranczer of the Metropolitan Life Insurance Company provided us with unpublished data. Christine de Fontenay at the Brookings Institution helped us to manipulate the Retirement History Survey.

1. U.S. Department of Health and Human Services, Social Security Administration, Office of the Actuary, *Social Security Area Population Projections, 1984,* Actuarial Study 92 (Government Printing Office, 1984), table 9b.

2. Calculations are based on data in table 1. Mortality rates for nonwhites show an even greater decline, although they may be contaminated by measurement errors. These data problems are discussed in Ansley Coale and Ellen Kisker, "Mortality Crossovers: Reality or Bad Data?" (Princeton University, Office of Population Research, 1985).

particularly high for "marginal survivors"—those who would have died at earlier ages were it not for recent progress in reducing mortality. A more optimistic view is also possible. It would argue that the same forces that have led to recent declines in mortality might also be expected to lead to reduced morbidity and increased ability to function. Mortality reductions lower the number of the aged who are within a year or two of death. Since these are the years when support costs are highest, especially for health care, the social burden per aged person might actually decline.

The relative importance of these two effects is an empirical question that cannot be resolved by a priori argument. The choice of which view is more appropriate is, however, clearly an important policy issue. Projections of future medicare costs are extremely sensitive to the number and expected needs of potential beneficiaries. While much attention has focused on efforts to reduce medicare costs by reforming reimbursement procedures and changing the health care delivery system, there are limits to the savings available from these individual devices. Moreover, because of the typically one-shot character of individual cost-reduction measures, their impact on projected future costs is ultimately smaller than demand-related factors, such as health status, which cumulate year after year.

This paper surveys some relevant evidence and presents some new calculations bearing on the effects of mortality improvements. While the available data permit only tentative conclusions, it appears that reductions in morbidity associated with declining mortality have been counterbalanced by high morbidity rates among marginal survivors. As a consequence, the health needs of elderly persons at given ages have not changed very much.

Mortality Trends among the Aged

Mortality among the aged has declined dramatically since 1950. Life expectancy for white women at age 65, after rising by 1.9 years between 1950 and 1970, rose by 1.6 years between 1970 and 1980. For white men the change was 0.2 years between 1950 and 1970 and 1.2 years between 1970 and 1980 (see table 1). These increases in life expectancy were caused by dramatic reductions in mortality rates at all ages. Between 1950 and 1980 the death rate of male 85-year-olds fell from 221 per 1,000 to 178 per 1,000, or nearly 20 percent.

The table describes progress in reducing mortality among the aged over

Table 1. Death Rates and Life Expectancy, by Age and Sex,
Selected Years, 1950–80

Measure	1950	1960	1970	1980
Crude death rate (per 1,000 people)				
Men				
55–59	18.8	17.8	17.7	13.9
65–69	40.7	40.5	40.5	33.2
75–79	90.1	87.0	86.9	80.7
85 and over	221.2	217.5	185.5	178.2
Women				
55–59	10.2	8.3	8.3	7.2
65–69	25.2	21.5	19.2	16.5
75–79	69.9	60.8	53.5	45.6
85 and over	196.8	194.8	159.8	140.4
Life expectancy (years)				
Men				
55	19.1	19.5	19.5	21.2
65	12.8	13.0	13.0	14.2
75	7.8	7.9	8.1	8.8
85	4.4	4.3	4.6	5.0
Women				
55	22.6	23.8	24.9	26.5
65	15.0	15.9	16.9	18.5
75	8.9	9.3	10.2	11.5
85	4.8	4.7	5.5	6.3

Sources: Death rates for 1950–70 from U.S. Department of Health, Education, and Welfare, National Center for Health Statistics, *Vital Statistics of the United States*, vol. 2: *Mortality*, pt. A (Government Printing Office, 1950, 1960, and 1970 issues). Death rates for 1980 and all life expectancies from Department of Health and Human Services, NCHS, *Vital Statistics of the United States, 1980*, vol. 2: *Mortality*, pt. A, sec. 6. Data are for white men and women only.

the past thirty years. We present data on white men and women, because demographic data for nonwhites at extreme ages are somewhat unreliable. Several patterns emerge from the mortality data. First, mortality reductions have been greater for women than for men, despite convergence between the sexes in patterns of employment, life-style, and rates of smoking. Second, mortality reductions do not exhibit any pattern across age groups, and there have been significant reductions even among the extreme aged. Despite forecasts of ultimate limits on life expectancy and the rectangularization of the life table, there is no evidence of rising mortality rates as more and more people reach extreme ages.[3] Third, the pace of mortality reductions has accelerated, with especially rapid progress being made during the 1970s.

3. For a discussion of the evidence on mortality among the extreme aged, see Kenneth G. Manton, "Changing Concepts of Morbidity and Mortality in the Elderly Population," *Milbank Memorial Fund Quarterly*, vol. 60 (Spring 1982), p. 192.

The second part of the table illustrates the substantial changes in life expectancy during this period. For women aged 75, life expectancy increased from 8.9 to 11.5 years between 1950 and 1980, an increase of 29 percent. The gain for men at age 75 was only 1 year during this period. Even at age 85, there were dramatic improvements: a 14 percent increase for men and a 31 percent gain for women. In 1950 an 85-year-old woman's life expectancy was only 0.4 years greater than that of an 85-year-old man. In 1980 the difference was 1.3 years.

The sources of these dramatic declines in mortality are not well established. The bulk of the increase in life expectancy at older ages appears to be the result of reduced death rates from cardiovascular diseases. The most recent report of the Social Security Administration's Office of the Actuary indicates that between 1968 and 1980 mortality from heart disease among men 65–69 declined at a 2.2 percent annual rate and mortality from vascular disease fell at a 4.9 percent rate. For women 65–69 the corresponding improvement rates were 2.5 and 4.9 percent. There have also been substantial reductions in death rates from digestive disease and diabetes for both sexes. Partially reflecting these changes, cancer death rates actually rose during this period at a 1.0 percent annual rate for men aged 65–69 and a 1.4 percent rate for women this age.[4]

The cause of these mortality reductions is far from clear. One possible explanation is improvements in access to medical care due to the enactment of medicare and medicaid in 1965. The timing of the acceleration in the mortality rates' decline supports this possibility. An alternative possibility is improved medical procedures for treating hypertension and heart attacks. Still another possible cause is improved diet and exercise among the aged. In all likelihood the decline in mortality can be traced to some combination of these and other factors.

Declines in mortality have potentially important effects on the composition of the aged population. The most obvious effect is that the average age of the elderly population will increase as more and more people survive to older ages. A more subtle but probably more important effect of reduced mortality is that the population at any given age will include marginal survivors who will be less healthy and less self-sufficient than the rest of the population.

The magnitude of the mortality declines is well conveyed by the percentage of the 1980 population at various ages who, if they reached age

4. Social Security Administration, *Projections, 1984*, p. 25.

50, would not have been alive had they faced the mortality rates of cohorts born ten, twenty, thirty, or forty years earlier. We focus on persons who would have reached age 50 to highlight changes for the elderly and to avoid contaminating our results with changes in infant mortality or other factors affecting younger persons.

The shares of marginal survivors are calculated using cohort life tables for persons born in the first year of each decade between 1850 and 1910. These data should be distinguished from those in synthetic life tables, the type commonly used in calculating life expectancies. In a synthetic table, the death rates at each age correspond to the probability that a person of that age in year t would die in year t. The death rates for different ages therefore correspond to different birth cohorts. In a cohort life table, a single birth cohort is followed throughout its life. The entry for age 65 in the 1910 cohort table would report the fraction of 65-year-olds in 1975 who died within one year.

We calculated the number of marginal survivors as follows. Let q_t^w denote the probability that a person born in year w dies between birthdays t and $t + 1$, conditional on living to age t. The probability of living to age t in birth cohort w, conditional on reaching age 50, is therefore:

$$S^w(t) = \prod_{i=50}^{t-1} (1 - q_i^w).$$

For persons of age $a > 50$ in 1980, a fraction $S^{1980-a}(a)$ of the members of the birth cohort who reached age 50 are still alive. If these persons had been born m years earlier, the comparable fraction would have been $S^{1980-a-m}(a)$. The proportion of the 1980 population that is accounted for by marginal survivors relative to the cohort m years earlier, $MS(a,m)$, is therefore:

$$MS(a,m) = \frac{[S^{1980-a}(a) - S^{1980-a-m}(a)]}{S^{1980-a}(a)}.$$

The results of the calculations are shown in table 2. Particularly at old ages, the share of marginal survivors in the population is very high. Fifteen percent of the 80-year-old men alive in 1980 and 35 percent of the 80-year-old women would have reached age 50 but not have been alive at 80, given the mortality experience of the cohort that preceded them by

**Table 2. Percentage of Persons Alive in 1980 Who Would Not Have Been
Alive Given Mortality Rates of Earlier Birth Cohorts, by Age and Sex**

Earlier birth cohort (number of years preceding)	Age in 1980							
	60		70		80		90	
	Men	Women	Men	Women	Men	Women	Men	Women
10	3.9	0.9	3.4	2.9	5.0	10.8	16.2	30.4
20	3.8	1.4	6.0	8.0	8.0	22.2	36.3	53.0
30	5.4	3.6	8.5	14.4	15.1	35.2	58.4	72.3
40	6.5	6.1	10.5	20.7	25.1	46.2	58.7	76.2

Sources: Authors' calculations based on cohort life tables provided by Metropolitan Life Insurance Company, and supplemented with data from DHEW, NCHS, *Vital Statistics of the United States*, vol. 2: *Mortality*, pt. A, for years since 1974. Data are for white men and women only.

thirty years. The share of marginal survivors rises rapidly with age. For example, given the mortality experience of the cohort that preceded them by ten years, 0.9 percent of the 60-year-old women would not have been alive in 1980, 2.9 percent of the 70-year-olds, 10.8 percent of the 80-year-olds, and 30.4 percent of the 90-year-olds.

The dramatic importance of marginal survivors at extreme ages may be somewhat misleading, since the number of individuals alive at these ages is much smaller than at earlier ages. We therefore calculated the fraction of the population over 60 who would not have been alive if they had faced the life table of the cohort thirty years before them. Aggregating across age groups, more than 9 percent of the men and 16.9 percent of the women over age 60 in 1980 were marginal survivors. If people had faced the life table of those born forty years earlier, 12 percent of the men and 22 percent of the women would not have reached their current ages.[5]

Changes in mortality rates or other indicators of health status for the very old are difficult to interpret. The composition of the population has changed quite dramatically through time. Without general improvements in health, we would expect the large number of marginal survivors to reduce indices of health status at any given age. Of course, the dramatic reductions in mortality could have been accompanied by progress in lowering morbidity rates as well. We consider this possibility below. First we consider some implications of continuing reductions in mortality.

Demographic forecasts are notoriously difficult. The substantial mor-

5. We calculate the share of people alive in 1980 who would not have been alive if they faced the life table of m-years earlier as $[MS(60,m)*N_{60} + MS(70,m)*N_{70} + MS(80,m)*N_{80} + MS(90,m)*N_{90}]/(N_{60} + N_{70} + N_{80} + N_{90})$, where N_i is the number of persons of age i alive in 1980. We use data for every ten years because these are the only cohort life tables available to us.

tality gains of the last decade were largely unforeseen. Most observers expected a leveling off in the rate of decline of death rates among the elderly. Nonetheless, it is useful to consider the potential effects on the future population of continued mortality reductions. We rely on the Social Security Administration's Office of the Actuary, which computes three alternative scenarios reflecting different degrees of optimism about future mortality reductions. Alternative II assumes the continuation of current trends, with a gradual adjustment to moderate rates of progress in reducing mortality. Alternatives I and III, respectively, consider slower and faster progress.

Table 3 displays information on projected death rates under Alternative II. If current trends continue, the death rate at ages 75–79 for women is expected to decline 24 percent by 2000. At this point, it will be fully 48 percent below its 1960 level. By 2080 the death rates for women at all ages over 75 are projected to be approximately half their current level. For men progress is less dramatic but still implies a 40 percent mortality reduction at high ages between 1980 and 2080.

Table 4 shows the forecasts for life expectancy at age 65 under all three mortality scenarios. Dramatic improvements are clearly a possibility. Under Alternative II, the life expectancy for men at age 65 will rise by 22 percent, to nearly twenty years, by 2040. For women, even the pessimistic projections suggest life expectancies at 65 of more than twenty years by 2040. The optimistic scenario suggests more than twenty-five years by 2040 and over twenty-nine years by 2080.

These reductions in mortality have important implications for the size and structure of the aged population. In 1982 there were 27.5 million

Table 3. Actual and Projected Death Rates per 1,000 People, by Age and Sex, Selected Years, 1982–2080

Age	1982[a]		2000[b]		2040[b]		2080[b]	
	Men	Women	Men	Women	Men	Women	Men	Women
60–64	20.9	11.2	16.2	9.7	13.8	8.2	11.9	7.0
65–69	33.7	16.9	28.0	14.8	23.8	12.5	20.6	10.6
70–74	49.0	25.3	41.4	20.5	35.2	17.1	30.2	14.4
75–79	74.8	41.1	63.9	31.2	53.9	25.5	46.2	21.1
80–84	106.2	65.7	90.7	49.0	76.2	39.5	64.9	32.3
85–89	158.4	112.2	135.1	84.8	112.5	67.6	95.2	54.7
90–94	225.9	177.6	191.6	140.9	157.7	111.1	131.8	88.9

Source: U.S. Department of Health and Human Services, Social Security Administration, Office of the Actuary, *Social Security Area Population Projections, 1984*, Actuarial Study 92 (GPO, 1984). Projections assume continuation of current trends (Alternative II).

a. Actual.
b. Projected.

Table 4. Actual and Projected Life Expectancy at Age 65, by Sex, Selected Years, 1980–2080

	1980		2000		2040		2080	
Alternative[a]	Men	Women	Men	Women	Men	Women	Men	Women
Alternative I	14.0	18.4	14.8	19.5	15.6	20.6	16.4	21.5
Alternative II	14.0	18.4	15.7	20.7	17.1	22.5	18.5	24.3
Alternative III	14.0	18.4	16.6	21.8	19.9	25.5	23.3	29.1

Source: SSA, *Projections, 1984*, table 9b.
a. Alternative I assumes slower progress in mortality reduction than current trends; Alternative II assumes continuation of current trends; and Alternative III assumes faster progress than current trends.

persons aged 65 and over; this constituted 11.4 percent of the total population and 19.5 percent as many people as the population aged 20–64. By 2040 the Alternative II projections imply that those aged 65 and over will number 68.8 million, or 21.1 percent of the total population and 38.2 percent as many as those aged 20–64. The average age of those over age 65 will also rise. Even in the case of the pessimistic projections, the share of the aged population who are over 85 will rise from 9.7 percent in 1985 to 16.2 percent in 2040. The population at older ages will contain many marginal survivors. Of the 65-year-olds alive in 1965, 23.8 percent of the men and 44.6 percent of the women were still alive in 1985. The intermediate projections of the Social Security Office of the Actuary suggest that 39.6 percent of those between 65 and 70 in 2000 will be alive in 2020.[6] Less dramatic increases in the proportion of 65-year-olds living to be 75 can also be projected.

These data suggest that progress in reducing mortality is now having and will continue to have an important impact on the composition of the aged population. These effects are potentially important because there are great differences among the aged in the medical and institutional resources they require. In 1982, the most recent year for which data are available, per capita medical expenditures for persons over 85 were about twice as great as those for persons between 65 and 66.[7] The rate of institutionalization was 11.3 times as great for men over age 85 as for those between 65 and 74. For women the comparable ratio was 14.6.[8] These figures suggest that the dependency burden of the elderly population could increase sub-

6. Based on data in Social Security Administration, *Projections, 1984*, table 7b.

7. U.S. Department of Health and Human Services, Health Care Financing Administration, Bureau of Data Management and Strategy, *Annual Medicare Program Statistics, 1982* (GPO, 1984), p. 226.

8. Unpublished data from the 1982 National Master Facility Survey provided by the National Center for Health Statistics.

stantially with time. It also seems reasonable to expect that the health status of marginal survivors will be worse than that of the rest of the population.

The adverse effect of increased survivorship on the health status of the elderly population may of course be offset by improvements in the ability to treat chronic illness. We present a formal framework for thinking about the effects of reduced mortality on the health status of the population, and then examine the relative importance of improvements in managing chronic illness.

A Formal Model of Mortality Reductions

The interactions between reductions in mortality and the health status of the surviving population are complex. On the one hand, measures that lower mortality may also improve health status. Reductions in smoking, improvements in diet, and improved control of hypertension probably improve health at all ages. On the other hand, reductions in mortality may also raise morbidity by changing the composition of the surviving population. An obvious example is those whose lives have been extended through the widespread availability of kidney machines. Mortality reductions also raise morbidity by increasing the average age of the population.

The relative importance of these two effects has been the subject of some dispute. Victor Fuchs and James Fries take the optimistic view that health progress is likely to be associated with reduced morbidity.[9] Other authors, notably Kenneth Manton, take the opposite view and suggest that the burden of caring for the elderly population will rise as mortality falls.[10] The question of which view is correct depends on the source of mortality reductions. Kidney machines and exercise programs will differ in their effects on the health status of the aged population. Ideally, an analysis of

9. Victor R. Fuchs, " 'Though Much Is Taken': Reflections on Aging, Health, and Medical Care," *Milbank Memorial Fund Quarterly,* vol. 62 (Spring 1984), pp. 143–66; James F. Fries, "Aging, Natural Death, and the Compression of Morbidity," *New England Journal of Medicine,* vol. 303 (July 17, 1980), pp. 130–35; and James F. Fries and Lawrence M. Crapo, *Vitality and Aging: Implications of the Rectangular Curve* (San Francisco: W. H. Freeman, 1981).

10. Manton, "Changing Concepts of Morbidity and Mortality." A similar viewpoint is found in Lois M. Verbrugge, "Longer Life but Worsening Health? Trends in Health and Mortality of Middle-Aged and Older Persons," *Milbank Memorial Fund Quarterly,* vol. 62 (Summer 1984), pp. 475–519.

recent trends would focus on the differential sources of reduced mortality. However, it is notoriously difficult to isolate the reasons for declining mortality among the elderly. We therefore present a general framework that formalizes the effects of lower mortality rates on health status.[11]

Population Heterogeneity and Mortality

We present a model developed by Vaupel, Manton, and Stallard that permits decomposition of observed changes in death rates into two components: one due to health progress, which affects all individuals, and one due to the changing average frailty of the population.[12] The model is stylized in assuming that each individual is endowed with a "frailty" at birth that remains constant throughout life. While this assumption may be unrealistic, it successfully captures the notion that health progress that reduces the risk of death for all individuals will reduce the strength of the surviving population, especially at very advanced ages. This composition effect may partly mask mortality improvements. It may also lead increasing morbidity to be associated with mortality reductions.

We assume the force of mortality for individual i, in cohort j, at age t, $\mu_i^j(t)$, is the product of two terms:

$$(1) \qquad \mu_i^j(t) = z_i \mu^j(t),$$

where $\mu^j(t)$ equals the cohort-specific force of mortality for persons of age t, and z_i is person i's frailty at birth.[13] The age-specific death rate, $q_i^j(t)$, is defined as the probability that person i in cohort j dies between ages t and $t + 1$, conditional on reaching age t. The force of mortality and $q_i^j(t)$ are linked by the approximation

$$(2) \qquad \mu_i^j(t) = -\log[1 - q_i^j(t)].$$

---

11. The issues here closely parallel those in the labor economics literature on heterogeneity versus state dependence. An overview of these questions may be found in James J. Heckman and George J. Borjas, "Does Unemployment Cause Future Unemployment? Definitions, Questions and Answers from a Continuous Time Model of Heterogeneity and State Dependence," *Economica*, vol. 47 (August 1980), pp. 247–83.

12. James W. Vaupel, Kenneth G. Manton, and Eric Stallard, "The Impact of Heterogeneity in Individual Frailty on the Dynamics of Mortality," *Demography*, vol. 16 (August 1979), pp. 439–54.

13. We normalize the average frailty at birth to equal 1, as in ibid.

The probability that a type z_i individual will survive to age m, $S_i^j(m)$, is

(3) $$S_i^j(m) = \exp\left[-\int_0^m \mu_i^j(t)dt\right] = \exp\left[-z_i \int_0^m \mu^j(t)dt\right].$$

The population force of mortality at each age, $\bar{\mu}^j(t)$, is just a weighted average of individuals' $\mu_i^j(t)$'s. It depends upon both the distribution of frailties among those who are alive and the cohort-specific force of mortality $\mu^j(t)$. From equation 1,

(4) $$\bar{\mu}^j(t) = \bar{z}^j(t) \cdot \mu^j(t),$$

where $\bar{z}^j(t)$ equals the mean frailty of survivors in cohort j at age t. The rate of morbidity, $\bar{\nu}^j(t)$, can also be modeled as a function of average frailty and a cohort-specific morbidity function, $\nu^j(t)$:

(5) $$\bar{\nu}^j(t) = \phi[\underset{\sim}{z}^j(t)] \cdot \nu^j(t).$$

The ϕ function translates mortality-relevant frailties into morbidity-relevant ones. The cohort-specific morbidity function is designed to capture various factors that affect morbidity, such as medical progress.

To make this model operational, we must make some assumption about the distribution of frailties at different ages. We define $f^j(z,t)$ as the probability density function for frailties of individuals in cohort j at age t. Vaupel, Manton, and Stallard assume that frailties at birth follow a gamma distribution.[14] The gamma is sufficiently flexible to allow for a wide variety of distribution patterns. It also has the appealing property that if frailties at birth are gamma distributed, then so are frailties of the survivors at all subsequent ages. We postulate that

(6) $$f^j(z,0) = \lambda_j^k z^{k-1} e^{-\lambda_j z}/\Gamma(k),$$

which is the gamma density with parameters λ_j and k. Its mean is k/λ_j, which equals 1, the average frailty of individuals at birth. This implies $k = \lambda_j$. The variance equals k/λ_j^2. Vaupel, Manton, and Stallard show that the density of frailties for age t survivors is

(7) $$f^j(z,t) = [\lambda_j(t)]^k z^{k-1} e^{-\lambda_j(t)z}/\Gamma(k).$$

14. Ibid., p. 442.

The parameters of this gamma distribution are $\lambda_j(t) = \lambda_j - \log \bar{S}^j(t)$ and k. $\bar{S}^j(t)$ is the fraction of cohort j surviving to age t. Using equation 7, the average frailty of age-t survivors is therefore

(8) $\bar{z}^j(t) = k/[\lambda_j - \log \bar{S}^j(t)] = k/[k - \log \bar{S}^j(t)]$,

and the variance in frailties at age t is

(9) $\sigma_j^2(t) = k/[\lambda_j - \log \bar{S}^j(t)]^2$.

Average frailty declines as a cohort ages, since death is more likely to remove frailer members of the population at earlier ages. The variance of frailties is also a declining function of age. This is intuitively reasonable, since at very advanced ages only the strongest members of the original population, those with the lowest z's, will remain alive.

The effect of selection-induced changes in average survivor frailty is largest at extreme ages. This can be illustrated by considering a reduction in mortality that lowers the cohort-specific force of mortality by a constant fraction (δ) at all ages:

(10) $\bar{\mu}(t) = \delta \cdot \mu(t)$ $\delta < 1$.

This mortality improvement will affect the mean frailty of the very old by more than that for other groups, but since the average frailty of people who survive to very old age has been raised, the age-specific death rates for the very elderly will show least improvement as a result of the general mortality gain. This is because the change in mortality at each age has two components:

(11) $\dfrac{d\bar{\mu}(t)}{d\delta} = \dfrac{d[\delta\mu(t)\bar{z}(t)]}{d\delta} = \bar{z}(t)\mu(t) + \mu(t)\,\dfrac{d\bar{z}(t)}{d\delta}$,

where $\delta = 1$ initially. The first term yields a reduction in mortality rates as δ falls. It corresponds to the direct reduction in the mortality rate for persons who survive to each age. The second term has the opposite effect; as δ falls, it shows that average frailty at each age will rise, causing some *increase* in the observed age-specific death rate. At all ages average frailty rises as δ falls. This effect is largest at old ages. Since the direct reduction in mortality rates is a constant proportion at all ages, the observed response to an improvement such as equation 10 will be smallest at high ages. This is what one would expect intuitively. The selection effect of mortality improvements cumulates through time, and so has its greatest impact at high ages.

The model we have sketched imposes several strong restrictions on the nature of mortality reductions. For example, a reduction in the cohort's baseline mortality, $\mu^j(t)$, affects very frail individuals much more than those who were initially healthy. There are undoubtedly some forms of medical progress that affect healthier individuals more than those who are extremely frail, and it would be desirable to allow for such progress in a more general framework. There also may be errors introduced by our assumptions about the functional form of the frailty distribution, although it is difficult to assess their impact. Finally, when we make comparisons across cohorts born at different ages, we assume that the average frailty at birth is the same for each cohort. This seems a natural starting point, although further work might examine the extent to which changing patterns of neonatal care could influence the value of $\bar{z}^j(0)$ across cohorts.

Application to Recent Mortality Gains

We now apply this framework to the analysis of recent mortality gains.[15] It allows us to measure the extent of true progress in reducing mortality at different ages by removing the effects of reduced mortality on the frailty of the remaining population.

When we normalize the mean cohort frailty to unity at birth, parameterizing the frailty distribution reduces to the problem of choosing k. The variance of frailties at birth is equal to $1/k$. As k rises, the dispersion of frailties declines until in the limiting case of $k = \infty$, there are no differences among cohort members. Manton, Stallard, and Vaupel analyze mortality data on the cohorts of white men and white women born in the United States in five-year intervals between 1850 and 1880. They estimate that k equals 3.93 for the male population and 2.84 for women.[16]

15. Parallel issues arise in analyzing the efficacy of medical techniques. These are discussed in Donald S. Shepard and Richard J. Zeckhauser, "The Choice of Health Policies with Heterogeneous Populations," in Victor R. Fuchs, ed., *Economic Aspects of Health* (University of Chicago Press, 1982); and Shepard and Zeckhauser, "Long-Term Effects of Interventions to Improve Survival in Mixed Populations," *Journal of Chronic Diseases,* vol. 33 (1980), pp. 413–33.

16. Kenneth G. Manton, Eric Stallard, and James W. Vaupel, "Methods for Comparing the Mortality Experience of Heterogeneous Populations," *Demography,* vol. 18 (August 1981), pp. 389–411. The authors also found some cases with much more heterogeneity, corresponding to k of less than 1.

Figure 1. Death Rates for Cohort and Constant-Frailty Person

Death rate per 1,000 persons

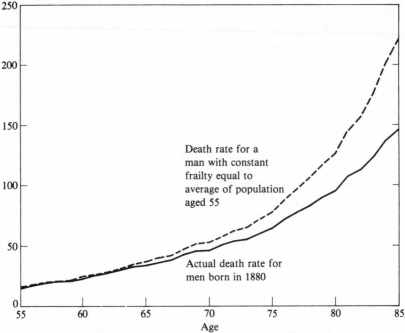

Our analysis assumes $k = 4.0$ for both men and women; this probably overstates k and understates the dispersion of frailty.[17] These parameters imply that 81.5 percent of men at birth have frailties between one-half and twice the average frailty. To illustrate the difference between the population mortality experience and that facing an individual of constant frailty, we compute for each year the probabilities of dying for a man who was born in 1880 with a frailty of 0.56, the average frailty for those who survived to age 55. We then compare the probabilities that he will die in each year after age 55 with the observed cohort death rates for these ages. The two sets of death rates, denoted $\bar{q}^j(t)$ and $q^j(0.56, t)$, are plotted in figure 1. As time elapses after age 55, the difference between the constant frailty individual's probability of dying and that for the cohort as a whole

17. We tried to make our own estimates of k, the parameter that determines the variance of frailties at birth, using our data on cohort-specific mortality rates. When the maximum likelihood algorithm converged, the estimates always implied $k = \infty$, suggesting the complete absence of heterogeneity and contrasting starkly with the results of Vaupel, Manton, and Stallard using American and Swedish mortality data. The differences in our findings may have resulted from our particular assumptions about the functional forms of the individual hazard functions. Further research should attempt to resolve these differences.

widens. At age 60, for example, the observed death rate is 23.7 per 1,000 persons, while that for the constant-z individual is 24.5. By age 75, the difference is more dramatic: 64.5 versus 77.8 per 1,000 persons. These trends reflect the declining average frailty of the surviving population; the constant-frailty person is increasingly among the frailest members of the surviving cohort. At age 60, he is frailer than 58.3 percent of the surviving cohort; by age 75, 68.3 percent are less frail.

We use the Vaupel-Manton-Stallard technique to analyze changes in mortality rates and life expectancy for individuals born in 1880 and 1910. First, we calculate the observed change in mortality rates and compare it with the change that would have taken place if the average frailty of survivors in the 1880 cohort had applied to similar-aged survivors in the 1910 cohort. The underlying logic of our calculation can be illustrated graphically. Mortality rates are lower at each age for members of the 1910 cohort than for those born in 1880, so the distribution of frailties among those surviving to any particular age in the two cohorts differs. For example, the average frailty among survivors aged 65 in the later cohort is *higher* than that for 65-year-olds in the earlier cohort. Figure 2 is a stylized representation of the difference in frailty distributions at a particular age.

It shows two gamma distributions with the rightward-shifted one corresponding to the 1910 cohort. Given the cohort-specific force of mortality, $\mu^{1880}(t)$ and $\mu^{1910}(t)$, the two frailty distributions imply different observed mortality rates. The distribution of mortality hazards looks the same as the frailty distribution, since $\mu_i^j(t) = z_i \cdot \mu^j(t)$. Our calculations ask what the observed mortality rate at particular ages would have been for the 1910 cohort if it had had the same mortality distribution at those ages as the 1880 cohort did.

We also compute the changes in life expectancy at each age between the two cohorts, again making corrections for movements in average frailty. This enables us to identify the ages at which substantial mortality gains have taken place. Computing life expectancies requires data on the probability of death at ages up to 100 because the exact age at which people die is important. Unfortunately, the maximum age reported in our cohort life tables is 85. For the 1910 cohort, data are available on persons up to 72 years of age. We extended our tables to age 100 by fitting a Gompertz curve, a standard functional form relating age and the force of mortality, to our data on each cohort's death rates at ages 55–85.[18] We then use this

18. A discussion of the Gompertz function and its uses may be found in Shiro Horiuchi and Ansley J. Coale, "A Simple Equation for Estimating the Expectation of Life at Old Ages," *Population Studies*, vol. 36 (July 1982), pp. 317–26.

Figure 2. Change in Frailty Distribution at Age 65 as a Result of Mortality Improvements at Earlier Ages

Probability density

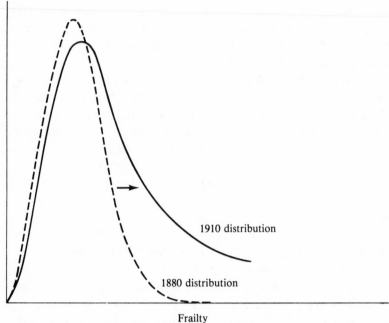

Frailty

curve to predict values of death rates at ages greater than 85. The Gompertz curve specifies that the force of mortality rises exponentially over time: $\mu^j(t) = \mu^j(a)e^{\beta(t-a)}$, where a in our estimates equals 55. This specification implies a simple regression model for mortality rates:

$$(12) \qquad \log\{-\log[1-q^j(t)]\} = \alpha_j + \beta_j(t-55) + \epsilon_{jt}.$$

The results of our estimates for each cohort are shown in table in A-1.

The probabilities of death that would have been observed for the 1910 cohort if average frailty at each age had equaled that for the 1880 cohort are

$$(13) \qquad \bar{q}^{1910}(\bar{z}^{1880}(t), t) = 1 - \exp\{-k\log[1-\bar{q}^{1910}(t)]\bar{z}^{1880}(t)/\bar{z}^{1910}(t)\}.$$

This expression depends upon $\bar{z}^{1910}(t)$, the average frailty at age t for the survivors in the 1910 cohort, and $\bar{z}^{1880}(t)$, the average frailty for survivors from the 1880 cohort when they were t years old. These average frailties are functions of survival probabilities at earlier ages; see equation 8 above.

The results of the mortality rate calculations are shown in table 5, which reports the actual and the frailty-adjusted death rates at five-year intervals for both men and women. The table shows that for men the death rates at age 65 declined from 34.1 to 29.1 between the 1880 and 1910 cohort. At age 80 the decline was more pronounced, from 95.4 to 57.8. The table also shows that the decline would have been even larger at both ages if the average frailty of the respective populations had remained constant at its 1880 level. The change at age 65 would have been 6.7 persons per 1,000, compared with the actual 5.0, while at age 80 the constant-frailty decline in death rates equals 43.0, rather than 37.6. Figure 3 shows the reductions in death rates, with and without our frailty adjustment, for men of all ages between 55 and 85. The figure vividly demonstrates that the largest reductions in mortality occurred at very advanced ages. While a male survivor's probability of dying falls by nearly one-fourth at age 55, it is reduced by roughly 50 percent at all ages above 80.

The table shows that even more pronounced changes have occurred for women. At age 65 the observed mortality rates declined from 22.9 to 13.5 between 1945 and 1975, the dates when women in the 1880 and 1910 cohorts turned 65. Adjusting for changes in frailty yields a relatively small additional improvement, converting the 1975 mortality rate to 12.5. At older ages, the frailty adjustment matters somewhat more. At age 85, for example, observed death rates fell from 119.8 to 36.3, while keeping the 1880 cohort's frailty level would have lowered the death rate to 30.2.

Studying changes in death rates is one way to identify the ages at which the most progress has been made against mortality. However, the claim that substantial gains have occurred at extreme ages may be of little significance if the fraction of the population that lives to these ages is trivial. An alternative measure of where gains have been made is the change in life expectancy at a given age between two cohorts.

Table 6 shows the actual and adjusted life expectancies at ages 55 through 85 for individuals born in 1880, 1890, 1900, and 1910. The changes in life expectancy for both men and women occur disproportionately between the last two cohorts. For example, a man born in 1880 who lived to age 75 had a life expectancy of 8.3 years. If he had been born in 1900 and reached age 75, his life expectancy would have been 9.3 years. However, an individual born just ten years later, in 1910, would have a life expectancy of 12.5 years at age 75. The absolute gain in life expectancy is

Table 5. Actual and Frailty-Adjusted Death Rates per 1,000 Persons, 1880–1910 Birth Cohorts, by Age and Sex

| | Death rate, 1880 cohort | | Death rate improvements | | | | | | Death rate 1910 cohort | |
| | | | 1880–90 cohort | | 1890–1900 cohort | | 1900–1910 cohort | | | |
Age	Men	Women	Men	Women	Men	Women	Men	Women	Men	Women
Actual death rate										
55	16.5	11.7	0.9	2.3	2.1	2.5	-0.1	0.4	13.6	6.5
60	23.7	15.7	1.6	3.5	1.4	2.3	-0.3	0.4	21.0	9.5
65	34.1	22.9	2.5	5.4	0.2	2.3	2.3	1.7	29.1	13.5
70	46.6	30.7	1.3	4.5	-1.1	2.5	8.4	5.1	38.0	18.6
75	64.5	45.0	-1.1	4.8	1.2	4.4	15.4[a]	9.3[a]	49.0[a]	26.5[a]
80	95.4	72.1	0.4	9.4	6.1	9.4	31.1[a]	21.9[a]	57.8[a]	31.4[a]
85	146.1	119.8	18.0	24.5	20.0[a]	29.4[a]	41.5[a]	29.6[a]	66.6[a]	36.3[a]
Death rate assuming 1880 frailty level										
55	16.5	11.7	1.1	2.5	2.5	2.7	0.2	0.5	12.8	6.1
60	23.7	15.7	1.9	3.7	2.0	2.6	0.1	0.6	19.8	8.8
65	34.1	22.9	3.0	5.8	1.1	2.8	2.7	1.9	27.3	12.5
70	46.6	30.7	2.0	5.2	0.2	3.3	8.9	5.2	35.5	17.0
75	64.5	45.0	-0.2	6.1	2.9	5.6	16.4[a]	9.4[a]	45.4[a]	23.9[a]
80	95.4	72.1	1.7	11.7	8.5	11.4	32.8[a]	21.5[a]	52.4[a]	27.6[a]
85	146.1	119.8	20.2	29.0	24.0[a]	31.8[a]	44.3[a]	28.8[a]	57.6[a]	30.2[a]

Source: Authors' calculations based on cohort life table data for white men and women provided by Metropolitan Life Insurance Company. See text for details of calculations.
a. Based on extrapolated death rates.

Figure 3. Actual Death Rates for White Men Born in 1880 and 1910, and 1910 Rates Assuming 1880 Frailty Distribution

Death rate per 1,000 persons

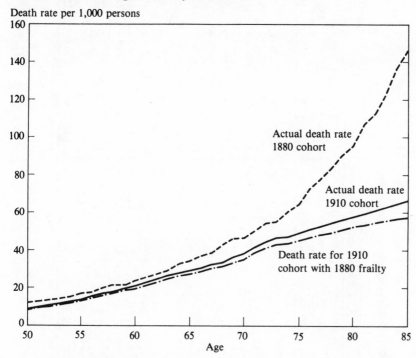

a smoothly declining function of age, while the percentage gain rises with age.

The difference between actual and frailty-adjusted life expectancies can be seen by comparing the top and bottom sections of the table. If the average frailty of the 1910 cohort at each age had equaled the same-age average frailty of the 1880 cohort, life expectancy would have been roughly one year greater. At age 55, for example, it would have raised male life expectancy from 22.4 to 23.5 years. At age 80 changes from 10.66 to 11.60 years for men and 13.92 to 14.87 years for women would be observed. Put another way, the marginal survivors at each age have lower life expectancies than those who would have lived to that age in the previous cohort. Since the difference between the actual and frailty-corrected estimates is approximately the same at all ages, the proportionate change induced by the frailty correction is largest at old ages.

These data cast doubt on the view of Fries and Crapo and others that

Table 6. Actual and Frailty-Adjusted Life Expectancies, 1880–1910 Birth Cohorts, by Age and Sex
Years

| | Life expectancy, 1880 cohort | | Life expectancy improvements | | | | | | Life expectancy, 1910 cohort | |
| | | | 1880–90 cohort | | 1890–1900 cohort | | 1900–1910 cohort | | | |
Age	Men	Women	Men	Women	Men	Women	Men	Women	Men	Women
Actual life expectancy										
55	19.06	22.55	0.46	1.94	0.59	2.14	2.29	3.48	22.41	30.12
60	15.87	19.01	0.36	1.71	0.51	1.97	2.55	3.60	19.29	26.28
65	13.03	15.75	0.25	1.43	0.50	1.85	2.87	3.72	16.65	22.75
70	10.56	12.76	0.25	1.27	0.53	1.74	2.98	3.68	14.32	19.45
75	8.31	10.04	0.33	1.16	0.70	1.77	3.10[a]	3.68[a]	12.45[a]	16.65[a]
80	6.52	7.78	0.45	1.15	0.84	1.77	2.84[a]	3.21[a]	10.66[a]	13.92[a]
85	5.44	6.37	0.57	1.01	0.61[a]	1.43[a]	2.21[a]	2.30[a]	8.83[a]	11.11[a]
Life expectancy assuming 1880 frailty level										
55	19.06	22.55	0.61	2.30	0.93	2.66	2.85	3.89	23.45	31.40
60	15.87	19.01	0.50	2.06	0.82	2.46	3.12	4.00	20.31	27.54
65	13.03	15.75	0.38	1.78	0.80	2.34	3.44	4.10	17.66	23.96
70	10.56	12.76	0.37	1.61	0.81	2.21	3.57	4.03	15.31	20.61
75	8.31	10.04	0.45	1.49	0.96	2.21	3.71[a]	3.98[a]	13.42[a]	17.72[a]
80	6.52	7.78	0.57	1.46	1.10	2.18	3.42[a]	3.45[a]	11.60[a]	14.87[a]
85	5.44	6.37	0.70	1.30	0.84[a]	1.75[a]	2.68[a]	2.43[a]	9.66[a]	11.86[a]

Source: Authors' calculations based on cohort life table data for white men and women provided by Metropolitan Life Insurance Company. See text for details of calculations.
a. Based on death rate extrapolations.

longevity is currently pushing an upper limit.[19] Taking account of heterogeneity, it appears that life expectancy is increasing more at old than young ages. It is increasing more for women than for men, even though women already have longer life expectancies. We find little evidence to confirm the view that mortality is increasingly bunched at some specific age. When we remove the selection effect of reduced mortality at earlier ages on mortality at older ages, clear evidence against rectangularization emerges.

Our results suggest that if the framework sketched here is roughly accurate, the changing frailty mix between the 1880 and 1910 cohorts reduced the gains in both lower mortality rates and higher life expectancies that would have taken place if the survivors were of the same frailty as those in the 1880 cohort. These substantial changes in average frailty should also have had other effects. If a larger fraction of the population survives until age 65, then the variance of frailties at that age will increase. This should imply an increase in the variance of longevities after age 65. For men reaching age 65 in 1925, the variance of the remaining years of life was 40.7; for those reaching 65 in 1965, it was 66.5. The comparable figures for women in these two years were 45.2 and 87.0, respectively. This accords with the predictions of the heterogeneity model.

Evidence on Changing Morbidity and Health Needs

While it is difficult to assess the extent of heterogeneity in the population, the preceding analysis suggests that changes in mortality rates could result in important changes in the composition of the surviving population. If this were the only force acting on the health status of the aged, one would expect to see substantial deterioration, especially among those at high ages. This supports the pessimistic view of health progress. Another explanation could also be proposed to account for reductions in health status. Episodes of morbidity may weaken individuals. Recent progress may have allowed people to become more ill, and less resilient, without causing their death. If illness-induced reductions in resilience are persistent, then health progress may raise the average frailty of the surviving population.

Victor Fuchs's optimistic analysis of changes in health status does not

19. Fries and Crapo, *Vitality and Aging*.

consider the changing composition of the aged population.[20] Rather, he focuses on the effects of broadly defined health progress on the health status of a given aged person. He proposes an intriguing model for thinking about the linkages between aging and health. He argues that for medical care costs, disability, and institutionalization, age is better measured *backward* from death rather than forward from birth. Medical care costs, for example, have been shown to be highly concentrated in the year or two immediately preceding death. Since death rates at all ages have been declining, raising the average number of years till death, Fuchs's view would lead to the expectation that the health status of the elderly population should actually be improving. The fraction of the population at each age who are within one or two years of death has declined, as evidenced by changing death rates. Fuchs's view predicts that there should be greater improvements in health status at old ages than at younger ages because of the greater absolute reduction in death rates among the elderly. Any other view emphasizing the importance of medical developments or changes in life-style in reducing morbidity would also lead one to expect trend improvements in the health of the elderly.

These two views thus offer dramatically opposite predictions about trends in the health status of the elderly population and about the relative health status of persons at different ages. One cannot doubt the existence of both positive developments that reduce morbidity and changes in the composition of the population that tend to increase illness and disability. The central question is which effects predominate. To investigate this issue, we examine a number of indices of the health status of the elderly. When possible, we look at age-specific measures to avoid biases due to the aging of the population.

Table 7 reports the fraction of the aged population residing in nursing homes as reported in the five most recent surveys. While the overall level of nursing home usage is probably driven more by supply than demand factors, differences in institutionalization trends across different groups can provide information on their relative health status. For both men and women under 85, the data show a steady upward trend in the rate of institutionalization from 1963 until 1977 and then a small decline in 1982. There is a substantial increase in institutionalization rates at all ages between 1963 and 1969. The pattern among very old men and women, those over 85, is quite different, however. The rate of institutionalization

---

20. Fuchs, " 'Though Much Is Taken.' "

Table 7. Percentage of Population in Nursing Homes, by Age and Sex, Selected Years, 1963–82

| | Age and sex | | | | | |
| | 65–74 | | 75–84 | | 85 and over | |
Year	Men	Women	Men	Women	Men	Women
1963	0.68	0.88	2.91	4.75	10.56	17.51
1969	0.99	1.29	3.60	6.23	13.08	24.76
1973	1.13	1.31	4.08	7.11	18.04	29.06
1977	1.27	1.59	4.74	8.06	14.00	25.15
1982	1.23	1.55	4.17	6.89	13.93	22.69

Sources: For 1963–77, NCHS, *Characteristics of Nursing Home Residents: Health Status and Care Received*, Vital and Health Statistics, series 13, no. 115 (DHHS, 1981), p. 4. For 1982, calculations are based on data from the National Master Facility Survey provided by the National Center for Health Statistics.

rises steadily until 1973 and then declines sharply through 1982. This pattern is rather surprising. Nonhealth determinants of the rate of institutionalization, such as the availability of public assistance or increased viability of remaining at home, would be expected to exhibit similar trends for all age groups. Thus these data suggest that the health status of the very old is improving relative to that of their younger counterparts.

An interesting feature of the data is that at all ages women have considerably higher rates of institutionalization than men, despite their longer life expectancy. This probably reflects their much greater likelihood of being widowed. The data also reject popular stereotypes about the pervasiveness of institutionalization. Even for the extremely aged, less than one-fifth of the population is in a nursing home. Only about 5 percent of the elderly population is institutionalized at any given time.[21]

An alternative indicator of health status is expenditures on medical care among persons of different ages. In our heterogeneous population model, the survivorship gains of the last two decades should have raised the average frailty among the extremely aged by more than that of the "young old" (those aged 55–70). This should correspond to increases over time in the relative health care needs of the extremely aged, provided more frail individuals experience both higher mortality and higher morbidity, as we have suggested. Data on medicare expenditure trends are presented in table 8. Because the overall level of medicare spending is driven by economic and noneconomic forces beyond the scope of this paper, we

21. However, one-fifth of all elderly persons will be in a nursing home at some point. See ibid., p. 161.

Table 8. Medicare Expenditure Ratios, by Age and Sex, Selected Years, 1966–82[a]

	1966		1971		1977		1982	
Age	Men	Women	Men	Women	Men	Women	Men	Women
65–66	1.00	1.00	1.00	1.00	1.00	1.00	1.00	1.00
67–68	1.11	1.20	1.36	1.34	1.05	1.03	1.10	1.10
69–70	1.15	1.18	1.43	1.43	1.13	1.10	1.19	1.21
71–72	1.28	1.30	1.52	1.57	1.22	1.18	1.30	1.29
73–74	1.40	1.40	1.59	1.73	1.34	1.32	1.45	1.41
75–79	1.57	1.58	1.76	1.91	1.48	1.52	1.62	1.64
80–84	1.74	1.80	2.01	2.21	1.64	1.77	1.85	1.93
85 and over	1.97	2.02	2.09	2.24	1.87	1.97	1.96	2.10

Sources: Authors' calculations based on U.S. Department of Health and Human Services, Health Care Financing Administration, *Medicare Program Statistics*, annual issues, and *Health Care Financing: Program Statistics*.

a. Ratio of average medicare expenditure per enrollee to expenditures per enrollee aged 65–66. Data are for white men and women only.

focus only on relative levels of expenditure on persons of different ages. The table reports the average medicare reimbursement per enrollee in each age group, scaled by the average reimbursement per enrollee aged 65–66. The data show very little variation over time in the age pattern of medicare expenditures. In 1966 the ratio of expenditures on enrollees over 85 to those between 65 and 66 was 1.97 for men and 2.02 for women. In 1982 the comparable values were 1.96 and 2.10, respectively. Similar patterns emerge in other years and at intervening ages.[22] Movements in the fraction of enrollees who receive some medical services also show a similar pattern. In 1966, 30.2 percent of medicare enrollees aged 65–66 received service, compared with 48.2 percent of those over 85. In 1982 the rates were 57.5 percent and 73.3 percent, respectively. The growth in utilization was larger for those at younger ages than for the very old.[23]

These data on both utilization and care levels suggest that the effects of health progress and the changing composition of the population have largely offset each other. They do not support the view that health progress inevitably carries with it huge expenditure burdens for marginal survivors, as the heterogeneity model would suggest. While close to half of the 1982 population of persons over 85 were marginal survivors, compared with a

22. One exception is 1971, when the unusual results appear to be due to unusually low expenditures on persons aged 65–66. Relative levels of expenditures between other ages are not out of line with the data from other years.

23. Data are drawn from the Health Care Financing Administration, *Annual Medicare Program Statistics, 1982*, and from U.S. Department of Health, Education, and Welfare, *Health Care Financing: Program Statistics, 1966*.

Table 9. Restricted Activity and Bed Disability among Aged, by Age and Sex, Selected Years, 1961–80

Health indicator and year	Average days per person			
	Age and sex			
	65–74		75 and over	
	Men	Women	Men	Women
Restricted activity days				
1961	31.9	34.8	36.1	46.2
1963	31.3	36.3	41.4	49.6
1965	30.9	30.7	36.0	41.9
1968	31.2	30.3	35.0	47.6
1971	26.6	30.6	38.8	44.9
1975	31.1	36.2	40.7	49.4
1980	34.2	39.2	36.0	46.6
Bed disability days				
1961	11.4	12.5	14.6	23.6
1963	10.8	11.3	17.6	20.0
1965	11.5	11.1	14.5	16.0
1968	12.0	11.6	16.3	20.9
1971	9.0	10.9	17.9	18.9
1975	9.8	10.6	17.0	17.7
1980	10.9	12.9	13.4	19.1

Source: NCHS, *Disability Days*, Vital and Health Statistics, series 10 (DHHS, various issues).

lower fraction in earlier years, relative medicare costs remained roughly constant.

Data on medicare expenditures and institutionalization have the virtue of being objective, but also have the problem of being influenced by a variety of factors other than the health status of the elderly. Another source of health status information is the extent of activity limitation and disability in the elderly population. Data on these health measures for the civilian noninstitutional population are collected in the Health Interview Survey, and tabulations are periodically published by the National Center for Health Statistics.[24] Table 9 presents information on the number of restricted activity days and bed disability days per year for subgroups of the elderly population for various years. Because the numbers refer only to the noninstitutionalized population, they may be heavily influenced by

24. Martin Neil Baily's chapter in this volume reviews a number of limitations of these data.

fluctuations in the institutionalization rate, especially since persons in institutions are likely to have substantial amounts of restricted activity.[25]

In general, the data on restricted activity display no clear trend. The reduced morbidity and frailty-composition effects of medical progress again seem to offset each other. The incidence of restricted activity days for both men and women aged 75 and over is nearly the same in 1980 as in 1961.[26] For those aged 65–74, there is slight evidence of an increase in restricted activity days in the 1980 data. These data confirm the inference drawn from the data on institutionalization: the health of the elderly has not worsened and may have improved in recent years. In particular, they offer no support for substantial reductions in health at extreme ages where the incidence of marginal survivors is greatest.

Similar conclusions are suggested by information on the incidence of bed disability days also shown in table 9. They also appear to be relatively constant between 1961 and 1980. For all age groups except women aged 65–74, the incidence of bed disability days was lower in 1980 than in 1961. In some cases, such as women aged 75 and over, the improvement suggests an average reduction of nearly one week per year of disability. For men over 75 a substantial improvement in health status is observed between 1975 and 1980, paralleling the observations made above. The principal gains for extremely old women occurred during the 1960s. An interesting aspect of the data is that the disability rate is higher for women than for men, particularly in the over-75 category. This tends to contradict Fuchs's view that time until death is a good indicator of health status, since women have longer life expectancies than men. It is consistent with the heterogeneity view, since a much larger fraction of women than men reach the age of 75.

These data suggest that improvements in morbidity associated with increases in life expectancy largely offset changes in the composition of the surviving population due to reduced mortality. As a result, improvements in life expectancy appear to have little effect on indicators of health status at advanced ages. While each of the indicators that we have

25. This may explain the presence of some outlying observations, such as the one for restricted activity days for women aged 75 and over in 1965.

26. One contrary finding on the incidence of disability is the fraction of new male social security recipients aged 62–64 who report health factors as the main reason for leaving their last job. This fraction has fallen from 54 percent in 1968 to 29 percent in 1982; see Sally R. Sherman, "Reported Reasons Retired Workers Left Their Last Job: Findings from the New Beneficiary Survey," *Social Security Bulletin,* vol. 48 (March 1985), p. 25. These data are unfortunately difficult to interpret because of the dramatic changes in retirement probabilities during this period.

examined—institutionalization, medical expenditures, restricted activity days, and bed disability days—are flawed as measures of health status, their problems are somewhat independent. As a result, this consistency provides fairly strong support for our basic conclusion that the "heterogeneity" and "reduced morbidity" effects of medical progress roughly cancel each other.

Microeconometric Evidence

The data presented thus far suggest that the health of the elderly population has not changed much through time despite the changing composition of the elderly population and progress in reducing morbidity. This suggests that these two effects have been roughly offsetting. We now present some very crude microeconometric evidence bearing on this question. We test Fuchs's hypothesis that "relevant age" should be measured backward from death rather than forward from birth by making use of longitudinal data from the Retirement History Survey.[27] A finding that years until death rather than age was the best predictor of health status would provide strong support for the optimistic view that increases in life expectancy will be associated with improvements in the health status of the aged. Conversely, a finding that controlling for time until death had little effect on the impact of age on health would support the more pessimistic view that increased morbidity will come with reduced mortality.

The Retirement History Survey includes information on individuals' ages as well as dates of death for the quarter of the original sample that died between 1969 and 1979. We compare the power of the age and time-till-death variables in explaining health-related activity limitations. Since this is only one indicator of health status, we also compare the performance of the two age variables as predictors of retirement decisions.

The Retirement History Survey suffers from several drawbacks as a source for an investigation of this type. First, it provides data on only the youngest part of the aged population.[28] Even at the end of the sample, the

27. The RHS data are described in Lola M. Irelan and others, *Almost 65: Baseline Data from the Retirement History Study,* U.S. Department of Health, Education, and Welfare, Social Security Administration, Office of Research and Statistics, Research Report 49 (GPO, 1976).

28. We initially tried to estimate equations for hospital costs. Unfortunately the limited age variation in our sample rendered the age effect on these costs statistically insignificant, precluding our test of whether any significant relationship is spuriously due to the time-till-death effect.

oldest person in the sample was only 73. Second, the information on activity limitation is self-reported and may therefore be subject to a number of biases.

We estimate activity-limitation equations of the form:

(14) $LIMIT_i = \alpha_0 + \alpha_1 MARRY_i + \alpha_2 EDUC_i + \alpha_3 SMSA_i$

$+ \alpha_4 RACE_i + \alpha_5 AGE_i + \alpha_6 YTD_i$

$+ \alpha_7 SURVIVOR_i + \epsilon_i,$

where
LIMIT   = a 0-1 variable that equals 1 if the respondent reported that health limitations restricted the kind or amount of work or housework that he could perform;
MARRY = a dummy variable equal to 1 for persons who were married;
EDUC   = years of schooling;
SMSA   = a dummy variable equal to 1 for persons residing within an SMSA;
RACE   = 1 for nonwhites;
AGE   = chronological age;
YTD   = years to death.

Our goal is to compare the effect of increases in age with the effect of time until death on health-induced activity limitations. We control for several exogenous individual characteristics in an attempt to improve the precision of our estimates. The survey records both month and year of death, so we are able to measure this variable quite accurately. We also include SURVI-VOR, a dummy variable equal to 1 if the respondent survived until the end of the sample period. We assigned these individuals the maximum value for YTD as well. No economic variables, such as wealth, were included in the equation because of the possibility that they were affected by individual choices based on knowledge of health status.

The results of several specifications of the activity-limitation equation are shown in table 10.[29] Increases in age and reductions in the number of years to death both raise the probability that a respondent would report health limitations. A one-year reduction in years to death has roughly the

29. All estimates were obtained using the Brookings Retirement History Survey extract, provided by Christine de Fontenay. We omitted one observation which claimed that the respondent had died in 1958.

Table 10. Estimates of Equations Explaining Health-Related Activity Limitations[a]

Variable	Equation 1	Equation 2	Equation 3
Constant	−0.588	0.926	−0.051
	(−0.186)	(0.031)	(−0.186)
MARRIED	−0.097	−0.090	−0.089
	(−0.016)	(−0.015)	(−0.015)
EDUCATION	−0.022	−0.021	−0.021
	(−0.001)	(−0.001)	(−0.001)
SMSA	−0.052	−0.047	−0.049
	(−0.011)	(−0.010)	(−0.010)
RACE	−0.004	−0.008	−0.003
	(−0.019)	(−0.018)	(−0.018)
AGE	0.021	. . .	0.016
	(0.003)	. . .	(0.003)
YEARS TO DEATH	. . .	−0.023	−0.023
	. . .	(−0.004)	(−0.004)
SURVIVOR	. . .	−0.088	−0.085
	. . .	(−0.022)	(−0.022)
SSR	1,729.3	1,676.4	1,670.5
R^2	0.046	0.075	0.079

a. All equations are estimated with 8,011 observations from the Brookings 1969 Longitudinal Retirement History Survey Extract File. Numbers in parentheses are standard errors.

same effect on the probability of reporting such limitations as one additional calendar year of age. The most important finding, however, is that the effects of age and time-till-death are largely independent. Although equations including the time-till-death variable fit significantly better than those with only age in the specification, controlling for time-till-death reduces the coefficient on the age variable by less than 25 percent. This suggests that the relationship between health limitations and age is not a spurious one, due solely to an underlying relationship between health care needs and time until death. It does suggest, however, that increases in life expectancy will reduce the age-specific activity limitation rates in the elderly population.

We extended our analysis of health status to consider also the effect of the two age measures on retirement decisions. Because the 1969 survey includes a relatively small fraction of retired persons, we report results for both it and the subsequent 1973 survey. The equation we estimate corresponds exactly to that for activity limitations above, except that the dependent variable now equals 1 if the person has retired and 0 otherwise. The results of estimating the retirement equation are shown in table 11. As one would expect, both AGE and YTD have significant effects on the probabil-

Table 11. Estimates of Equations Explaining Retirement Decisions[a]

Variable	1969 sample			1973 sample		
	Equation 1	Equation 2	Equation 3	Equation 1	Equation 2	Equation 3
Constant	-1.326	0.480	-1.030	-3.658	0.726	-3.529
	(-0.131)	(0.022)	(-0.133)	(-0.212)	(0.036)	(-0.088)
MARRIED	-0.098	-0.096	-0.095	-0.091	-0.093	-0.088
	(-0.011)	(-0.011)	(-0.011)	(-0.016)	(-0.017)	(-0.017)
EDUC	-0.009	-0.009	-0.008	-0.016	-0.015	-0.014
	(-0.001)	(-0.001)	(-0.001)	(-0.001)	(-0.002)	(-0.001)
SMSA	0.004	0.008	0.005	0.032	0.040	0.032
	(0.008)	(0.007)	(0.007)	(0.011)	(0.012)	(0.011)
RACE	0.016	0.010	0.016	-0.063	-0.078	-0.063
	(0.013)	(0.013)	(0.013)	(-0.020)	(-0.020)	(-0.020)
AGE	0.026	...	0.024	0.067	...	0.065
	(0.002)		(0.002)	(0.003)		(0.003)
YEARS TO DEATH	...	-0.002	-0.002	...	3.4×10^{-4}	3.0×10^{-4}
		(-0.002)	(-0.002)		(7.3×10^{-4})	(7.1×10^{-4})
SURVIVOR	...	0.008	0.013	...	-0.116	-0.097
		(0.016)	(0.015)		(-0.031)	(-0.030)
SSR	870.6	870.2	856.0	1,665.3	1,749.2	1,657.6
R^2	0.042	0.042	0.058	0.072	0.025	0.077
N	8,011	8,011	8,011	7,332	7,332	7,332

Source: See table 10.
a. Numbers in parentheses are standard errors. See text for further description.

ity of retirement. The 1973 estimates imply that an extra year of age increases the probability of retirement by 6.5 percent. Being a year closer to death has a trivial positive effect on this probability. This effect is also statistically insignificant. The important result is again that controlling for time until death does not change the effect of *AGE* on retirement for either the 1969 or 1973 samples, again suggesting that there is a genuine link between age and retirement. In results that are not reported here, we found that the *YTD* variable in both the retirement and activity-limitation equations had a highly nonlinear effect. Imminent death has a strong positive effect on the probability of retirement. Further research could usefully explore these effects in greater detail.

Conclusions

Our analysis of several types of data suggests that neither an extremely optimistic nor an extremely pessimistic view of the impact of declining old-age mortality is appropriate. Increased survivorship among relatively unhealthy members of the population has in the past been offset by general reductions in morbidity, leaving the age-specific health status of the population largely unchanged. While projections are difficult, there is no obvious reason to expect this pattern to change.

This suggests that future medicare costs or the costs of institutionalization can be estimated using current age-specific information. Projections of this type are somewhat ominous. On the basis of 1982 age-specific rates of institutionalization and intermediate mortality assumptions, one can forecast a 53 percent increase in the population of institutionalized men and a 67 percent increase for women by the year 2000. By 2020 the increase will be nearly 120 percent. Under the optimistic mortality assumptions, the corresponding figures are 64 percent for men and 79 percent for women by 2000, and by 2020 both populations would rise to more than 150 percent of their 1982 level. On the basis of the most recent profile of medicare costs by age, one can forecast a cost increase of 37 percent by the year 2000 under the intermediate mortality assumptions.[30] The increase would be 43 percent under optimistic assumptions. Since the

30. We calculated this value using the Office of the Actuary's Alternative II population projections, weighing the number of persons in each age group by the age-specific medicare costs shown in table 8.

intermediate mortality assumption implies that the population aged 65 and over will increase by 32 percent by the year 2000, these findings suggest that 22 percent of the increase in male institutionalization and 35 percent of the female increase will result from aging of the elderly population. For medicare, the comparable figures are 4 and 7 percent.

These increases in costs seem large relative to the savings attainable through improvements in the delivery of health care or the savings that might be possible through making consumers bear a larger fraction of health care costs. This suggests that we must inevitably plan on increases in the resources devoted to taking care of the dependent elderly, even if substantial improvements in the delivery of care are achieved.

Proposals to redefine the elderly are frequently advanced. The proponents suggest that the age of 65, originally set by Bismarck, is no longer an appropriate demarcation point for defining old age. More important, it is often argued that with increases in life expectancy the normal age of retirement should be increased so as to preserve the ratio of working years to retirement years for the average member of the population. Indeed, this principle was enshrined in the 1982 social security reform package, which calls for future increases in the social security retirement age. Our analysis suggests that these policy prescriptions are inappropriate. The data do not support Fuchs's view that age should be measured backward from death. Reductions in mortality do not seem to be associated with reductions in morbidity at each age. There is little reason to think that the health status of the typical 65-year-old twenty years from now will be better than it is now. Hence there is little basis for proposing a redefinition of the elderly.

Reductions in mortality, however, will be associated with increases in the variance of health status at any given age. Medical progress will make the best-off members of any given cohort still better off, while marginal survivors are likely to be in very poor health. This suggests the desirability of flexible policies when dealing with the aged population. Policies based on necessarily arbitrary age thresholds will become less and less satisfactory as the variance of health status in the population increases.

Our analysis has focused on the effects of mortality reduction taken as a whole, without distinguishing the cause. Further detailed investigations would be extremely valuable, since different types of reductions in mortality will have different effects. Reductions in accidents, for example, may not change the composition of the population in an unfavorable way, while the implantation of artificial hearts will increase dependency among the surviving population. At the margin, it would probably be desirable to tilt medical progress toward policies of the first type. The criterion of maximizing total years of lifespan tends to favor policies directed at persons who, if saved, will be in good health. Maximizing the number of lives saved in the current year, another criterion, is more likely to lead to saving individuals who will be unhealthy and have a high risk of death.

Table A-1. Estimates of Gompertz Models for Mortality Rates, Age 55 and Over[a]

Birth cohort	Constant(α)	Age − 55 (β)	R^2	N
Men				
1880	−4.103	0.073	0.997	31
	(−0.013)	(0.0007)		
1890	−4.169	0.075	0.999	31
	(−0.009)	(0.0005)		
1900	−4.247	0.077	0.997	26
	(−0.013)	(0.0009)		
1910	−4.215	0.067	0.986	16
	(−0.019)	(0.0022)		
Women				
1880	−4.531	0.077	0.992	31
	(−0.023)	(0.0013)		
1890	−4.786	0.081	0.996	31
	(−0.016)	(0.0009)		
1900	−5.017	0.085	0.999	26
	(−0.006)	(0.0004)		
1910	−5.001	0.069	0.996	16
	(−0.011)	(0.012)		

a. Estimates are based on cohort life table data provided by the Metropolitan Life Insurance Company. The estimating equation is:

$$\log\,[-\log\,(1 - q_t)] = \alpha + \beta \times (t - 55) + \epsilon_t,$$

where t corresponds to chronological age. Estimation is by ordinary least squares; numbers shown in parentheses are standard errors.

Comment by Joseph Newhouse

Poterba and Summers have explored some consequences of the decline in mortality rates among the aged. In recent years the decline has been striking; for example, they calculate that almost one-fourth of white women who were age 80 in 1980 would not have survived if mortality rates had remained unchanged between 1960 and 1980.

It is not surprising that such a large demographic change—perhaps comparable to the postwar baby boom in both its unexpectedness and its consequences—would have potentially large implications for public policy. To take but one example, in 1982 nearly one-fourth of women over 85 resided in nursing homes and roughly half of nursing home expenditures are paid for by medicaid. In part because of the decline in mortality rates, the number of women over 85 approximately tripled between 1960 and 1980 and is expected to double again by the year 2000. Little wonder that real expenditures on long-term care have risen by a factor of twelve in twenty years.

The decline in mortality among the elderly, although of obvious importance, has been little explored by economists. (Victor Fuchs is a clear exception.) The Poterba and Summers analysis is therefore welcome. Poterba and Summers reach a number of striking conclusions:

1. There continues to be considerable debate within the health policy community about what might be called the "one-hoss-shay" model of aging. This hypothesis, first put forward by Fries, suggests that there is a natural limit to the life cycle that we are beginning to approach.[31] Fries argues that we can therefore look forward to rather modest future gains in life expectancy. Medical progress, however, will continue to reduce morbidity and to improve the quality of life before that limit. Concomitant with the improvements in morbidity, there may well be reductions in medical care spending. In effect, disability and the costs of illness will become compressed into a brief interval near the end of life.

There is an opposite view, which holds that life expectancy will continue to increase as medical progress keeps alive individuals who would otherwise have died. These individuals, however, may not have very high-quality lives and may have above-average medical expenditures.[32] Thus, in marked contrast to the one-hoss-shay model, medical progress may be steadily extending life at increasing marginal cost and decreasing marginal quality of life. This view implicitly suggests that the return on biomedical research is steadily falling.

Poterba and Summers suggest that both these positions have some validity. Medical progress can both reduce costs and improve health for those who would have survived in any event, while it simultaneously may keep alive those who would have died ("marginal survivors") in a rather poor state of health and at high cost. Indeed, they go even further and suggest that quantitatively these two effects approximately offset. As a result, they conclude that future age-specific medical care costs can be projected using current age-specific information.

31. Fries, "Aging, Natural Death, and the Compression of Morbidity."

32. Joseph P. Newhouse, "The Erosion of the Medical Marketplace," in Richard M. Scheffler, ed., *Advances in Health Economics and Health Services Research,* vol. 2 (Greenwich, Conn.: JAI Press, 1981), pp. 1–34.

Their projections using current age-specific information are quite ominous. The number of institutionalized persons is estimated to grow around 60 percent by the year 2000. They point out the low likelihood that the costs of such large growth could be offset either by greater efficiencies in the delivery system or by greater cost sharing. (I agree, although some might argue that a more efficient delivery system could in fact offset them.)

2. Because Poterba and Summers argue that the health status of the average aged person is not likely to change (health status gains among those who would have survived anyway are offset by increased survival of those with greater risk of death, or to use their term, greater frailty), they conclude that there is little basis for increasing the retirement age to more than 65 years.

3. Finally, they point out that it would be desirable to "tilt medical progress" to take account of the quality of lives saved by medical advances; moreover, the maximal number of lives saved may not be an appropriate criterion in appraising proposed innovation. Reductions in accidents from improved highway safety, for example, may not increase the average frailty at any given age, but implantations of artificial hearts may well do so; if the cost and benefits of a measure to reduce accidents equals those of an artificial heart, the former would be preferred.

The Argument

I suspect many of Poterba and Summers's conclusions are correct, although the supporting evidence is far from compelling. The first evidence introduced is the Vaupel, Manton, and Stallard model of heterogeneity of risks. This model illustrates how, if mortality rates fall generally, the surviving population will contain a higher fraction of those at greater risk (higher average frailty) than if mortality rates are constant. Poterba and Summers use this model to suggest what life expectancies might have been if the average frailty in the population did not tend to rise over time (that is, if selection did not operate). The difference between actual life expectancies and frailty-corrected life expectancies is about the same in absolute terms at all ages; hence the percentage gains are greater at older ages (where life expectancies are less). In the context of the Vaupel, Manton, and Stallard model, these percentage gains reflect the percentage fall in mortality rates facing a cohort at a given point in time; actual mortality rates also include the selection effect and hence show less of a fall. Because the percentage gain in frailty-corrected rates is greater at older ages, Poterba and Summers infer that "these data cast doubt on the view of Fries and Crapo and others that longevity is currently pushing up against an upper limit." Put another way, corrected for the selection effect, the greatest percentage improvements in mortality rate appear to be at older ages, contrary to the one-hoss-shay hypothesis.

The difficulty with Poterba and Summers's quantitative conclusion from the Vaupel, Manton, and Stallard model is that it is dependent on both the structure of the model and the parameter used to operationalize it. Although it will seem plausible to almost any economist that there is some heterogeneity, so that the qualitative argument of Poterba and Summers is correct, the conclusion of offsetting effects obviously depends on the amount of heterogeneity. Here it is somewhat disconcerting that their own estimates suggest an absence of heterogeneity, a result they dismiss as unreasonable. The quantitation in the paper, therefore, uses an estimate of heterogeneity made by Vaupel, Manton, and Stallard. This estimate may, of course, be correct (Poterba and Summers regard it as conservative), but no formal estimate of the uncertainty surrounding this parameter is given. In light of Poterba and Summers's independent estimate of no heterogeneity, however, the uncertainty appears to be considerable. Uncertainty surrounds not only this parameter, but also whether the structure of the model is correct; that is, whether frailty is in fact distributed with a gamma distribution. This is important because one must specify how much the frailty of the marginal survivor increases as death rates fall. Because the quantitative conclusion leans heavily on that assumption, it would be better if the argument that the factors offset could be sustained on the basis of other evidence, and Poterba and Summers offer some.

They note that if heterogeneity is present, the increase in average frailty, all else being equal, increases morbidity—although of course medical progress could also be working to reduce morbidity as well as mortality. They contrast this view with a recent analysis by Fuchs, which did not account for heterogeneity (or selection). Fuchs argued that health may be better measured by years until death rather than by age. The basis of his argument was that medical expenditure is concentrated in the two years before death; essentially the argument is that health dramatically worsens just before death. Because years till death is increasing among the aged, this argument implies that average health should be increasing. Fuchs went on to suggest that the conventional retirement age of 65 might be increased as a result. Poterba and Summers point out that Fuchs has ignored the selection effect.

The data they cite do not show much of a trend in morbidity: (1) the institutionalization rate generally increased after 1963 but fell from 1977 to. 1982 (and in some age groups from 1973 to 1977); (2) age-specific medicare expenditures showed little trend between 1966 and 1982: the percentage of the medicare population seeking care increased at all ages between 1966 and 1982, but increased more for the young than the old; and (3) disability days showed little trend between 1961 and 1980. Poterba and Summers conclude from this relative constancy that the selection effect and medical progress in reducing morbidity may be offsetting.

Again I am sympathetic to their general point that heterogeneity may be important and should be accounted for, but I find their empirical evidence less than compelling. Essentially, the argument centers around whether one would have observed a fall in morbidity had not improved life expectancy led to survival of the less fit.

The problem with the evidence at hand is, as Poterba and Summers acknowledge, that many factors that are not controlled for affect the measures of morbidity; thus interpretation is difficult. For example, coverage of long-term care services by medicaid undoubtedly increased institutionalization rates, whereas the increased availability of home health services probably decreased them. The spread of supplementary insurance policies (medigap) has undoubtedly contributed to the percentage of medicare enrollees who obtain services. Disability days may reflect primarily the incidence of acute illnesses and have little to do with frailty or medical progress. It is not clear that any of these omitted variables are age-neutral. As a more nitpicking comment, table 8, which presents age-specific medicare expenditure patterns, should probably also include expenditure on long-term care. Even with long-term care included, however, I doubt that the patterns would look very different. The main point, however, is straightforward: because changes in factors other than average frailty were occurring, the data are simply not very decisive one way or the other.

Finally, Poterba and Summers consider data from the Retirement History Survey to examine Fuchs's claim that years to death may be a better measure of health status than age. They use both years to death and age to explain hospital costs in 1968 for the sample included in this survey. They find that age and years to death exert independent and marginally significant effects on hospital costs. They derive a similar (but statistically stronger) finding for the retirement decision.

As a minor technical suggestion, I think they might do better using the log of hospital costs, given the strong skewness of the distribution of hospital expenditure. But I find their conclusion that there are independent effects of these variables quite plausible. Age may be a proxy for accumulating chronic conditions from the aging process, while proximity to death may indicate a sudden worsening of one's health. These effects, however, can occur independently of selection; thus they cannot be used to infer selection.

The Conclusions

I find Poterba and Summers's conclusion that future medicare costs and costs of institutionalization can be predicted from current age-specific information consistent with the model and the empirical work, but in practice too sweeping because it ignores the advent of the medicare prospective payment system. First, and quite mundanely, the federal government is attempting to cap outlays on medicare, whereas previously it had been rather passive. Future medicare expenditure patterns and even age-specific patterns may thus be quite different, depending on the details of the payment system. For example, if a procedure used heavily by the younger aged (such as surgery) is downweighted, age-specific patterns would be affected. Second, and with greater economic content, the previous cost reimbursement method of financing hospital use may have induced much of the technological change that Poterba and Summers find of dubious merit. Because insurance paid almost fully for any marginal test or procedure, the economic calculus that previously applied to an innovation in inpatient care was (approximately) whether its expected benefit was greater than zero.[33] The advent of prospective payment changes this calculus; cost-saving innovation is rewarded, but innovation of new products (such as the artificial heart) may or may not be rewarded, according to government decisions about how to reimburse for these new technologies. Such uncertainty may well retard new product innovation and hence the rate of expenditure increases. Moreover, this too may not be age-neutral. Thus there is a high degree of uncertainty surrounding any predictions of future medicare costs simply because of the changed reimbursement system; current age-specific patterns may not be a good guide.

33. Edward L. Schneider and Jacob A. Brody, "Aging, Natural Death, and the Compression of Morbidity: Another View," *New England Journal of Medicine,* vol. 309 (October 6, 1983), pp. 854–56.

Second, Poterba and Summers argue that there is little basis for proposing a redefinition of the elderly because the health status of the typical 65-year-old twenty years from now is likely to be about the same as it is now (rather than better, in which case one might advance the conventional retirement age to some higher figure). I also have some doubts about this argument. First, it seems to accept that 65 is the appropriate retirement age given current health status. In light of how the convention surrounding age 65 arose, however, this is a doubtful proposition. But suppose one accepts that at current levels of health status 65 is the optimal retirement age. Then if their premise is correct that average health status will remain unchanged, should the retirement age stay fixed? I am not persuaded for two reasons. The first is Poterba and Summers's own emphasis on heterogeneity, which straightforwardly seems to imply that the retirement age should not be uniform. The second is that the effect of selection on frailty may weaken. Continued increases in frailty at age 65 depend on continuing reductions in mortality rates before age 65, but mortality rates cannot fall below zero (or more realistically, there is probably some irreducible minimum above zero). Hence the increase in frailty is bounded. Moreover, depending on the actual distribution of frailty in the right tail, as mortality rates fall toward zero, the increase in average frailty can in principle fall (that is, the second derivative can be negative), although this is not the case if frailty follows a gamma distribution, as Poterba and Summers assume. Although the increase in frailty is bounded, improvement among the health status of those aged 65 who survive—whether from improvements in medicine such as the artificial hip or from changes in life-style such as changed diets—is not obviously bounded. Thus, even if one accepts the argument that selection and medical progress have approximately offset each other in the past twenty years, they may well not do so in the next twenty.

Third, Poterba and Summers argue that at the margin it would be desirable to reorient medical progress toward policies that are less selective in their effects on mortality. It is not clear that this is possible; that is, it is not clear whether existing allocations already account for this, so that what they are talking about is a reduction in research and development. In any event, one must consider willingness to pay for these advances; it is possible that individuals (including frail individuals) are willing to pay for progress that has selective effects. This certainly may be true of individuals' willingness to pay in their own behalf. Additionally, it appears difficult for the American political process not to save identifiable lives when the means are available to do so. This implies that there is likely to be a market for technology that saves such lives, once developed, and in turn research on such technologies may be supported by private monies—witness the current support of the artificial heart by a private firm. Thus any attempt to reorient federal research and development policy may be ineffective in reorienting the total research and development effort.

Although these comments have emphasized the uncertainties that surround these issues, I close by emphasizing that the issues Poterba and Summers are dealing with are difficult empirically—indeed, it is hard to offer constructive suggestions that would make major improvements in their analyses—and their principal point concerning the importance of selection effects is quite likely to be correct.

Martin Neil Baily

Aging and the Ability to Work: Policy Issues and Recent Trends

The relations between health and retirement, and the extent to which there have been trends in the health status of the population that have affected the ability to work and the need to retire, are important issues for policymaking. Various changes in the social security system have recently been proposed or enacted that would alter the age when retirement benefits can first be collected and that affect the disability program. Given the current pressure on the federal budget and the size of social security expenditures, it is vital to have a firm, factual basis for decisions in this area. In particular, if it is true that the population is becoming less able to work over time, then it is natural to expect social security expenditures to expand to meet the increased need. If the population is becoming healthier and more able to work, then the program could contract unless expansion is justified for other reasons.

Analytical Issues in Health and Retirement

A simple model of retirement (model 1) can be developed to examine how changes in disability, mortality, and the ability to work among the population might affect the optimal retirement age, or other aspects of the social security program. There is an extensive literature on retirement theory, and I have particularly drawn from the work of Diamond and Mirrlees and Nalebuff and Zeckhauser.[1] Several of the results obtained

Nathaniel Levy and Alice Keck provided invaluable research assistance. Comments from Thomas A. Gustafson, Henry J. Aaron, and Alice M. Rivlin were most helpful. Jacob Feldman and his colleagues at the U.S. Department of Health and Human Services gave substantial help with the data.

1. P. A. Diamond and J. A. Mirrlees, "A Model of Social Insurance with Variable Retirement," *Journal of Public Economics,* vol. 10, (December 1978), pp. 295–336; and Barry Nalebuff and Richard Zeckhauser, "Pensions and the Retirement Decision," NBER Working Paper 1285 (Cambridge, Mass.: National Bureau of Economic Research, March 1984).

here will parallel those obtained elsewhere; I will describe such results only briefly, pointing up their relevance to the issues of health and retirement. More novel is an analysis of how changes in the "take-up" rate (the proportion of disabled who apply and receive aid from a disability program) would affect the optimal retirement age.

Model 1: Initial Assumptions

The first model serves as a starting point for the analysis and is structured as follows:

—Workers are identical and can choose either to be employed full-time and to receive a wage $W - T$ net of social security taxes or to be retired and to receive a social security retirement benefit B.

—Workers start work at "age" zero, retire at age R, and die at age E.

—As workers get older, they suffer a decline in their ability to work— their marginal productivity declines. The wage is therefore, a decreasing function of time or age, $W(t)$. In addition to declining wages, a worker also experiences an increasing disutility of work. Completing forty hours of work, particularly of blue-collar work, becomes more onerous as workers reach 50, 60, or 70 years of age. The disutility of work is therefore an increasing function of time or age, $D(t)$.

The disutility of work figures prominently in the model. It will serve as a proxy for the effects of aging and health on the capacity to work; specifically, aging causes the disutility of work to rise, so that people in poor health are assumed to have a greater disutility of work than people in good health.

The adult lifetime utility of a representative worker is given by

$$(1) \qquad V = \int_0^R [U(C_W) - D]e^{-rt}dt + \int_R^E U(C_R)e^{-rt}dt.$$

It is assumed in this specification that utility is separable in work and consumption and that both the time and age discount rates are r. The levels of consumption while working, C_W, and during retirement, C_R, are simply

$$(2) \qquad C_W = W - T - S \qquad \text{(during work years)}$$

$$C_R = B + P \qquad \text{(during retirement years)}$$

$$\int_0^R Se^{-rt}dt = \int_R^E Pe^{-rt}dt \qquad \text{(no inheritances or bequests).}$$

S is the level of private saving during work, and P is the level of "dissaving" (private pension) when retired.

With Present Value of Benefits and Taxes Equal

If, in addition to the conditions already stated, it is also the case that social security benefits received and taxes paid are actuarially fair on an individual basis, then model 1 becomes unsuitable as a framework for analyzing social security. The magnitude of the benefit and the minimum age for collecting it are irrelevant to the retirement decision and to the levels of consumption during both work and retirement years. This is because workers have been assumed to make fully rational decisions with complete freedom to borrow or lend and to have perfect foresight.[2] They can offset any change in the retirement age or in the benefit and tax levels by adjusting their own saving behavior. If the system were to set the tax and benefit levels too high, workers could borrow for additional consumption during preretirement years. If the minimum age for receipt of benefits were too great, they could retire earlier and use their savings or could borrow against their future benefits. The assumption of actuarial fairness on an individual basis ensures that there is no distortion of private decisionmaking.

Although social security drops out, model 1 is still a useful benchmark for setting optimal retirement behavior. Because the model assumes that the interest rate and the discount rate for utility are the same, it implies that consumption remains constant during the lifetime, and the optimal retirement age is set by

(3) $$U'(C)\ W(R) = D(R).$$

A worker will choose to retire when the disutility of work has risen and the wage has fallen to the point where there is equality between the disutility of work and the utility benefit of the additional wage income from postponing retirement.

Two results are obvious from condition 3. First, the longer people live, the older is the optimal retirement age. For a given R, consumption C will

---

2. This point is developed by Vincent P. Crawford and David M. Lilien, "Social Security and the Retirement Decision," *Quarterly Journal of Economics*, vol. 96 (August 1981), pp. 505–29.

be reduced, and the marginal utility of consumption $U'(C)$ increased, by an increase in E. Thus R must increase if condition 3 is to hold.

Second, the greater is the disutility of work, the earlier is retirement. For example, suppose that the disutility function is given parameters as follows:

$$(4) \qquad\qquad D = D_0 e^{\delta t}.$$

Equation 4 is quite tractable and says that disutility increases at a constant rate with age. The equation is oversimplified in that δ probably rises with age, but for most modeling purposes δ can be thought of as the rate of increase in work disutility near the retirement age.

Changes in the health status of the population can affect both parameters D_0 and δ of equation 4. If improvements in medical care reduce the adverse effects of aging, then δ will decline, and the optimal retirement age will increase. Alternatively, an increase in the effects of aging, because of life-style or environmental changes, would lower the retirement age.

A change in D_0 might come about because better nutrition or child health care raised the capacity of persons to work throughout their adult lives. An increase in D_0 will also lower the optimal retirement age. Alternatively, poor health may strike some individuals during their lifetimes, causing an increase in D_0 and a drop in retirement age.

It is not possible to make a general statement about the effect of changes in the wage. For example, if the rate of decrease in wages over time were to be reduced, this reduction would not be equivalent to a reduction in the effect of aging (a decline in δ) because there would be a wealth effect. Even though the higher wage would have made work more attractive, workers would be richer at any given retirement date and would desire more leisure time and earlier retirement. The same offsetting wealth and substitution effects would also apply to a general increase in wages, such as that resulting from rising productivity in the economy as a whole. As the economy gets richer, the retirement age may increase or decrease.

Model 2: With No Private Saving and with a Constant Wage

Model 1 had no place for a compulsory savings system. Optimal retirement and savings were achieved without it, and a compulsory system could distort private decisions. For example, if the system displaces private saving but does not accumulate assets itself, then national saving will be reduced, as Martin Feldstein has argued.[3] But a system that rewards early retirement could distort the labor-leisure choice and actually encourage too much saving, as Diamond and Mirrlees have pointed out.[4]

An appropriate framework for analyzing a compulsory savings program is one in which people do not save enough for retirement when left to make a free choice. There may be several reasons for the savings shortfall: lack of foresight, concern about the safety of investment opportunities or lack of knowledge about how to invest, and distortions brought about by the tax system. To simplify the exposition, I will make the extreme assumption of no private saving. Comparing the results of such a model with results from the model with perfect foresight just described may provide a guide to the realistic case in which there is some private saving. High-income, high-education workers usually do save and have well-developed private pension programs, but many other workers do not plan ahead.

Another simplifying assumption made at this point is that the wage remains constant throughout the working life. The change in the disutility of work with age, therefore, becomes the main factor leading to retirement. With increasing age it becomes harder for an employee to perform the tasks required by the job. Again this is not an ideal assumption, but it may approximate the situation of blue-collar employees whose wages and productivity are largely determined by work rules and technology. Work itself is fairly arduous and does become more difficult with age.

The assumption that taxes paid and benefits received are equal in present value (on an individual basis) is retained:

$$(5) \qquad \int_0^R Te^{-rt}dt = \int_R^E Be^{-rt}dt.$$

To simplify notation, define $e(x)$ as follows:

$$(6) \qquad e(x) = 1 - e^{-rx}.$$

3. Martin Feldstein, "Social Security, Induced Retirement, and Aggregate Capital Accumulation," *Journal of Political Economy*, vol. 82 (September–October 1974), pp. 905–26.

4. Diamond and Mirrlees, "Model of Social Insurance." See also Henry J. Aaron, *Economic Effects of Social Security* (Brookings, 1982), for a review of the issues.

Note that $e(x)$ and $e'(x)$ are positive for positive values of x. Then equation 5 gives

(7)
$$B = \frac{Te^{rR} e(R)}{e(E - R)},$$

where tax and benefit levels do not vary over time. People then choose to retire at age R, given from the necessary condition for maximizing lifetime utility (see equation 1):

(8)
$$U(B) - [U(W-T) - D(R)] = \frac{U'(B)Be(E)}{e(R)}.$$

The left-hand side of this condition is the difference in the levels of instantaneous utility just after retirement and before retirement. Consumption is B after retirement and $W - T$ before. Because the right-hand side of condition 8 is positive, it follows that utility rises as people retire. They feel better off because they no longer experience the disutility of work. If the benefit and tax levels are set exactly right, then consumption remains constant over the lifetime. (In this case, equation 8 reduces to equation 3.) Depending on the policy choice, however, consumption may rise or fall at retirement. In practice, consumption falls for those retiring on social security alone. If the benefit and tax rates are not set optimally, then condition 8 sets a second-best optimal retirement income level that is contingent on the prior choice of the level of the program.

The term on the right-hand side of condition 8 reflects the fact that by postponing retirement each worker raises the benefit level he or she will receive when retired. Workers do not retire the minute $U(B)$ is equal to $U(W - T) - D$ because they take account of the effect of their decision on their own benefits. Of course if workers are shortsighted and do not save for retirement, they may also understate the effect that postponing retirement might have on their own future utility. They will not include a full evaluation of the term on the right-hand side of condition 8. Voluntary retirement will then occur before the socially optimal age set by condition 8. This occurrence provides a rationale for including a minimum age for receiving benefits in the social security program.[5]

---

5. There are other possible reasons. General income taxation also opens up a gap between the social and private return to work.

The first health-related question for model 2 concerns changes in mortality. Other things being equal, does an increase in life span (an increase in E) result in an increase in the optimal age of retirement? If the benefit level is always adjusted optimally, the answer is already known from equation 3. Retirement is postponed when the age of death is advanced. In general this relation will also hold in other cases. For example, if the benefit level is too low and consumption falls on retirement, and if the policy response to an increase in life expectancy is to maintain the level of benefits but to raise taxes, then the optimal retirement age does increase. This effect can be seen by differentiating condition 8, holding B constant, and using equation 7:

$$(9) \qquad [U'(W-T) - U'(B)] \frac{Be'(E)}{e(R)}$$

$$+ \frac{dR}{dE} \left[D'(R) + \frac{U'(B)Be(E)e'(R)}{[e(R)]^2} \right] = 0.$$

From this expression it follows that dR/dE is positive when $W - T$ is greater than B. In other cases, however, the sign may be ambiguous or reversed.

The response of the optimal retirement age to a change in the ability to work is simpler and more robust. The faster is the rate of increase in the disutility of work (the larger is δ), the lower is the optimal retirement age. Rapid aging reduces the retirement age.

The conclusions from this model are straightforward. If workers are myopic and do not save optimally, then a compulsory government savings program can be a utility-increasing policy. If workers choose their retirement optimally even though their saving behavior was not so chosen, then they will voluntarily retire later if life expectancy increases, or if the ability to work is sustained into later years, or if both occur. These commonsense results are fairly, but not totally, robust when tested against alternative assumptions.

The historical evidence does show that many workers would not save enough for retirement if left to themselves.[6] A need therefore exists for policies to increase saving, either by a compulsory social security system or by incentives for private saving and pensions. In practice, this is not the only reason for a compulsory system. An important rationale for social

6. Robert J. Lampmann, *The Share of Top Wealth-Holders in National Wealth, 1922–56* (Princeton University Press, 1962).

security rests in the heterogeneity of workers and the consequent insurance component of the system. This is the next topic.

Model 3: With Uncertainty in the Ability to Work

Model 2 assumed identical workers, all with the same pattern of aging; the disutility of work therefore rose at a common rate δ. In practice, people differ substantially in their ability to work, and everyone faces considerable uncertainty about the ability to work in the future. This uncertainty is modeled in the following way. The disutility of work, $D(t)$, is given by

$$(10) \qquad D(t) = D_0^g e^{\delta t} \quad \text{[with probability } P(t)\text{]}$$

$$= D_0^b e^{\delta t} \quad \text{[with probability } 1 - P(t)\text{]}.$$

Bad health may strike at any age, and the disutility of work rises with its onset ($D_0^b > D_0^g$), where D_0^b is associated with bad health and D_0^g *with good health*. $P(t)$ is the cumulative probability that a worker has not been stricken with poor health by age t.

If this specification of the disutility term is combined with the assumptions of model 2, then workers will sort themselves by health status. Substituting equation 10 into condition 8 will give three possible outcomes:

—Workers who have been stricken early with poor health retire at an age that is optimal, given their high disutility of work D_0^b. This poor-health retirement age is R^b and is determined from

$$(11) \qquad U(B^b) - [U(W-T) - D_0^b \exp{(\delta R^b)}] = \frac{U'(B^b)B^b e(E)}{e(R^b)}.$$

In this expression B^b is the benefit level financed by contributions made up to age R^b.

—Workers who remain in good health retire at R^g, which is defined by an equivalent condition with D_0^g instead of D_0^b.

—Some workers are stricken with poor health when they have already passed the age R^b. They retire between R^b and R^g, at the time when they are stricken.

Model 3 raises two problems for retirement policy. First, if there is a compulsory social security program that sets a single age at which benefits can be received, then workers in poor health will retire later than is optimal, and workers in good health will be encouraged to retire too early.

For example, suppose that the common retirement date were determined by maximizing the expected utility of a representative worker:

$$(12) \quad \max_R \left[\int_0^R \{ U(W-T) - P(t)D_0^g e^{\delta t} - [1 - P(t)]D_0^b e^{\delta t} \} e^{-rt} dt \right.$$
$$\left. + \int_R^E U(B)e^{-rt} dt \right].$$

The optimal retirement age R from this maximization then lies between R^b and R^g.

The second potential problem arises from the condition that the tax and benefit levels be equated on a present-value basis. The condition means that even if workers choose different retirement ages, they will not be able to optimize retirement because of uncertainty. Workers who receive in benefits only what they contributed in taxes will have benefits that are too low if they are stricken with poor health or will have benefits that are too high if they remain healthy. Workers would prefer to be insured against the adverse outcome of becoming ill.

Model 4: With Benefits Conditional on Health

There is no perfect way to deal with the problems raised by model 3, and the current provisions of the retirement and disability programs of social security try to solve them as best they can. The disability program tries to confront the problem of heterogeneity directly by attempting to measure state of health. If this could be done, one could in principle design a very efficient program. Consider how it would look. If the benefit and tax rates were set optimally, then consumption would be the same for all persons regardless of occupational or health status. Call this level of consumption C^*. Then workers would be allowed to retire with benefits when their disutility of work had risen to a critical level $\overline{D}$, where $\overline{D}$ is given by

$$(13) \qquad\qquad U'(C^*)W \equiv \overline{D}.$$

Model 4 is closed by the condition that total wage income has to be sufficient to finance consumption level C^*.

The information requirements for this fully optimal solution are unattainable, so it is worth thinking about where the most important slippage occurs and how changes over time might have affected optimal parameters of the current program. The basic difficulty is that individual states of health are not fully observable. The problem cuts in two directions. Some workers with a taste for leisure may present themselves as disabled when they are not. Other workers who are truly disabled either do not apply or are erroneously denied benefits because the extent of their disability is incorrectly measured.

The extent of malingering is intrinsically hard to assess. A few cases of fraud can generate great animosity among taxpayers—no one wants to subsidize the lazy. But it is not clear that malingering is a quantitatively important problem. I will argue later in this paper that, given the history of the social security disability program, the most likely hypothesis is that the propensity of the disabled to apply for benefits was low when the program began in 1958 and has risen since then.

Model 5: With Variations in the Take-up Rate

Consider designing a retirement and disability program under the assumption that only a fraction θ of the disabled will actually apply for and receive special treatment. To achieve tractability, I will also assume that workers either have good health (with probability P) or poor health (with probability $1 - P$). Poor health does not strike randomly during working life. The task of the retirement or disability program is then to choose a retirement age, R^g, for those in good health and a retirement age, R^b, for those in poor health. These choices must take into account that some of those in poor health will actually work until R^g. The program parameters are then set to maximize expected utility, covering workers in good health as well as workers in poor health who either do or do not take advantage of the disability program.

The objective function to be maximized is then

(14)
$$\int_0^{R^g} P[U(W-T) - D_0^g e^{\delta t}]e^{-rt}dt$$

$$+ \int_0^{R^g} (1-P)(1-\theta)[U(W-T) - D_0^b e^{\delta t}]e^{-rt}dt$$

$$+ \int_0^{R^b} (1-P)\theta[U - (W-T) - D_0^b e^{\delta t}]e^{-rt}dt$$

$$+ \int_{R^b}^{E} (1-P)\theta\, U(B)e^{-rt}dt$$

$$+ \int_{R^g}^{E} [P + (1-P)(1-\theta)]\, U(B)e^{-rt}dt.$$

The maximum is taken subject to a program budget constraint. The optimal solution is to equate consumption in all states, and this condition will be assumed to hold and to yield a consumption level C^*. The retirement ages satisfy the following conditions:

(15a)
$$PD_0^g \exp(\delta R^g) + (1-P)(1-\theta)D_0^b \exp(\delta R^g)$$
$$= [P + (1-P)(1-\theta)] \, U'(C^*)W$$

(15b)
$$D_0^b \exp(\delta R^b) = U'(C^*)W.$$

The point of interest about conditions 15a and 15b is what they say about the response of the optimal retirement age R^g to changes in the take-up rate θ of the disability program. The result is a commonsense one, but it takes several steps to derive.

First, note the obvious result that R^g, the optimal retirement age for the good-plus-poor-health group, is greater than R^b, the age for the poor-health group. Second, I need the result that the optimal consumption level C^* declines as the take-up rate θ increases. This result follows because, as a larger fraction of the work force takes the earlier retirement age, the total labor supply and, hence, the income available for consumption both decline.

The effect of changing θ on R^g can now be shown. Differentiating conditions 15 with respect to θ gives

(16)
$$(1-\theta)D_0^b \, \delta \exp(\delta R^g) \frac{dR^g}{d\theta} = D_0^b \exp(\delta R^g) - U'(C^*)W$$
$$+ (1-\theta)U''(C^*)\frac{dC^*}{d\theta}.$$

From conditions 15 and $R^g > R^b$, it follows that the sum of the first two terms on the right-hand side of equation 16 is positive. The third term is also positive, so that R^g increases with θ. As more of the people who suffer poor health or disability opt for the early retirement age R^b, the optimal retirement age for those with good health increases. The program has been forced to compromise between those with good and poor health. As more workers shift to the disability program, the optimal retirement age for workers in good health obtains greater weight. This result follows quite simply from the model, but it may be a point of some importance in practice. If a disability program can successfully identify those workers who are unable to work, the retirement program can encourage healthy workers to retire later.

The retirement age for those in poor health—which also can be thought of as an index of the eligibility condition for the disability program—may rise or fall as the take-up rate increases. The increased number of people on disability drives down C^*, and this decrease in C^* tends to increase R^b. But the increase in R^g raises C^* and this decreases R^b.

Other Issues

State of health and the ability to work are not determined purely exogenously. Life-style, diet, and the use of alcohol, tobacco, or other drugs can alter the ability to work. Thomas Espenshade in his comment on this paper suggests that retirement and health should by analyzed together in a model of the allocation of time within the family. In such a model the time people allocate to their own health is an endogenous decision variable. This approach recalls an earlier point. If people look ahead rationally and make saving and life-style decisions optimally, then there is the likelihood that a retirement or disability program will distort private decisions. For example, if smoking induces disability, then a program that provides disability benefits will encourage both smoking and poor health.

The existence of a distortion problem—or a problem of moral hazard—does not mean that the optimal amount of insurance is zero. There is a familiar trade-off between the benefit of insurance provisions and the cost of distorted behavior. If health were made endogenous in the preceding models, it is clear where such endogeneity would lead. The disability program would be made stricter or less generous in order to encourage people to look after their own health. By design or accident, policy has done this to some degree. Consumption is not fully maintained for persons who retire on disability benefits. In addition, other policies of a different kind have been introduced, such as antismoking campaigns and campaigns to encourage use of automobile seat belts, in attempts to change life-styles.

The models analyzed here have assumed a common age of death for both the healthy and the unhealthy. Nalebuff and Zeckhauser stress that this is not correct and point out that people in poor health die earlier than those in good health.[7] Allowing for this morbidity effect would not change

7. Nalebuff and Zeckhauser, "Pensions and the Retirement Decision," p. 18.

the analysis of the preceding models by very much. In the optimal solution, consumption remains constant over the lifetime. A shorter retirement period for the disabled simply allows a higher constant level of consumption for everyone. Such is the rather cold-blooded logic of these models.

There are, of course, distributional implications in the early death of the disabled. The models developed here have implied that healthy workers are subsidizing the unhealthy. That may not be the case if the disabled workers die early. They may actually be subsidizing the healthy.

This same issue comes up in other contexts, and it often causes disagreement over policy. The expected-utility models of retirement imply that when the date of death is uncertain, all workers will prefer a retirement annuity that ensures a constant consumption stream. The models have no room for the idea of providing higher pensions for workers who discover that their expected lifetimes are short.

Trends in Mortality and Retirement

The models of the preceding section emphasized the importance of length of life and the disutility of work for the choice of an optimal retirement age. The first data I examine bearing on these parameters are data on mortality and life expectancy. How much have these changed since the inception of the social security program?

Declining Mortality and Increased Longevity

Death rates for men and women at various ages over the period 1960 to 1980 are shown in figures 1 and 2. For men the decline has occurred only in the past decade, although there were also declines before 1960. For women, the decline has been uniform over the twenty-year period. The figures on life expectancy illustrate perhaps more dramatically the extent to which the average retirement period has increased (figure 3). In 1930 someone 20 years old had a life expectancy of 46.1 years, so the expected age of death was 66—only a year beyond the standard retirement age of 65 (figure 3, part A). For men the life expectancy was 45.1 years in 1930, so the expected age of death was actually the same as the standard retirement age (figure 3, part B).

Given what was known about life expectancy in the 1930s, at the time the social security retirement program was being formulated, social secu-

Figure 1. Death Rates for Men, by Age Group, 1960–80

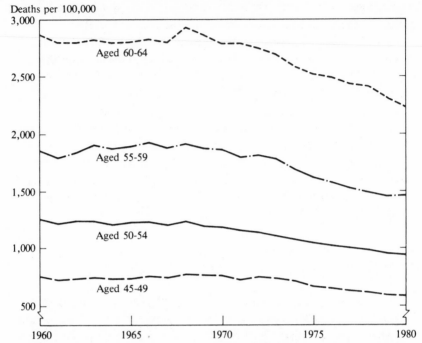

Deaths per 100,000

Source: U.S. Department of Health and Human Services, National Center for Health Statistics, *Vital Statistics of the United States*, vol. 2: *Mortality*, pt. A (Government Printing Office, various years).

rity was not at all conceived as a universal retirement program; rather, it was insurance against not dying young. Only those persons who lived longer than average would collect significant retirement benefits. For some subgroups of the population this insurance function pertained far beyond the 1930s. For example, black males in 1957 had a life expectancy of only 44.5 years at age 20, an expected age of death of only 64.5.[8]

By 1980 life expectancy for the population as a whole had increased substantially. Someone 20 years old had a life expectancy of 55.2 years, an expected age at death of 75, or some 10 years of retirement (figure 3, part A). For men the life expectancy was 51.6 years, or a lifetime of 71.6 years (figure 3, part B). Retirement has become a much more general phenomenon. The change in life expectancy can be broken into two parts.

8. U.S. Department of Health and Human Services, National Center for Health Statistics, *Vital Statistics of the United States*, vol. 2: *Mortality*, pt. A (Government Printing Office, various years).

Figure 2. Death Rates for Women, by Age Group, 1960–80

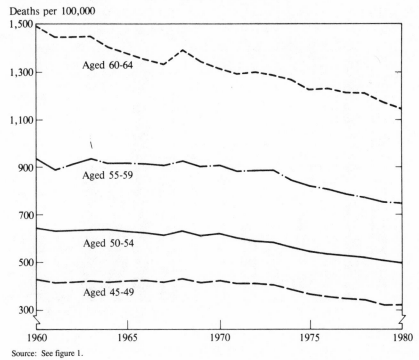

Deaths per 100,000

Source: See figure 1.

First, more people reach age 65; second, those who do reach age 65 live longer. In 1930 someone 65 years old had a life expectancy of 12.2 years; this had risen to 16.4 years by 1980, an increase of 4.2 years (figure 3, part A). Just under half of the total increase in life expectancy has come from the changed expectation of those who are 65 years old, and just over half from the increase in the number of people who reach the age of 65.

Effects on Optimal Retirement

What are the implications of declining mortality and increased life expectancy for the design of a social security retirement program? If the optimal retirement age for a representative worker in the 1930s was 65 years of age, then the mortality data alone unambiguously indicate that the optimal retirement age today is greater than 65. Even with no change in the disutility of work, it is optimal to keep working longer to finance a

Figure 3. Life Expectancy, by Age and Year

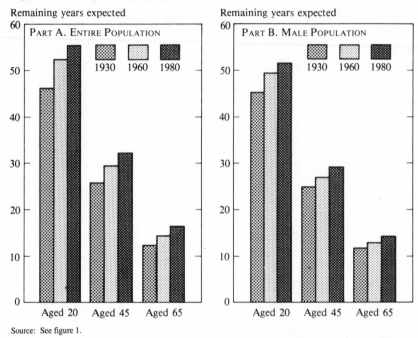

Source: See figure 1.

much longer lifetime. In addition, the decline in death rates is an indicator of improved health in the population and suggests that the disutility of work is lower at a given age than it was in earlier periods.

The implications of the mortality data are clear-cut, but two important qualifications are needed. First, the optimality of the original choice of retirement at age 65 is arguable. Social programs are usually introduced on a small scale and are then expanded. Increased life expectancy may have moved the retirement age of 65 closer to the optimal point. Second, there are other changes that have taken place and other indicators of health that may point in the opposite direction. In particular, there is some strong and puzzling evidence of deteriorating health.

Recent Trends in Health and the Ability to Work

There can be no disagreement that life expectancy has increased, but considerable controversy exists about whether this increase indicates improving health. With reference to the models, even though the age of death E has increased, it may be that the disutility of work D at a given age may be higher now than it was in the past. It has even been argued that increased life expectancy itself has been a major cause of a decline in the average health of the population, since advanced medical science is now prolonging the life of sick people, but not restoring them to full health.

In this section I first review the principal evidence given to support the hypothesis that the ability to work has declined. Then I analyze the hypothesis that our society is keeping sick people alive.

The Health Interview Survey

Almost every year since 1960–61 an extensive sample of the U.S. population has been interviewed about its health status and various other medical-related facts. These surveys have revealed a picture of health status that is quite startling in some of its dimensions.[9] Figure 4 shows the most striking result. The number of men aged 45–64 who reported that they were "unable to perform their major activity" because of a chronic health problem rose from 4.4 percent in 1960–61 to 10.8 percent in 1980. In almost all cases the major activity referred to was work. This increase in disability is the most forceful indication that health status may be declining that will be presented in this paper. There are reasons not to take it simply at face value, but it is a fact not easily explained away. The results for men aged 17–44 also show an increase in activity limitation. Although the disability rate is quite low for this group, it almost doubled over the period. The disability rate for men over 65 is quite high, and it rose by several percentage points. These results suggest that the ability of men to work is declining, and if this is correct, it would indicate a decline in the optimal retirement age.

Figure 5 shows the equivalent situation for women, and the picture is not clear. There is virtually no trend in the group aged 17–44, and the disability rate actually declined for women over 65. There is, however, an increase in disability among women aged 45–64, the age group most relevant to early retirement provisions. Note also the difference between the scales of figures 4 and 5. The percentage of women reporting that they

9. For an extensive review of the findings of the Health Interview Survey, see Deborah D. Newquist and Pauline K. Robinson, *Health and Extended Worklife* (University of Southern California, Andrus Gerontology Center, 1984).

Figure 4. Adult Men Limited in Major Activity, by Age Group, 1960–80

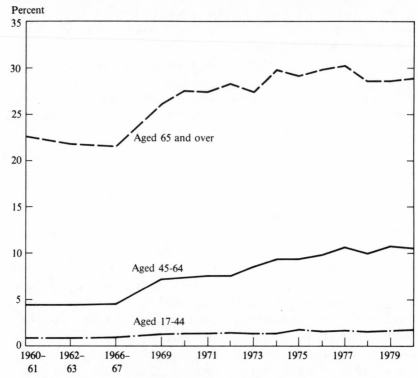

Source: Adapted from Ronald W. Wilson and Thomas F. Drury, "Factors Affecting the Use of Limitation of Activity as a Health Status Measure" (National Center for Health Statistics, undated memorandum).

were unable to perform their major activity is much smaller than that for men. Many women reported "keeping house" as their major activity. Housekeeping is not necessarily less arduous than work outside the home, but there may be no alternative for many women except to do housekeeping themselves.

Another perspective on these dramatic findings can be given because the percentages shown in figures 4 and 5 come from a broader question about activity limitations. Many respondents reported that they had such limitations but said that they still could perform their major activity. The totals for men and women aged 45–64 who reported that they had some limitations are shown in figure 6. For men the percentage with some activity limitation did rise over the period, but only by about one-third. By contrast, the percentage unable to perform the major activity more than

Figure 5. Adult Women Limited in Major Activity, by Age Group, 1960–80

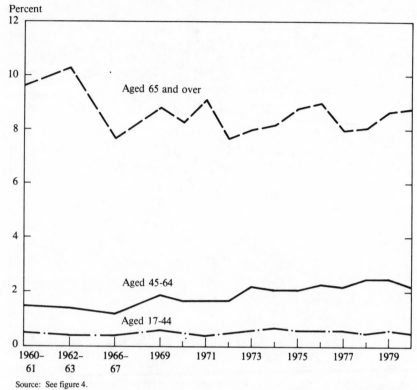

Percent

Aged 65 and over

Aged 45-64

Aged 17-44

1960–61 1962–63 1966–67 1969 1971 1973 1975 1977 1979

Source: See figure 4.

doubled. To a considerable extent, people who used to report milder limitations are now reporting that these limitations are more severe. The results also show that the percentage of women with limitations on activity is only a little less than that of men, even though the percentage of women reporting that they were unable to perform their major activity is much less than that of men. Women have limited activity because of chronic health problems at a rate close to that of men, but women report their health problems to be less severe. These sets of results show that the actual incidence of health problems is fairly constant over time or between the sexes, although there are changes over time and differences between the sexes in the reported severity of the problems.

CHANGES IN THE SURVEY. The issue, of course, is whether the apparent decline in the reported ability to work of men and women aged 45-64—a

Figure 6. Adults Aged 45–64 with Limited Activity, 1960–80

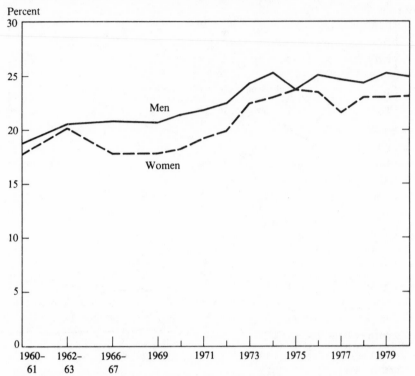

Percent

Source: National Center for Health Statistics, *Vital and Health Statistics: Current Estimates from the National Health Interview Survey,* series 10 (DHHS, various years).

decline that conflicts with trends in life expectancy—is real or simply a change in the way in which respondents answered the survey questions. A large increase in the number of people reporting that they were unable to perform their major activity occurred between the 1966–67 and the 1969 surveys. The percentages of men and women aged 45–64 in that category both went up by a factor of about 1.6 between the two surveys. This increase coincided with a change in the design of the survey.[10] Compared with the 1966–67 survey, the 1969 survey differed in two important respects. First, all persons surveyed were asked the questions about chronic activity limitation regardless of whether they had reported a

10. This draws on Ronald W. Wilson and Thomas F. Drury, "Factors Affecting the Use of Limitation of Activity as a Health Status Measure" (U.S. Department of Health and Human Services, National Center for Health Statistics, undated memorandum).

chronic condition; second, instead of the respondent selecting the severity of the limitation from a printed card, the interviewer read the options to the respondent. It appears that it was the latter change that altered the results. There was virtually no change in the total of persons reporting limited activity (see figure 6), but there was a sharp increase in the reported severity of the limitation. It is indicative of the fragility of survey data that such a minor procedural change could have such drastic consequences.

To estimate the effect of the change, separate regressions were run for the percentages of men and of women who were unable to perform their major activity, on a constant and a time trend and with a shift variable to capture the change in survey design. With a fixed time trend imposed over the time period, the regressions implied that the percentage of men who reported that they were unable to perform their major activity rose by only about a percentage point (0.97), and for that of women by only about a tenth of a percentage point (0.13), as a result of the survey change. These numbers are smaller than one would guess from looking at the data—the percentage of men who were severely limited jumped from 4.5 to 7.2 between 1966–67 and 1969. With a constant time trend imposed, the regression line implies that the 1966–67 figure was far below its expected value. Much of the 2.7-point jump between surveys is then attributable to a return to the regression line, not to the change in survey design.

To see whether the imposed constancy of the time trend was responsible for this result, the regressions were rerun in a way that also allowed the trend to break between 1966–67 and 1969. These revised regressions do indeed show different results. For men it was found that the changed survey design accounted for 2.20 percentage points of the increase in reported disability between 1966–67 and 1969. The corresponding figure for women was 0.54. This specification with a broken time trend is probably the correct one, and I conclude that a substantial part of the reported increase in disability is simply a survey effect. The conclusion that there has been a trend of deteriorating health, however, is not eliminated. For men it was found that between 1969 and 1980, on average, the percentage of those aged 45–64 unable to perform their major activity was increasing by 0.35 of a percentage point a year. There was almost no trend between 1960–61 and 1966–67. For both men and women the increases in the trend after 1969 were strongly statistically significant.

THE SOCIAL SECURITY DISABILITY PROGRAM. The finding from the Health Evaluation Surveys of a rising trend of disability is corroborated by the experience of the social security disability program. There has been a tremendous increase in the number of people collecting disability benefits. Figure 7 shows both the number of male and female beneficiaries and the rate per 1,000 men and women covered. All the series are expressed as index numbers equal to 100 in 1960.

The number of beneficiaries rose extremely rapidly through 1978. There were over five times as many male beneficiaries in the late 1970s as in 1960. Part of this increase, particularly in the number of female beneficiaries, represented the increase in the number of persons covered by the program. The rate per 1,000 insured workers also rose, however, to a peak that was about three and one half times the 1960 level by 1977. There has been discussion in the press of efforts by the Reagan administration to tighten eligibility requirements. Figure 7 indicates, however, that the decline in the rates per 1,000 eligible began after 1977, during the Carter administration.

Figure 7. Social Security Disability Beneficiaries, by Number, Rate, and Sex, 1960–82

Index numbers
(1960 = 100)

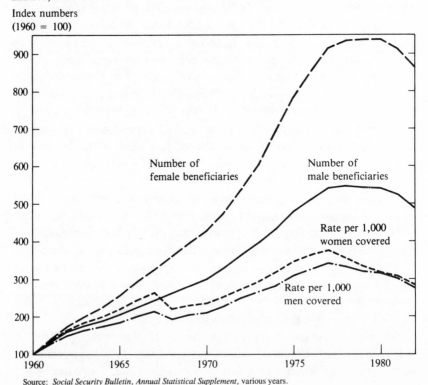

Source: *Social Security Bulletin, Annual Statistical Supplement,* various years.

There were some changes in the eligibility rules over the period. When the program began in 1958, disability was defined as "inability to engage in substantial gainful activity because of any medically determinable permanent physical or mental impairment."[11] This definition was eased in 1965 to include any disability expected to last for at least a year.[12] In addition, the blind were eligible if they were unable to engage in their usual occupation. In 1967 the rules were tightened so that a person able to perform "any substantial gainful work existing in the national economy" could not collect benefits.[13] This tightening is evident in figure 7 in the dip in the disability rates of both males and females in 1967–68.

According to Hans Weill, a longtime examining physician for the disability program,[14] the medical requirements that must be met for a declaration of disability have not become less stringent over time—on the contrary, somewhat the reverse has been true, and these requirements are stated in rather detailed and objective terms. In practice, however, the judges, physicians, and administrators of the program have become more lenient over time in interpreting the rules. This tendency has recently been reversed, with the reversal accounting for part of the decline in disability rates since 1977.

Is Society Keeping the Disabled Alive?

The declining trend in mortality and the rising trend in disability present a paradox. One way to resolve this paradox is to argue that improved medical treatment has kept people alive without restoring them to full health. The additional disabled today are those who would have died in past decades. I tested the quantitative scope of this hypothesis in the following way.

Men 25–49 years old in 1960 were 45–69 years old in 1980 if they were still alive. The period 1960–80 is chosen because this is when the paradox emerged. It is the decline in the self-reported ability to work of men between the 1960 and 1980 Health Interview Surveys that is so puzzling. The probability of death for a man, say, 35 years old in 1970 is known from published mortality tables. The same is true (with some extrapola-

11. *Social Security Bulletin, Annual Statistical Supplement, 1977–79*, p. 16.
12. The first check could be received, however, only after six months of disability. This restriction was changed to five months in 1972.
13. *Social Security Bulletin, Annual Statistical Supplement, 1977–79*, p. 16.
14. Dr. Weill was a visiting scholar at Brookings, and this paragraph is based on a conversation with him.

tion) for each age in each year over the period 1960–80. The probability of death also implies the probability of survival, so that the probability that a man 25 years old in 1960 would survive until 1980 can be computed. Similarly, survival rates can be computed for men aged 26, 27, and so on up to age 49. From this information, the fraction of the cohort of men aged 25–49 who survived to become the cohort aged 45–69 in 1980 can be computed.

The mortality rates and associated survival probabilities reflect the improvement in death rates described earlier. Suppose this improvement had not taken place. Suppose that the age-specific mortality rates that had existed in 1960 had simply continued unchanged. Then the associated survival probabilities can be computed, and the fraction of the cohort that would have survived until 1980 with these lower survival probabilities can be calculated. Comparing this fraction with the previous calculation allows an estimate to be made of the fraction of the cohort kept alive.

Algebraically, the calculation is as follows. Define $S_{t\tau}$ as the survival probability of a man τ years old in year t. The probability P of this man surviving from year t to year $t + T$ is given by

$$(17) \qquad P_\tau(t, t + T) = \prod_{i=0}^{T-1} S_{t+i,\tau+i}.$$

The fraction of men aged 25–49 in 1960 who survived until 1980 is then given by

$$(18) \qquad F_{60}(25\text{–}49) = \sum_{\tau=25}^{49} \alpha_\tau P_\tau \, (1960, 1980),$$

where α_τ is the proportion of the cohort of men aged 25–49 that is age τ.[15] F was calculated by using mortality rates available for each age group. If survival probabilities had remained at 1960 levels, probabilities of survival would be given by

$$(19) \qquad \bar{P}_\tau(t, t + T) = \prod_{i=0}^{T-1} S_{t,\tau+i}.$$

15. The values for α are taken from population estimates.

With these unchanged survival rates it was calculated that a smaller percentage of the cohort would have survived.

The survival probabilities (in percent) from these calculations were as follows:

	Age in 1980		
Survival probability	45–69	45–64	65–69
Actual	84.3	87.3	66.7
Hypothetical (1960)	83.1	86.2	64.8

It follows, therefore, that if *all* of the men kept alive were actually disabled, the disability rates (in percent) for the above age groups would have risen as follows:[16]

	Age in 1980		
Increase in disability rate	45–69	45–64	65–69
Maximum addition	1.44	1.25	2.83

As indicated, these possible additions to the disability rates are the maximum increases that could come from keeping disabled people alive. It is hardly likely that all of those kept alive were actually disabled. If half of the group were disabled, this would mean that only 0.625 was added to the disability rate of males aged 45–64 as a result of this phenomenon. Thus the hypothesis that the disabled are being kept alive cannot fully explain the rise in reported disability of this group.

Additional Evidence on Health and the Ability to Work

The data reported so far point in conflicting directions. Improving mortality suggests better health, but the Health Interview Surveys indicate increasing health problems. One way of resolving the puzzle, the keeping-people-alive hypothesis, did not work out. Therefore I now turn to additional data sources that may inform the issue of whether the population's ability to work has changed and, hence, what may have happened to the optimal retirement age.

The Health Evaluation Surveys

One would think that an objective doctor's evaluation of a person's state of health would provide a more reliable measure than self-reported evalua-

16. For example, the figure for men aged 45–69 is calculated as $(84.32 - 83.11)/0.8432$.

tions of health. A series of such objective Health Evaluation Surveys have been conducted since the first one that was done over the period 1960–62. A trailer went around the country with doctors, nurses, and examination rooms. A sample of adults and children were examined by these health professionals, and those examined also filled out questionnaires. The survey was repeated in 1971–75 and again in 1976–80, with additional information collected about nutrition (becoming, thereby, the Health and Nutrition Evaluation Surveys, or HANES in the literature).

I had intended to use the results of these surveys as an objective measure of health over time for a sample of the population. This intent was thwarted by the lack of comparability among the surveys and by the fact that the survey results remain unprocessed or semiprocessed and hence impossible to analyze.

There is one piece of time-series evidence from the surveys that is available. Figure 8 shows that the incidence of high blood pressure has declined in the adult population. Better diagnosis and more widespread treatment with antihypertension drugs are responsible for the decline. This evidence shows the population to have become healthier. The change occurred between the 1971–75 and 1976–80 surveys, when widespread use of new drugs began. High blood pressure is quite dangerous and can lead to cerebral hemorrhage, or stroke, which is disabling or fatal. This piece of evidence, however, is slim at best.[17]

The paucity of information from the Health Evaluation Surveys is frustrating. Much information is simply not available. Lung capacity, for example, is a good general measure of health. But lung capacity was not measured in the 1960–62 survey. Moreover, much information has not been released in a form that would enable comparisons to be made.

Relative Validity of Self-reported and Doctor's Ratings

Although it seems reasonable a priori that a doctor's examination can reveal a person's health more effectively than self-evaluation, there is some evidence that this is not so. A 1973 study by George Maddox and

---

17. Henry Aaron of Brookings has suggested to me that the evidence is even slimmer than I state. He says that high blood pressure is not disabling in itself, and that the success in treating hypertension may be one way in which people who are less healthy than average are kept alive, thereby raising the overall disability rate.

Figure 8. Trends in High Blood Pressure and Hypertension, 1960–80

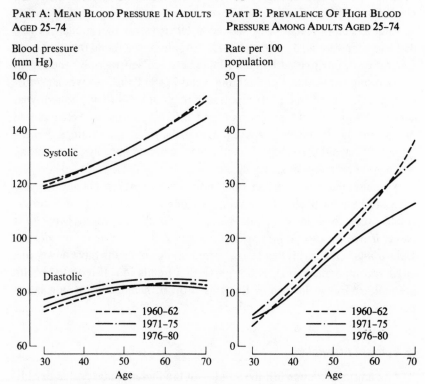

PART A: MEAN BLOOD PRESSURE IN ADULTS AGED 25–74

PART B: PREVALENCE OF HIGH BLOOD PRESSURE AMONG ADULTS AGED 25–74

Source: National Center for Health Statistics, "Advance Data no. 84: Blood Pressure Levels and Hypertension in Persons Aged 6 to 74 Years, United States, 1976–80" (October 8, 1982).

Elizabeth Douglass[18] reported on 270 noninstitutionalized persons aged 60 and over who were asked to rate their own health. They were then given an extensive medical and psychiatric evaluation by a project physician. The subjects were followed over a fifteen-year period during which the procedure was repeated six times. The final sample consisted of 83 persons.

The results indicated the following: (1) there is a persistent, positive congruence of self-reported and physician's ratings; (2) when divergence occurs, people overestimate their own health; (3) there is substantial sta-

18. George L. Maddox and Elizabeth B. Douglass, "Self-Assessment of Health: A Longitudinal Study of Elderly Subjects," *Journal of Health and Social Behavior*, vol. 14 (March 1973), pp. 87–93. This study also contains references to earlier works on the subject.

bility in both kinds of ratings; (4) self-reported health ratings predict future physician's ratings better than the reverse.

Another, more recent study looked at 69 survivors of a group of twins that had been followed since 1947–49.[19] Again it was found that there was a significant, positive correlation (0.42) between self-reported and physician's ratings of health. For the group aged 77–84 there also was a significant correlation between self-reported ratings of health and the five-year survival probability (0.81 for men and 0.67 for women). Self-reported ratings did slightly better in this regard than the physician's ratings. For the group of very old (aged 85–93) neither self-reported nor physician's rating was a good predictor of survival.

Although these studies had small numbers of participants and the participants were fairly old, it is striking that self-reported ratings of health do contain substantial information. *When the self-reported rating was off the mark, it was because a person had a medical problem he or she did not know about.* Of course, that self-reported ratings of health have power in a cross-sectional analysis does not prove that trends in self-reported health are valid.[20] But it does show that this form of health information is not purely subjective.

Causes of Disability

An additional way to test the validity of the increase in reported disability is to look at the causes of activity limitation or disability—first in the Health Evaluation Surveys. A study by Alain Colvez and Madeleine Blanchet reported all of the declared causes of limited activity in men and women aged 45–64 that had changed significantly over the period 1966–74 (table 1).[21]

The causes that changed significantly all increased in incidence, and they do not appear to have been exaggerated or imaginary problems. Cancer, diabetes, heart and other circulatory problems are serious ailments diagnosed by doctors, not simply reported by individuals. Other causes

19. Asenath LaRue and others, "Health in Old Age: How Do Physicians' Ratings and Self-Ratings Compare?" *Journal of Gerontology,* vol. 34 (September 1979), pp. 687–91.

20. The self-reported ratings do predict the future, but this is still a cross-sectional result—which persons in the cross section have higher or lower survival probabilities.

21. Alain Colvez and Madeleine Blanchet, "Disability Trends in the United States Population, 1966–76: Analysis of Reported Causes," *American Journal of Public Health,* vol. 71 (May 1981), pp. 464–71.

Table 1. Causes of Limiting Activity

Cause	Incidence and percentage change	
	Men	*Women*
Malignant neoplasm	62(104)	89(158*)
Diabetes	136(151*)	142(144*)
Cardiovascular condition		
Heart	612(38*)	359(21)
Hypertension	150(85*)	271(64*)
Other	173(197*)	157(224*)
Musculoskeletal condition	197(89*)	182(156*)

Source: Alain Colvez and Madeleine Blanchet, "Disability Trends in the United States Population, 1966–76: Analysis of Reported Causes," *American Journal of Public Health,* vol. 71 (May 1981), pp. 467. Incidence refers to specific cause of disability per 10,000 men and women aged 45–64 in 1974; percentage change, in parentheses, refers to increases in reported cause in the same group between 1966 and 1974.

*Statistically significant. Tests of significance used the standard errors estimated by the survey administrators.

that had not shown significant increases were tuberculosis, benign neoplasms, psychological and neurological conditions, asthma, other respiratory problems, gastrointestinal conditions, genitourinary conditions, arthritis and rheumatism, visual impairment, hearing impairment, and musculoskeletal conditions. If anything, causes in this latter group are more prone to self-reported exaggeration—for example, psychological problems or rheumatism.

The same kind of information on causes of disability is also available for the recipients of disability benefits. The results are somewhat different, as shown in figures 9 and 10. Gastrointestinal, psychological, and neurological problems have become causes of substantially greater importance for social security disability, whereas cardiovascular and musculoskeletal problems have diminished in relative importance. Despite the differences, figures 9 and 10 taken together do not indicate a great increase in malingering. A common complaint about the disability program is that people exaggerate their musculoskeletal problems to become eligible. This cause of disability has actually diminished in importance.

The Framingham Disability Study

The Framingham Heart Study of the National Heart, Lung, and Blood Institute was begun in 1950.[22] The original cohort ranged in age from 28 to

22. This subsection draws heavily on William S. Cartwright and others, "The Framingham Disability Study: Age Functional Disability and Work Status" (National Institute on Aging, undated memorandum).

Figure 9. Cause of Disability in Men, 1966 and 1978

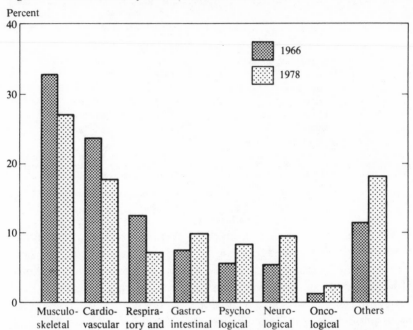

Percent

Sources: 1966 data from Kathryn H. Allan and Mildred E. Cinsky, "General Characteristics of the Disabled Population," *Social Security Bulletin,* vol. 35 (August 1972), pp. 24–37; 1978 data from Mordachai E. Lando, Richard R. Cutler, and Edward Gamber, *The Survey of Disability and Work: Data Book* (DHHS, 1982), pp. 102–05.

62 years and comprised 5,209 individuals. In 1976 the Framingham Disability Study was begun as a substudy, and the surviving members of the original cohort were then 55 to 88 years old. Participants were interviewed, and information was collected on self-reported health status, functional disability, and work status. Functional disability was determined on the basis of whether the participants reported that they were able to climb stairs, walk half a mile, and do heavy work around the house. Of the original cohort, 1,649 had died, and 1,209 had moved away or were unavailable for various reasons. The final sample was 2,351.

The first interesting findings from this study concerned comparisons made between those aged 62–64 and those aged 65–68. Participation in the work force was sharply lower in the older group: 66 percent of the younger group were working compared with 34 percent of the older group. *There was essentially no difference between the two groups in either self-*

Figure 10. Cause of Disability in Women, 1966 and 1978

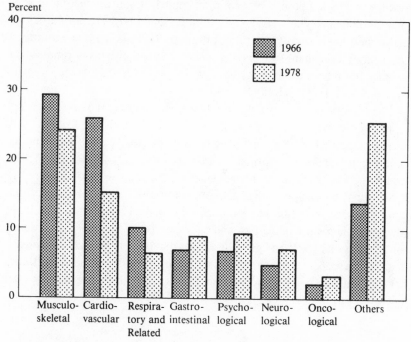

Percent

Sources: See figure 9.

reported health status or functional disability. For example, among those 62–64 years old, 24.0 percent could not perform all three tests for disability; the figure for those 65–68 years old was 23.8 percent. In contrast to this result, people over age 68 did show a deterioration in health and functional ability. Thus, the study found that health and ability deteriorate with age, but that the age 62–68 is not one of particularly steep decline in these characteristics.

When the sample was divided by sex, it was found that women have a higher rate of functional disability than men at a given age. For men, however, the disability rate rises in those 62–64 years old compared with younger groups and then rises again for those over 75 years old. The rate for women begins to rise first among those 69–74 years old.

In addition to the study of the 2,351 survivors from the original sample, there is an ongoing effort in the Framingham Disability Study to make time-series comparisons by reviewing the files of participants over the entire period since 1950. The full results are as yet unavailable, but the patterns that have emerged so far are of great interest. When the doctors' evaluations made in the 1960s are reexamined, it appears that there were many individuals who were clearly disabled but who were not participating in the social security disability program. The take-up rate was apparently much less than 100 percent. This rate did rise over time in the sample, but recent evaluations have still found disabled individuals who were not collecting disability benefits.

The Framingham study covers only a small sample, and one that is not representative of the U.S. population. The participants are from a fairly narrow range of ethnic and socioeconomic groups. But the kind of detailed, longitudinal information that it offers is almost unique. The results reported here are highly relevant for the analysis of optimal retirement. First, they suggest that nonparticipation in the social security disability program is important. Parameter θ of model 5 is an important one; it was less than unity in the past and has been rising. Second, the comparison of age groups around age 65 indicates that there is no sudden decrease in ability to work at this age. The disutility of work, D, in the models does not jump at this point. It appears that D does begin to rise rapidly after age 68.

Changes in the Nature of Employment

The data presented so far bear on the health of the population and its ability to work. Trends in health, I have argued, will cause the optimal age of retirement to change. But the disutility of work, which entered the specification of the models, is the result of two forces. The ability of the population to perform a given job interacts with the demands of the jobs that the economy provides. Exogenous changes in technology can bring about shifts in job requirements, and endogenous responses by employees to the capabilities of the work force can do the same.

Job Requirements

The nature of jobs has been changing over time (figure 11). Factory workers (craft workers and operatives) and laborers have declined as a proportion of the employed. Professional and technical workers, sales, clerical and service workers have increased in employment shares.

The Department of Labor publishes a handbook that gives characteris-

Figure 11. Employment by Occupational Group, 1955 and 1979

Percent

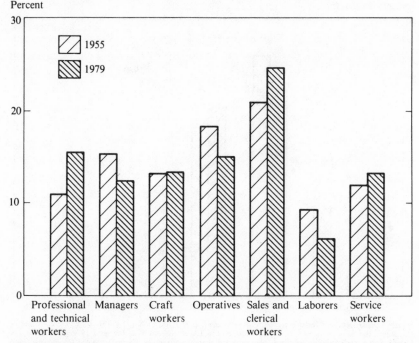

Source: U.S. Department of Labor, Employment and Training Administration, *Dictionary of Occupational Titles,* Supplement (GPO, various years).

tics of thousands of different occupations.[23] This information includes whether the occupation requires sedentary, light, medium, heavy, or very heavy labor. The classifications are based on the amount of lifting involved. The department also publishes data on employment by occupation for 114 job categories. I gave research assistants the task of using the information in the handbook to assign a rating to each of the 114 categories. The rating involved subjective judgment in estimating the average requirements of a job category on the basis of representative occupations in that category. Data on total employment in each of the 114 categories then provided the weights used in calculating the average physical demand of U.S. employment over time. Figure 12 shows a comparison of the physical demand of labor in 1950 and 1980 and it has clearly decreased

23. U.S. Department of Labor, Employment and Training Administration, *Dictionary of Occupational Titles, Fourth Edition Supplement* (GPO, 1982).

Figure 12. Physical Demand on Labor, 1950 and 1980

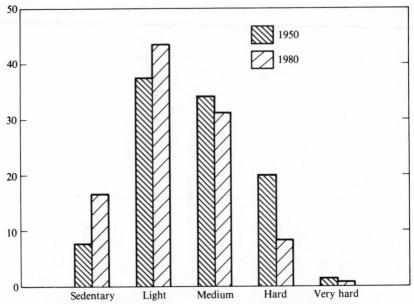

Percent of work force

Sources: *Employment and Training Report of the President, 1982* (GPO, 1983), pp. 181–82; U.S. Department of Commerce, Bureau of the Census, *Historical Statistics of the United States: Colonial Times to 1970* (GPO, 1976), pp. 140–45; and U.S. Department of Labor, Manpower Administration, *Selected Characteristics of Occupations: 1966 Supplement to the Dictionary of Occupational Titles,* 3d ed. (GPO, 1966).

over this period. Jobs requiring little or light physical effort have increased from 45 percent of the total in 1950 to 60 percent by 1980. Jobs requiring heavy or very heavy physical effort have declined from 21 percent to 9 percent. This result is explained in part by the decline in agricultural employment.

These data therefore suggest that, for a given level of health in the population, the ability to work should have increased. Fewer jobs demand strenuous physical effort. People who wish to change jobs to avoid heavy physical demands should find it easier to do so now than in the past.

Education

The conclusions just described are reinforced by data on educational attainment. In a cross section of people, those with more years of education have much lower social security disability rates than those with fewer

Table 2. People Aged 18–64 with Work Disability in 1970
Percent

Extent of disability	Years of schooling completed						
	Elementary			Secondary		College	
	0	1–7	8	1–3	4	1–3	4 or more
	Men						
Total	34.5	19.4	14.1	11.7	8.8	9.2	5.9
Partial	9.4	10.9	9.3	8.3	6.9	7.5	5.1
Complete	25.1	8.5	4.8	3.4	1.9	1.7	0.8
	Women						
Total	28.6	18.9	13.6	10.9	6.8	6.3	4.7
Partial	5.4	7.1	6.2	5.5	3.9	4.0	3.2
Complete	23.2	11.8	7.4	5.4	2.9	2.3	1.5

Source: *Social Security Bulletin*, vol. 38 (December 1975), p. 20, table 4. Groups were standardized by age.

years of education (table 2), and the population has also become more educated steadily over time (table 3). The overall picture presented by figure 12 and tables 2 and 3 is rather clear. The nature of U.S. employment has been changing. Heavy, blue-collar manual jobs performed by workers with a high-school education or less have diminished in importance. These positions have been replaced by increased automation and by rising productivity in agriculture. Professional and technical jobs with greater edu-

Table 3. Educational Level of Employees in Private Sector, 1959, 1964, 1973, and 1979
Percent

Year	Years of schooling completed						
	Elementary			Secondary		College	
	0–4	5–7	8	1–3	4	1–3	4 or more
	Men						
1959	5.8	10.8	16.5	20.4	28.3	9.0	9.3
1964	4.2	8.9	14.1	19.8	32.5	10.2	10.2
1973	2.5	5.7	8.2	17.5	38.2	14.0	13.9
1979	1.6	3.7	5.5	14.4	39.2	17.3	18.3
	Women						
1959	2.4	7.2	13.4	19.9	43.9	9.2	4.1
1964	2.0	5.9	11.7	19.6	46.0	10.1	4.6
1973	1.2	3.6	6.2	17.5	51.0	14.0	6.6
1979	0.9	2.4	3.6	14.3	49.6	18.6	10.6

Source: Edward F. Denison, *Accounting for Slower Economic Growth: The United States in the 1970s* (Brookings, 1979), table 3-10, p. 43; and Denison, *Trends in American Economic Growth, 1929–1982* (Brookings, 1985), table 3-10, p. 91.

cational requirements, and sales, clerical, and service jobs that are not manual in nature have grown in importance. Other things being equal, this trend of changing employment should have reduced the incidence of disability.

Interpreting the Evidence

I have presented a composite model of optimal retirement and evidence about the parameters of health, mortality, and the ability to work that are central to the model. Fitting the pieces together poses a serious challenge. Perhaps the first and most obvious issue of interpretation is the question of whether reported disability is rising because more people now collect disability benefits.

Economic Incentives

The disability rate reported by the social security program is inherently more suspect than the one from the Health Evaluation Surveys because the applicants for social security disability benefits have an incentive to make the most of their health problems. The Health Interview Surveys are not free from this problem either. Someone receiving benefits or thinking of applying for them will certainly respond to the official interviewers of the Health Evaluation Surveys in a manner consistent with the interviewers' approach to the social security program. The trend since 1969 of rising reported inability to work, which was found in the Health Evaluation Surveys, corresponds closely to an increase of 20 percent in the level of inflation-adjusted social security disability benefits during 1969–73.

Recent research by Bazzoli and by Anderson and Burkhauser has confirmed the interaction between self-reported health status and the economic cost of retirement.[24] These studies found that the apparently powerful predictive effect of self-reported health on the decision to retire that had been found in earlier studies is weakened when the economic variables relevant to retirement are fully specified.

24. Gloria J. Bazzoli, "The Early Retirement Decision: New Empirical Evidence on the Influence of Health," *Journal of Human Resources*, vol. 20 (Spring 1985), pp. 214–34; and Kathryn H. Anderson and Richard V. Burkhauser, "The Retirement-Health Nexus: A New Measure of an Old Puzzle," *Journal of Human Resources*, vol. 20 (Summer 1985), pp. 315–30.

The changes that have taken place in the economic pressure on workers to keep working have come about not only as a result of government transfers. Increasing affluence and the increased participation of women in the work force are also important. In 1960 only 7 percent of married men aged 45–64 were not in the work force. This figure had more than doubled, to 15.2 percent, by 1980 and rose further, to 18.2 percent, by 1984. Over the same period married women aged 45–64 in the work force increased from 34.2 percent in 1960 to 46.9 percent in 1980 and to 48.9 percent in 1984.[25]

From both of these studies and common sense, it is clear that changing economic incentives have altered the participation of older men in the work force and are part of the reason for the rise in the disability rate. But this conclusion tells only part of the story.

Are People Really Disabled?

Suppose it is true that people retire early when they have the economic resources to do so and keep working when they do not. Does that mean that people are lying when they give health as the reason for retirement? Does it mean that people are faking disability to get benefits? Not at all. Disabled or not, unless people have the economic resources to retire, they are not going to do so. Blue-collar families typically have few assets that can sustain consumption. If someone has a pension, or disability benefits, or other family members working, then poor health will lead to retirement. Without these alternatives, someone with a high disutility of work will nonetheless continue to work.

Examination of the causes of disability, demonstration of the validity of self-reported ratings of health, and the findings of the Framingham Disability Study all point to the conclusion that most of the people who have reported disabling health problems actually have them. Of course there are a few malingerers, but the more frequent finding is the reverse—that people overestimate the state of their own health.

A Possible Interpretation of Health and Mortality Data

None of the evidence examined allows a clear-cut resolution of conflicting trends in the ability to work. But one hypothesis makes much more

25. Bureau of the Census, *Statistical Abstract of the United States, 1986* (GPO, 1985), p. 398, table 673.

sense than any other. Improvements in nutrition and medical care have raised levels of general health and life expectancy. Combined with a reduction in the physical demands of employment, these improvements have meant that most people have a greater ability to work today than in past decades. In terms of the models, $D^g(t)$, the disutility of work for those in good health, is lower for a given age t.

The rising trend in the number of social security disability recipients reflects an increase in the take-up rate of the program, as a larger and larger fraction of those who are disabled apply for benefits. The economic incentive of rising benefit levels, plus the increased willingness of doctors in the certification process to grant approval, have spurred this increase. In addition, changing social attitudes have encouraged more people to apply. One person retires on disability benefits, so a friend or relative also decides to apply.

The rising trend in the percentage of persons with self-reported disability parallels trends in the disability program. People collecting benefits, or hoping to, will certainly report themselves as limited in activity. Even for others, the availability of early retirement pensions and the presence of other family members who work allow people to retire. Health problems provide a socially acceptable explanation for retirement and one that is essentially correct.

Directions for Retirement Policy

To make sound policy for the social security system requires far more systematic research into the health and ability to work of the population in the years near retirement. It is absurd that such an enormous social program should have policy decisions based on inadequate and incomplete information. The first conclusion of this paper is that the data are inadequate.

On the basis of what I have described as the most likely hypothesis about trends in the ability to work, some policy recommendations can be made. Increased life expectancy and improved ability to work for people in good health indicate that the normal range of retirement can be increased from the age of 62–65 to 65–68. This policy change is already going into effect. Of course it is possible that when the age range 62–65 was first introduced it was too high relative to optimal retirement. But the results of the Framingham study show no sharp decline in the ability to work up to the age of 68. It is therefore reasonable to expect people without specific health problems to continue working until the age of 68.

The second policy recommendation is that the disability program should be seen as a vital part of the retirement program. The increase in the take-up rate is removing from the work force those people with serious health problems. This is an important reason for raising the general retirement age. An effective disability program improves the efficiency of the retirement program and may even save money if it allows later retirement for the majority. This positive perspective, however, does depend on the capacity of the disability program to measure accurately applicants' ability to work. Incorrect decisions in either direction will undermine the program.

In the models and in the actual disability program, only two states—good health and poor health—were distinguished. In practice there are different degrees of disability. A future direction for research in modeling and in empirical analysis, and a topic for policy discussion, should be the concept of partial disability. Even people with serious health problems may be able to work at certain jobs or to work part-time. A designation of partial disability, with supplementary benefits, might be appropriate for some. Within the limits of administrative feasibility, increased flexibility in setting the retirement age is clearly desirable.

Comment by Thomas J. Espenshade*

This paper on aging and the ability to work attempts to shed light on some rather difficult but important issues of public policy. As elderly people make up an increasingly larger proportion of the population over the next several decades, it becomes critical for those who design our retirement and disability programs to have an accurate understanding of such questions as the factors that cause people to retire early or to postpone retirement, the socially optimal retirement age and how it might be changing, and consideration of health and disability factors in the operation of the social security system.

*Tracy Ann Goodis, Susan Kalish, and Terri Murray provided much-appreciated technical assistance in the preparation of these remarks.

Summary

Baily's paper divides into two parts. The first develops a model of the factors that contribute to retirement decisions in order to explore how changes in disability, mortality, and the ability to work among the population affect the socially optimal retirement age and other aspects of the social security program. The second part analyzes several studies providing empirical evidence on the health status of the population in order to interpret the significant increases in disability rates that have occurred among men in recent years.

Baily's model arrives at the optimal age of retirement in terms of the interaction of such factors as wages, the disutility of work, and the utility value of consumption. Elaborating on this model, Baily considers the possible effects of several factors—including changes in life expectancy, variations in disability rates with age, and the presence of voluntary or compulsory savings arrangements—on retirement age. He factors in workers' uncertainties about their ability to work in the future. He also attempts to model the difference in age of retirement between workers in good health and those in poor health, and to analyze the financial impact of those who retire earlier because of poor health on healthy workers who postpone retirement.

Among the public policy issues that this analytical section touches on are (1) the efficiency of having a common retirement age for all workers, (2) the question of whether the early retirement of workers in poor health places an unfair burden on healthy workers who typically retire later, (3) questions about the potential for abuse that exist in the disability system, and (4) the possible efficacy of a compulsory government savings program to be imposed throughout the working life.

One of the important variables in his model is the ability of the adult population to participate in gainful employment, and as Baily turns to examine the empirical evidence on trends in the ability to work, he reaches a paradox. The number and rate of people collecting disability benefits have greatly increased in recent years; yet to conclude that the population's ability to work is therefore declining would be counterintuitive. Such factors as increasing longevity, the wider availability of health care, an increase in educational level in the population, and the trend toward a more automated service economy in which the physical strength of workers is not a determinant of job performance—all argue for an increase, not a decline, in the population's ability to work. Still, as Baily points out, at least one longitudinal study of health status seems to show an increase in disability. The Health Interview Survey conducted by the National Center for Health Statistics shows rising trends between 1960 and 1980 in the proportion of men and women aged 45–64 who said that they were "unable to perform their major activity" because of chronic health problems. The impairments that contributed to this declining ability to work included increased reports of such objectively diagnosable conditions as cancer, diabetes, and heart and circulatory problems.

Baily observes that increases in longevity and the decrease in the typical physical demands of employment have increased the optimal retirement age. Although somewhat more tentative in his interpretation of the increase in the reporting of disabilities, Baily suggests that these increases may not indicate a real decline in the ability of the population to work. He suggests that the true extent of disability in the population has probably always been fairly high and may actually be falling at this time. He concludes that "the most likely hypothesis [for the reported rise in disability] is that the propensity of the disabled to apply for benefits was low when the program began in 1958 and has risen since then."

Critique

In undertaking this investigation, Baily is up against a difficult problem: although this is an area with important implications for public policy, it is also one in which there is unfortunately little hard evidence to go on. Three general comments might be made about this paper:

—I am in basic agreement with Baily's conclusion about the reason for the apparent rise in disability. But I would add that a much greater fraction of the disabled are not only willing but also able to report themselves as such. Not only has the range of disabilities qualifying for support been broadened, but both the quality and quantity of health care have improved. Better diagnoses and more extensive access to health professionals are the results. Both factors imply a tendency for reported disabilities to rise.

—Until evidence becomes much more persuasive, I am disinclined to believe that there has been a decrease in the ability to work. It seems more likely that economic incentives—including rising benefit levels—have raised the opportunity cost of working at older ages, discouraging some people from postponing retirement.

—Although I like the idea of starting off the paper with a model of the optimal age at retirement, the exposition of the model might be somehow better integrated with the presentation of the empirical evidence on changes in disability rates that now forms the second portion of the paper. Moreover, a more natural starting point for the model might be the "new home economics," in which good health, for example, is an endogenous variable formed partially by the inputs of time and purchased market goods and services.

One problem with Baily's model is that it assumes that workers possess perfect foresight with regard to their own health status, life expectancy, income, taste for work, social security taxes, and retirement benefits, and that workers make plans and decisions at the beginning of their working years concerning the optimal age at retirement on the basis of this information. It might be helpful to be more explicit about the considerable uncertainty surrounding each of these variables and about the fact that retirement plans made early in working life are constantly reevaluated over the life cycle as more information comes along to narrow the range of uncertainty about each of the determining factors. The model might also be adjusted to reflect the problem of life-cycle time allocation. One possible approach would be to incorporate the concept from new home economics that income does not yield utility directly, nor does leisure time yield utility (nor work time disutility). Instead, time and income—or time and market goods and services—are combined to produce more basic commodities, and it is these more basic commodities that enter into the utility function.

From some of the discussions of the optimal age for retirement it can be inferred that what is optimal for the individual may not be optimal for society. One of the interesting policy questions highlighted by Baily's paper is how to deal with instances in which this discrepancy exists.

The elaboration of the model makes an important contribution by recognizing that individuals are heterogeneous with regard to health status. Heterogeneity, however, extends to other variables as well—wages, taste for work, and so on. How to incorporate these other dimensions of heterogeneity into the model remains a challenge.

There are built-in difficulties in defining and measuring health or health status because such measurement necessarily includes both subjective and objective elements. The concept becomes perhaps even more elusive if one includes health in that basket of home-produced goods, as one of Gary Becker's basic commodities.[26] It is especially problematic to interpret

26. Gary S. Becker, "A Theory of the Allocation of Time," *Economic Journal*, vol. 75 (September 1965), pp. 493–517.

subjective self-reports of health status. These self-reports tend to be positively correlated with physician's ratings, but not strongly so ($\rho = .42$ in the one study Baily cites).[27] Moreover, two individuals with the same objective health status may evaluate their health differently depending on how healthy they expect to be. This raises problems similar to those that Easterlin attempts to overcome with his measure of relative income.[28] Perhaps we need a concept of "relative health status" to be used in interpreting self-reports of health.

Even objective measures of health status raise problems because the yardsticks do not remain constant. In this area of investigation, one typically lacks the conditions of other things being equal that reliable measures would require. For one thing, as the quantity of health care facilities expands over time, people have better access to health care. In addition, rising personal income makes doctor visits more easily affordable, and technological developments in medicine mean that disabilities are more readily detected. Even if intrinsic health status did not change, one would expect a population to become more aware of its infirmities because of these factors. For example, the rising proportion of teenagers with braces does not imply that dental hygiene is declining.

The conditions of other things being equal are missing in the two key data sets Baily cites to support the view that ability to work is declining. In the Health Interview Surveys, the most abrupt increase in the proportion of the population reporting that they were "unable to perform their major activity" occurred between 1966–67 and 1969, when there was also a change in survey design. In addition, in the social security disability program, the recorded rise in disability rates between 1960 and the late 1970s occurred at a time when coverage under the program was being extended, the definition of disability was altered, and the leniency with which the rules were interpreted fluctuated. Indeed, to measure trends in health status accurately, one would ideally like to give members of successive cohorts a battery of diagnostic health tests using a constant measuring rod.

On the basis of the evidence Baily presents, one must conclude that the marked increase in the rates of people receiving disability benefits does not necessarily indicate a real trend toward a decline in the health status of the population. One cannot discount behavioral responses to changing policy

27. LaRue and others, "Health in Old Age."
28. Richard A. Easterlin, *Birth and Fortune: The Impact of Numbers on Personal Welfare* (Basic Books, 1980).

and programmatic regulations as a possible source of these increases. These behavioral factors go beyond concerns about the potential that exists for personal abuse of the disability system, or "malingering." Institutional arrangements structured into the disability system that create an incentive for early retirement (by providing disability income) may create the appearance of a deterioration in health status. Conversely, it is interesting that disability rates reversed their steep increase in the late 1970s and started to fall when eligibility was being tightened (see figure 7 of Baily's paper).

Despite these caveats, this is an interesting and valuable paper. Perhaps its most important contribution is to begin to develop a theoretical model of the optimal age of retirement that might eventually be used to evaluate the desirability of legislatively changing mandated retirement ages.

Gary Burtless

Occupational Effects on the Health and Work Capacity of Older Men

The health status of older workers is a crucial determinant of their retirement age. Workers who are in poor health or who perceive themselves to be in poor health tend to retire earlier than workers with average or above average health. The association between poor health and early retirement has long been recognized. Retirement research during the 1950s and early 1960s established that, for wage and salary workers who retired voluntarily, poor health was the most frequently cited reason for leaving work. Among self-employed workers not subject to an employer's pressure to retire early, over half of retirees mentioned poor health as a reason for quitting work.[1] About a quarter of all male respondents in the Retirement History Survey (RHS) said they left a job for health reasons over the course of that ten-year panel study (1969–79).

Although it should be obvious that the health status of a worker might affect his decision to retire, some observers are skeptical that health plays the critical role assigned by retirees themselves. The observed trends in retirement and public health do not appear to support the view that poor health is the main reason for early retirement. At the turn of the century, retirement was relatively uncommon among older men. Two out of three men over the age of 65 were employed.[2] By 1980 only 20 percent of aged men were working.[3] It is difficult to believe that the health status of older

I gratefully acknowledge the suggestions and assistance of J. S. Butler, Robert H. Meyer, and Robert A. Moffitt. Cameran M. Lougy and Sheila E. Murray provided able research assistance.

1. See Erdman Palmore, "Retirement Patterns among Aged Men: Findings of the 1963 Survey of the Aged," *Social Security Bulletin,* vol. 27 (August 1964), pp. 3–10.

2. U.S. Department of Commerce, Bureau of the Census, *Historical Statistics of the United States: Colonial Times to 1970* (Government Printing Office, 1975), p. 132.

3. U.S. Department of Labor, Bureau of Labor Statistics, *Handbook of Labor Statistics,* Bulletin 2175 (GPO, 1983), pp. 9, 13.

men declined as precipitously as their participation in the work force between 1900 and 1980. On the contrary, health probably improved. It seems more likely that rising lifetime wages, wealth, social security, and pension benefits have made retirement an attainable goal for most workers. Changing tastes have made retirement more attractive as well. Some analysts have suggested that retirees justify their retirement by reference to poor health, but that the principal motivation for retirement is a taste for greater leisure combined with the wealth and pension resources to indulge it.

Economic research conducted in the 1970s and early 1980s has confirmed the importance of wealth, pensions, and social security in determining the age of retirement. Even the most elaborate economic models, however, explain only a small share of the observed variation in retirement ages. After controlling for the effects of wages, pension availability, social security, and other financial variables, most analysts typically find that self-reported health status explains some significant part of the remaining variation in retirement age.[4] General trends in lifetime wealth, social security, pensions, and tastes may explain the historical tendency for men to retire at earlier ages, but individual differences in health status continue to play an important role in explaining differences in retirement age within any given birth cohort.

In view of the important effect of health on retirement, it is reasonable to ask what factors affect health and the capacity to work. This question has taken on added significance in recent years as the nation considers fundamental reforms in the social security program. Such reforms have become necessary to protect the solvency of the system as the birthrate and the rate of productivity growth have fallen below their historical levels. One reform adopted in 1983 was a proposal to raise the normal age of retirement from age 65, where it has stood since 1935, to age 67. This reform will occur gradually and will not be fully implemented until 2022. Its effect will be to reduce significantly retirement benefits payable to

---

4. See, for example, Richard V. Burkhauser and Joseph F. Quinn, "Is Mandatory Retirement Overrated? Evidence from the 1970s," *Journal of Human Resources*, vol. 18 (Summer 1983), pp. 337–58; and Peter A. Diamond and Jerry A. Hausman, "The Retirement and Unemployment Behavior of Older Men," and Gary Burtless and Robert A. Moffitt, "The Effect of Social Security Benefits on the Labor Supply of the Aged," in Henry J. Aaron and Gary Burtless, eds., *Retirement and Economic Behavior* (Brookings, 1984), pp. 97–134 and 135–74, respectively.

workers who retire before age 67. Nearly all workers now begin receiving social security benefits well before that age, with an important fraction receiving benefits at age 62, the earliest age at which benefits are payable. Because of health impairments, many workers who start collecting benefits at age 62 might have scant ability to postpone their retirement if the normal retirement age were gradually raised. Hence the rise in the normal retirement age will result in sharply lower retirement incomes for these workers.

The purpose of this paper is to identify and estimate the effects of factors that contribute to health impairment and work limitations among older male workers. Four different measures of impairment will be used. Three are subjective self-assessments of health status; the fourth, mortality, is a cruder but far less subjective measure. A major focus of the paper is the association between a worker's industrial and occupational attachment and his health and work status as he enters old age. In examining the relation between health and work status, it seems natural to concentrate on the effects of industry and occupation. If certain lines of work cause more rapid deterioration in health or require greater physical well-being, there may be good reasons to adjust the compensation system—including social security retirement benefits—to reflect this fact. For example, the normal or early retirement age could be adjusted to permit earlier retirement in arduous lines of work.

It seems clear that a worker's industrial and occupational attachment can affect his health status. Industries such as coal mining and chemical production pose well-known threats to health and worker safety. We also know that different types of work require varying levels of physical effort. Given the effects of aging, someone 60 years old might be capable of performing most jobs but incapable of engaging in some others, such as heavy construction or underground mining. Both effects of industrial and occupational attachment can influence a worker's self assessment of health. An older worker might report a health limitation because his job has caused an actual deterioration in his health and because it requires better health than is typical for a worker his age. Although it would be desirable to distinguish between these two effects, it is quite rare to obtain sufficiently precise data to do so. Given the ambiguity in most self-reported measures of health status, it is difficult to determine exactly how much particular industries and occupations may cause objective health indicators to deteriorate. By using a variety of self-reported indexes of health, as well as information on actual mortality, I attempt to investigate this problem here.

The plan of the remaining paper is as follows. In the first section I describe the evolving health status and work capacity of respondents in the RHS. This survey was the largest and most detailed panel study of retirement ever undertaken, and it includes extensive information on the health, mortality, and work history of respondents. I perform simple statistical tabulations to show the relationship of industry and occupation, on the one hand, to health and retirement patterns, on the other.

The second section outlines a statistical model of the effect of industrial and occupational attachment on a variety of measures of health status and work capacity. The model must be general enough to account for two features of the health data in the RHS. First, the variables measuring health status are categorical rather than continuous. Hence simple statistical procedures such as ordinary least-squares analysis cannot be applied. Second, the RHS provides data covering a ten-year period, with interview information giving respondents' health and work status about every two years. Because the health status of each member of the sample is correlated across periods, the observations in the six interviews cannot be treated as independent. To account for these two features of the data, I describe and estimate a multiperiod ordered-probit model. In addition to industry and occupation, the model takes account of the effects of other variables that have traditionally been thought to affect health: income, age, race, educational attainment, and marital status. The results of the estimation confirm the importance of most of these variables in determining health status and work capacity. An important pattern, however, is evident. Industry and occupation have a much stronger influence on work-related health measures than on measures that are less directly related to work capacity. Thus industry and occupation have a large and significant effect on health indexes that reflect whether health specifically restricts work capacity. They have a smaller effect on some other health measures, including mortality.

The third section examines the effect of self-reported health status as well as other variables on work and retirement. The reduced-form equation that predicts a respondent's work status also includes variables reflecting his industry and occupation. The results show an important direct effect of industry and occupation on the timing of retirement as well as an indirect effect through the influence of industry and occupation on health. The paper concludes by offering a brief summary.

Industry, Occupation, and Work Capacity

Many workers experience declining health as they enter their late 50s and early 60s. For some older men, declines in health are reported to be sufficiently severe to prevent work altogether. Before considering the relation between health and the ability to continue working, I will describe several measures of health available from the RHS. The survey provides a longitudinal panel of approximately 11,000 families headed by a person aged between 58 and 63 when the study began in 1969. Each family head was interviewed at two-year intervals through 1979, although the sample had shrunk considerably by that year because of the death or institutionalization of many original respondents. Individuals were asked a wide variety of detailed questions about their health, income, pension entitlements, work status, and employment history.[5] In addition, the RHS contains records of earnings history comprising annual wages covered by social security up through 1974 and social security payments and mortality data for the period 1968–79. In this paper I use data on the 8,131 married and unmarried men who were originally interviewed in 1969. Because of sample attrition, data from fewer than six interviews will be available for some men.[6]

The RHS interviews contain a variety of data that can potentially be used to measure a respondent's health status. In addition to a series of direct questions on the respondent's health, the interviews contain detailed questions about hospitalization, physician expenses, and other medical outlays. In this study I investigate four basic measures of health status—three that are based on direct questions about the quality of a respondent's health, and one reflecting each respondent's mortality experience. Data on hospitalization and medical outlays were not used because respondents faced a wide range of prices for medical care as a result of widely varying health insurance plans. Hence differences in consumption of health care might reflect systematic differences in copayment rates as well as underlying differences in the quality of health.

5. See Lola M. Irelan, "Retirement History Study: Introduction," in U.S. Department of Health, Education, and Welfare, Social Security Administration, Office of Research and Statistics, *Almost 65: Baseline Data from the Retirement History Study,* Research Report 49 (GPO, 1976).

6. The attrition rate was 11 percent by the second interview (in 1971), 21 percent by the third, 30 percent by the fourth, 39 percent by the fifth, and 46 percent by the seventh. Slightly more than half of the missing men were dead by the time of the sixth interview.

The simplest measure of health status used here is the response to the question "Are you handicapped or disabled?" The question was not directly linked to a respondent's work status, so there is no necessary correlation between possessing a handicap and being limited in one's capacity to work. The second health measure is based on the respondent's assessment of his health compared with that of others his age. Three responses were possible: "better than average," "average," and "worse than average." Again, these responses were not in any way linked to the respondent's work or retirement status. Responses were elicited from all men in the sample, regardless of their employment status. The third health measure reflects the respondent's assessment of his own work capacity. Men in the sample were asked if health limited their capacity to work. Those responding "yes" were asked whether this health limitation prevented full-time work. Men responding affirmatively to that question were asked whether the health limitation prevented work altogether. On the basis of responses to this series of questions, men can be divided into four groups: those without work limitations; those with limitations on the type of work performed, but not on the amount of work; those limited to part-time work; and those prevented from working. As mentioned above, the fourth measure of health was obtained from the data on mortality compiled by the Social Security Administration. Those data, which appear to be highly accurate, permit one to determine the date of death within about a month of its occurrence. In this study I simply consider whether a particular respondent was alive or dead as of each scheduled interview date (spring 1971, spring 1973, and so on.)

The first three measures described above have been criticized as indexes of health status. These criticisms have recently been summarized by Gloria J. Bazzoli, who points out that individuals may report poor health after they retire in order to justify reduced work effort. Retired men may tell an interviewer that they are in poor health because poor health is a more socially acceptable reason for retirement than the desire for increased leisure.[7] This problem may be more pronounced for early retirees than for men who retire around or after the normal retirement age, since retirement is more acceptable after that age. Of the three self-reported measures I consider, the respondent's assessment of health-related limitation on his capacity to work is probably the measure that invites the greatest skepti-

7. Gloria J. Bazzoli, "The Early Retirement Decision: New Empirical Evidence on the Influence of Health," *Journal of Human Resources*, vol. 20 (Spring 1985), pp. 214–34.

cism. It is certainly the measure that is most closely linked to current work status—two of the categorical responses are virtually indicators of work status as well as of perceived health status.

One way to circumvent the problems of self-reported health status is to rely on more objective measures of health. One such measure is mortality or age of death. If accurately measured, this index is undoubtedly objective, and it has begun to be used as an indicator of health in labor supply studies.[8] As a measure of health, however, mortality has several disadvantages. Many older men who die suffer no obvious work limitation up to the year or even the day of death. This would be true, for example, of men who die in accidents or of sudden heart attacks. Yet, some health problems, such as arthritis or partial paralysis, that impose stringent limits on work capacity may have no necessary effect on mortality. As an index of work capacity—or even of basic health—mortality therefore has important limitations. Men with poor mortality experience may have excellent health while alive, and men who live a long time may experience consistently poor health.

Whatever the shortcomings of the specific health measures investigated here, simple cross tabulations reveal that they are highly correlated. This correlation holds even if subjective health measures are compared with the presumably more objective measure provided by mortality. For example, of the 288 men who died before the second interview in 1971, half indicated in the 1969 survey that their health was worse than average for men their age. By contrast, fewer than 20 percent of men surviving past the 1971 interview reported worse than average health in the 1969 interview. Over 82 percent of men reporting better than average health in 1969 survived past the 1979 interview date; only 57 percent of men reporting worse than average health survived that long. Similarly, men reporting handicaps or work limitations had much higher death rates than men without disabilities or work limitations.

Table 1 provides a key to the terms and abbreviations for industrial and occupational categories used in subsequent tabulations. Table 2 contains summary statistics showing how health status varies among different industries and occupations with respect to the health indexes described

8. See Kathryn H. Anderson and Richard V. Burkhauser, "The Retirement-Health Nexus: A New Measure of an Old Puzzle," *Journal of Human Resources*, vol. 20 (Summer 1985), pp. 315–30; and Donald O. Parsons, "The Male Labour Force Participation Decision: Health, Reported Health, and Economic Incentives," *Economica*, vol. 49 (February 1982), pp. 81–91.

Table 1. Key to Industrial and Occupational Classifications

Term or abbreviation	Classification[a]
Agriculture	Agriculture, forestry, and fishing
Mining	Same
Construction	Same
Manufacturing	Same
Transportation	Transportation, communications, and other public utilities
Trade	Wholesale and retail trade
Finance	Finance, insurance, and real estate
Business	Business and repair services
Personal srv.	Personal services
Entertainment	Entertainment and recreational services
Professional or prof. (ind.)	Professional and related services
Pub. admin.	Public administration
Professional or prof. (occ.)	Professional, technical, and kindred workers
Farmers	Farmers and farm managers
Managers	Managers and administrators except farm managers
Clerical	Clerical and kindred workers
Sales	Sales workers
Craftsmen	Craftsmen and kindred workers
Operative	Operatives
Cfts. and opr.	Craftsmen, operatives, and kindred workers
Private h'hold	Private household workers
Service	Service workers except private household workers
Srv. and h'hold	Private household and service workers
Farm labor	Farm laborers and farm foremen
Nonfarm labor	Laborers, except farm laborers
Laborer	Farm laborers, farm foremen, and nonfarm laborers

a. Classifications are those used at the time the Retirement History Study (RHS) was first administered (1969).

above. Industries and occupations are described in accord with the standard two-digit classification current at the time the RHS was originally administered (1969). Each worker who responded to the relevant questions has been assigned to a single industry and a single occupation on the basis of the job he had held for the longest time up through the 1969 interview. The 1969 interview collected information on up to three jobs—a worker's current job, his previous job, and his longest-lasting job if that job was different from either of the other two. (For 50 percent of the respondents, the longest-lasting job was the job held in 1969; for 30 percent, it was the job held previously; and for the remaining 20 percent, it was a job held before the current or immediately previous job.) Note that by 1969 some men would not have been working in the industry or occupation in which they held their longest-lasting job.

Column 1 of table 2 shows the percentage of workers from each industry and occupation reporting a handicap or disability in the 1969 survey.

Table 2. Indicators of Health Impairment
Percent

Industry and occupation[a]		Handicapped or disabled, 1969 (1)	Worse than average health, 1969 (2)	Some health limit to working, 1969 (3)	Ever leave because of ill health, 1965–79 (4)	Dead by 1979 interview date (5)
Industry						
Agriculture	(n = 934)	30.7	27.4	44.1	31.4	21.4
Mining	(n = 182)	40.1	37.4	49.5	42.9	34.1
Construction	(n = 745)	32.9	24.8	38.7	29.9	28.7
Manufacturing	(n = 2,502)	27.4	24.3	32.9	26.3	26.7
Transportation	(n = 784)	27.8	24.6	32.9	24.9	21.6
Trade	(n = 1,150)	25.9	22.1	34.0	23.9	27.0
Finance	(n = 248)	23.8	16.9	30.6	17.7	26.6
Business	(n = 174)	28.7	23.0	36.8	24.1	28.7
Personal srv.	(n = 187)	25.7	22.5	33.7	29.9	27.8
Entertainment	(n = 50)	28.0	26.0	36.0	22.0	42.0
Professional	(n = 479)	23.4	16.9	24.8	15.0	23.0
Pub. admin.	(n = 496)	25.4	22.2	33.7	23.6	20.2
Occupation						
Professional	(n = 679)	20.5	13.8	19.6	12.2	21.1
Farmers	(n = 700)	29.6	25.4	43.4	28.3	21.4
Managers	(n = 1,308)	22.6	16.7	29.1	16.1	23.3
Clerical	(n = 405)	24.7	21.5	30.6	19.3	24.0
Sales	(n = 280)	20.7	17.9	32.1	20.4	28.9
Craftsmen	(n = 1,753)	27.7	22.9	33.6	26.9	25.5
Operative	(n = 1,595)	32.6	29.5	39.8	33.2	29.4
Private h'hold	(n = 14)	21.4	28.6	35.7	35.7	21.4
Service	(n = 429)	30.5	28.7	38.0	30.8	26.8
Farm labor	(n = 181)	35.9	37.0	49.2	38.7	20.4
Nonfarm labor	(n = 579)	35.8	33.5	43.7	38.7	29.2
Overall average		27.8	20.4	35.0	25.9	25.6

Source: Author's tabulations based on the 8,131 male respondents in the RHS.
a. The number *n* of respondents within each category (see the text) appears in parentheses.

The second column shows the percentage reporting health worse than the average for men their age (recall that respondents were 58 to 63 years old in 1969). The third column gives the percentage of men who had at least some health-imposed limit on their work capacity in 1969. For some of these men the health limit might have prevented full-time or even part-time work. Results presented in columns 1–3 are based solely on health information collected in the 1969 survey. Data from the later surveys were in general consistent with these patterns. Column 4 shows the percentage of workers who indicated on at least one of the six interviews administered between 1969 and 1979 that they had left a previous job for health reasons. The job left was probably—though not necessarily—in the industry and occupation of the worker's longest-lasting job. The last column provides information on mortality in each industry and occupation.

The statistics in table 2 are consistent with the view that industry and occupation have a systematic effect on both subjective and objective measures of health status. Although the alternative measures of health status do not distinguish identically between high- and low-risk industries and occupations, a few industries and occupations stand out consistently as posing greater threats to worker health and work capacity. Agriculture, mining, and construction are industries that appear to pose greater than average risks to an individual's work capacity. Mining, construction, and entertainment also pose serious risks to longevity. Among occupations, farmers and farm and nonfarm laborers seem to be at greater risk of suffering significant work limitations, whereas professional, technical, and kindred workers only rarely report health limits to work and experience lower than average death rates. Variations in health among different industries and occupations are more pronounced in columns 3 and 4 than in columns 1, 2, or 5 of the table. Note that the health limits reported in columns 3 and 4 are much more directly related to an individual's specific job requirements than are the measures in columns 1, 2, and 5. This pattern suggests that industry and occupation are somewhat less important in determining a worker's "objective" health status than in affecting the minimal health standards required for continued work.

Even though industry and occupation have less pronounced effects on objective than on subjective work-related indicators, the differences in mortality among industries and occupations remain quite striking. The odds of surviving two years, four years, six years, eight years, and ten years after the 1969 survey were considerably smaller for men in mining and construction than for men in professional industries and public administration. Similarly, the survival probabilities of operatives and nonfarm laborers were markedly worse than those for managers or professional, technical, and kindred workers.

It is tempting to attribute the observed differences in mortality to the effects of industry and occupation, but this inference is not warranted. Men attracted to different lines of work might have systematically different life chances before they begin the first day on their jobs. Average educational attainment, race, and rate of pay also vary among industrial and occupational categories. Because each of these factors may affect health status quite independently of industrial and occupational attachment, any conclusions about the net effect of industrial and occupational attachment on mortality should be deferred.

The health and mortality statistics displayed in table 2 can usefully be compared with retirement patterns observed among industries and occupations. Table 3 shows the retirement experience of men by industry and occupation. Retirement is defined in this table as a discontinuous drop in labor supply. For most men there was a definite age at which hours suddenly drop below the lowest level that could be considered full-time

Table 3. Retirement Experience by Industry and Occupation
Percent

Industry and occupation	Retired by		
	Age 60	Age 62	Age 65
Industry			
Agriculture	18.8	33.3	64.0
Mining	37.2	54.9	88.6
Construction	23.5	41.0	81.4
Manufacturing	19.8	38.7	82.1
Transportation	18.8	36.7	84.6
Trade	19.6	32.0	69.5
Finance	17.3	32.0	69.5
Business	20.4	34.8	75.7
Personal srv.	19.8	32.4	67.7
Entertainment	22.4	35.6	63.2
Professional	11.0	22.1	59.3
Pub. admin.	27.3	45.2	76.9
Occupation			
Professional	12.4	27.2	63.8
Farmers	16.1	28.9	61.9
Managers	16.3	30.4	69.3
Clerical	18.3	36.1	78.6
Sales	16.9	30.9	70.0
Craftsmen	20.3	37.0	79.9
Operative	23.5	41.9	83.3
Private h'hold	30.8	46.2	75.0
Service	22.7	39.2	77.3
Farm labor	28.3	48.3	70.4
Nonfarm labor	29.9	48.7	86.9
Overall average	20.0	36.5	75.9

Source: Author's tabulations based on the 8,131 male respondents in the RHS.

employment, here assumed to be thirty hours per week. For men who were involuntarily unemployed or who worked an indeterminate number of hours during a particular survey, I used information from the immediately preceding and succeeding interviews to determine whether retirement had occurred. Some workers resumed full-time work after a spell of retirement. For these men I defined the retirement age as the age of the first drop in work effort. Statistics displayed in table 3 show the fraction of men attached to a particular industry or occupation who had retired by ages 60, 62, and 65.[9]

In a significant number of industries and occupations, the frequency of early retirement seems linked to high mortality rates and to a high reported incidence of health limitations on work. For example, retirement occurred earlier in mining and construction than in other industries, and workers in those two industries had relatively high mortality rates and comparatively poor self-reported health. Similarly, nonfarm laborers and operatives retired earlier than average and had poorer reported health and survival rates. Early retirement and poor health are also linked in the case of farm laborers. At the other extreme, men engaged in professional industries and in professional, technical, and kindred occupations retired much later than average and appear to have enjoyed consistently better health than did men in other industries and occupations.

The variation in retirement patterns appears roughly consistent with other indicators of work capacity among industries and occupations. In the next section, I describe and estimate a formal statistical model of health and work capacity and of the effects of industrial and occupational attachment.

Statistical Model of Health Status

The indicators of health status used in this study are all categorical variables. That is, in describing their health, RHS respondents were permitted to choose among two to four categorical responses. For each indicator of health status there is a natural ranking of the categorical responses in terms of the underlying quality of a respondent's health. Suppose I_{it}^* designates the (unobserved) underlying degree of health impairment for

9. The statistics in table 3 overstate somewhat the fraction of men retired at each age because of the way in which missing data were treated. This overstatement should have no effect, however, on the pattern of retirement by industry and occupation.

the ith man in the tth time period. If there are three categorical health responses—say $H = 0$, 1, and 2, corresponding to "good," "average," and "poor"—then it is natural to assume that different values of I_{it}^* will be associated with different categorical responses. In particular, for levels of impairment I_{it}^* lower than a threshold value α_1, a respondent will identify himself in cateogry 0; for levels above α_1 but below the threshold α_2, he will identify himself in category 1; and for values above α_2, he will identify himself in category 2. (I ignore for a moment that the threshold values α_1 and α_2 might differ among individuals.) This relation between the continuous underlying index I^* and categorical responses can obviously be generalized to accommodate an indefinitely large number of ranked responses.

The level of a worker's impairment at a given time is affected by a variety of factors, as mentioned above. Age, education, race, marital status, and income, as well as industrial and occupational attachment, are variables widely believed to affect health. Even if all these variables were identical in a given sample, however, one would still observe variations in reported health. These variations arise from two sources. There are time-persistent differences in individual health, even controlling for the effects of observed variables. These persistent, random differences among men give rise to an individual-specific error term, μ_i. In addition, individual men may experience random fluctuations in underlying health, giving rise to a second error term ν_{it}, which varies both among individuals and over time for an individual.

The relation of the categorical health responses to these various factors and to the level of impairment can be summarized as follows:

$$
\begin{aligned}
I_{it}^* &= X_{it}\beta + \mu_i + \nu_{it} \\
&= X_{it}\beta + \epsilon_{it}
\end{aligned}
$$

(1)
$$
\begin{aligned}
H_{it} &= 0 \quad \text{if} \quad I_{it}^* \leq \alpha_1 \\
&= 1 \quad \text{if} \quad \alpha_1 < I_{it}^* \leq \alpha_2 \\
&= 2 \quad \text{if} \quad I_{it}^* > \alpha_2,
\end{aligned}
$$

where X_{it} is a vector of explanatory variables and β a vector of coefficients. (Some variables in X_{it}, such as race, remain constaint over time for a given individual; others, such as age, will vary.) If ϵ_{it} is distributed normally and observations are available for only a single period, equation

1 is a simple ordered-probit model.[10] Two normalizing assumptions are needed to yield a unique set of parameters for the model. The usual assumptions, which will be adopted here, are that $\alpha_1 = 0$ and $\sigma_\epsilon^2 = 1$. If data are available from more than one period, it is possible to determine the fraction of variance in ϵ_{it} that is due to individual-specific effects, denoted by μ_i, and the fraction that is due to purely transitory random effects, denoted by v_{it}. The individual-specific effect gives rise to a correlation between successive values of ϵ_{it}. The correlation term, denoted ρ, can be estimated if repeated observations on H_{it} exist for the same individual.

The RHS interviews provide up to six observations for each man in the sample. Because of death, not all men responded to all of the interviews, and some men failed to respond to interviews even though they remained alive. These problems can be handled in a natural way within the statistical model just outlined. Death is itself an indicator of health status—an extreme value indicator. To the three health states already described ($H = 0, 1, 2$), it is convenient to add a new category, $H = 3$, equivalent to death after the previous survey. Death occurs if $I_{it}^* > \alpha_3$. For men who were alive but did not respond in the tth period, $H_{it} = 4$, it follows that $I_{it}^* \leq \alpha_3$. Thus

$$(2) \quad \begin{aligned} H_{it} &= 0 &&if \quad I_{it}^* \leq \alpha_1 &&(\text{"good" health})\\ &= 1 &&if \quad \alpha_1 < I_{it}^* \leq \alpha_2 &&(\text{"average" health})\\ &= 2 &&if \quad \alpha_2 < I_{it}^* \leq \alpha_3 &&(\text{"poor" health})\\ &= 3 &&if \quad I_{it}^* > \alpha_3 &&(\text{deceased})\\ &= 4 &&if \quad I_{it}^* \leq \alpha_3 &&(\text{"alive but missing" health status}). \end{aligned}$$

Men who survived past the 1979 survey provided six observations on H_{it}. (Even if a respondent failed to respond to a particular survey, that he survived past that interview date provides some information on the state of his health at that time.) Men who died before 1979 supplied observations on H_{it} for each period while they remained alive plus an observation for the first interview date after their deaths. (Thus, someone who died in 1974—after the third interview but before the fourth—provides health status information for four periods.)

A simple diagram will illustrate the assumptions concerning the population distribution of health impairment. The top panel in figure 1 shows the

10. See Richard D. McKelvey and William Zavoina, "A Statistical Model for the Analysis of Ordinal Level Dependent Variables," *Journal of Mathematical Sociology*, vol. 4, no. 1 (1975), pp. 103–20.

Figure 1. Distribution of Health Impairment under Alternative Models

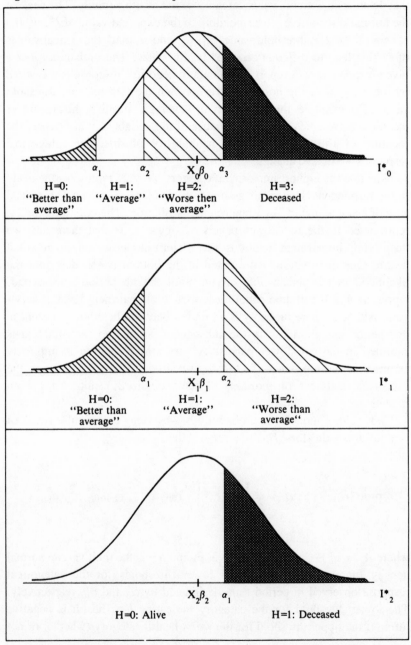

probability distribution of the impairment index I^* under the assumption that death is an extreme value category of the health variable. The peak of the normal distribution, corresponding to the expected value of I^*, occurs at $I^* = X_0\beta_0$. The threshold values α_1, α_2, and α_3 mark the critical values of I^* that lead to different reported health states. The probability that a given respondent will report a particular categorical response is measured by the area under the normal curve between the two relevant threshold values. For example, the probability of "average" health is the area under the curve between α_1 and α_2. As values of the variables in X_0 change, the location of the curve—and the probability of different categorical responses—will also change.

Note that the highest impairment category, $H = 3$, represents the death of the respondent. Under this assumption, death is conceived as a special case of a single underlying impairment distribution. The other possibility, represented in the two lower panels of figure 1, is that there are two underlying impairment relations that determine observed or reported health. One distribution, represented in the bottom panel, describes the likelihood that a person will survive until the tth period; the second, represented in the middle panel, describes the impairment level of survivors. Although there probably is a relation between health impairment in one period and mortality in the subsequent period, no such relation is assumed in the two lower panels. A very strong relation is implicitly assumed in the top panel. To test the sensitivity of my estimates to the statistical treatment of mortality, I have obtained results using both models.

Under either model, the probability of observing a particular string of health status indicators $(H_{i1}, \ldots, H_{iT})$ is then

$$(3) \quad \text{prob}(H_{i1}, \ldots, H_{iT}) = \int_{A_{i1}}^{B_{i1}} \ldots \int_{A_{iT}}^{B_{iT}} (\epsilon_{i1}, \ldots, \epsilon_{iT}) d\epsilon_{i1} \ldots d\epsilon_{iT},$$

where $A_{it} = \alpha_{it}^L - X_{it}\beta$, $\beta_{it} = \alpha_{it}^U - X_{it}\beta$, and $f(\cdot)$ is the multivariate normal density function. The upper and lower thresholds for the categorical response observed in period t are designated by α_{it}^U and α_{it}^L, respectively. The lower threshold for the category indicating *best* health is negative infinity; the upper threshold for the *worst* health category (whether or not it is death) is positive infinity; remaining threshold values are given in equation 2. The log-likelihood function for the model is

(4) $$L = \sum_{i=1}^{N} \log \left[\text{prob} \left(H_{i1}, \ldots, H_{iT} \right) \right].$$

Although the likelihood function appears deceptively simple, its maximization is quite formidable because of the T-fold integrals in probability statement 3. J. S. Butler and Robert Moffitt have proposed and implemented a computationally tractable method to evaluate the multiperiod probit problem, which is closely related to the model proposed here.[11] Their computer program was adapted to maximize the more complex likelihood function in equations 2–4.[12]

Before empirical results can be considered, an alternative interpretation of the effects of the X-variables on reported health status merits attention. Industry, occupation, and other exogenous variables are nominally represented in the specification by variables in the vector X_{it}. Such inclusion might suggest that these exogenous variables are assumed solely to be determinants of the unobserved individual impairment index I_i^*. That is, if X_i^j is the dummy variable representing occupation j, then β^j is the presumed effect of that occupation on a worker's underlying impairment index. The specification does not, however, identify the effect of occupation on impairment separately from the effects of occupation on the threshold values $\alpha_1, \alpha_2, \ldots$. It is conceivable, for example, that miners suffer much more frequent impairment than average, which would be confirmed by a significantly positive estimate of β^j. But it is equally plausible that miners establish significantly lower thresholds when categorizing their own health status. A higher fraction of them may describe their health as "poor" even though the true distribution of their health is no different from that in other industries. With reference to figure 1, miners might use

---

11. J. S. Butler and Robert A. Moffitt, "A Computationally Efficient Quadrature Procedure for the One-Factor Multinomial Probit Model," *Econometrica*, vol. 50 (May 1982), pp. 761–64. Robin C. Sickles and Paul Taubman have also adapted the Butler-Moffitt model in a paper treating a problem similar to the one analyzed here; see "An Analysis of the Health and Retirement Status of the Elderly," NBER Working Paper 1459 (Cambridge, Mass.: National Bureau of Economic Research, September 1984).

12. Butler and Moffitt generously provided me with their original computer code. Any errors in adapting it for this paper are of course my sole responsibility.

threshold values, or αs, that lie to the left of those used by workers in other industries. The model I estimate cannot distinguish between these two explanations of β^j. Objective measures of health, such as lung capacity or mortality, are of course not subject to this criticism.

The statistical model described above was used to estimate the effect of industry, occupation, and other relevant variables on the four measures of health and work capacity described in the previous section. In addition to dummy variables for most of the industrial and occupational classifications in the RHS, the basic specification included the following variables. Race is a dummy variable that takes the value of unity for black and of zero for white members of the sample. After some specification search, educational attainment was divided into four ranges: zero to seven years of schooling ($LT8$); exactly eight years of schooling ($EQ8$); nine to thirteen years of schooling; and fourteen or more years of schooling ($GT13$). (The coefficients on other variables did not appear to be sensitive to the exact specification of educational attainment.) Dummy variables were created for the first, second, and fourth categories of schooling, and these were entered into the basic specification. I hypothesize that better-educated men enjoy better health because education may train them to be better consumers of food, medicine, medical care, and other health inputs. Moreover, according to the well-known human capital paradigm, investment in one's health represents investment in human capital. Men with relatively high educational investments have a high revealed preference for investment in human capital. Hence, there may be a correlation between investment in education and investment in health capital.

Two variables were created to reflect the income from and the quality of the job held by each respondent. The first of these is potential annual earnings (measured in 1969 dollars). The purpose of this variable was to measure the typical preretirement earnings a respondent could hope to earn in 1969. The RHS provides at least four sources of information with which to measure this variable: a worker's current rate of earnings in 1969 if he was a full-time worker in that year; his rate of earnings on his preretirement job if that job provided full-time work; his total annual earnings in 1968 if he was a full-time worker in that year; and his annual earning levels from 1951 through 1974 as reported in the Social Security Administration's earning records. Information from these sources was combined with data about a respondent's retirement age to produce the best estimate of 1969 potential earnings. Even with these multiple sources of data, it appears that potential earnings for 389 of the RHS respondents were below

$1,000 per year—too low to be plausible for a preretirement worker. Either the data were exceptionally poor in these cases or the men had not worked in regular paid employment for several years. Whatever the reason for the low earnings, these observations were excluded from the estimation.

A second indication of the quality of a worker's job is his coverage by a private pension. If a worker was covered by a pension on either his current (1969) or his longest job, the pension dummy variable was set equal to unity. Conceivably, workers covered by a pension plan and eligible to receive a pension might be inclined to retire earlier than uncovered workers. According to the Bazzoli hypothesis (see footnote 5), those workers retiring early—possibly as a result of the availability of a pension—might report poor health to rationalize their early withdrawal from the labor market. The reason for including this variable, however, is not to detect questionable health reports but to provide an additional indication of the quality of a worker's job and the level of his permanent income. Coverage by a pension tends to be associated with other valuable fringe benefits— health and life insurance, disability plans, and so on. A pension might also be associated with better than average working conditions. An employer paternalistic enough to offer pensions might be concerned with other aspects of employment conditions. Finally, the availability of pensions— like the receipt of higher direct wage payments—raises the permanent income of workers. If the goods and services associated with obtaining better health are normal goods, then higher permanent income will lead to increased purchase of such goods.

The basic specification also includes each man's current age and marital status. Note that the age of each respondent rises by two years between interviews. Thus, if there is a steady rise in health impairment over successive interviews, the effect will be captured by the coefficient on age. The effects of sudden changes in health for particular individuals are captured in the disturbance term v_{it}. (The average values of all independent variables are reported in the appendix table.)

Statistical results from the maximization of equation 4 are reported in table 4. The results were obtained using 7,742 (or 95 percent) of the 8,131 men originally enrolled in the RHS. Slightly less than 5 percent of the original sample was excluded for reasons mentioned above. Of course, the RHS sample is representative only of the population of men that survived until ages 58 to 63. Hence the coefficients do not reflect the effects of income, industry, occupation, and other variables on men born between

Table 4. Multiperiod Ordered-Probit Estimates of Health-Impairment Models

Parameter or variable	Health disability (1)	Health compared with others (2)	Health limitation (3)
Constant	−4.838	−1.120	−4.526
	(−46.97)	(−12.10)	(−49.35)
Race	−0.052	−0.007	0.035
	(−1.99)	(−0.03)	(1.58)
Education LT8[a]	0.062	0.213	0.149
	(3.13)	(12.62)	(9.05)
Education EQ8[b]	−0.016	0.110	0.044
	(−0.92)	(7.49)	(2.95)
Education GT13[c]	−0.036	−0.094	−0.077
	(−1.59)	(−5.43)	(−3.95)
Potential earnings	−0.132	−0.153	−0.162
	(−10.74)	(−15.12)	(−14.42)
Pension	−0.058	−0.092	−0.136
	(−3.76)	(−7.46)	(−10.53)
Agriculture	−0.094	−0.059	−0.110
	(−2.57)	(−2.03)	(−3.63)
Mining	0.079	0.242	0.242
	(1.63)	(5.56)	(5.62)
Construction	0.021	0.073	0.101
	(0.74)	(3.16)	(4.20)
Manufacturing	−0.033	−0.038	−0.013
	(−1.50)	(−2.21)	(−0.69)
Transportation	−0.073	0.021	−0.043
	(−2.59)	(0.90)	(−1.87)
Personal srv.	−0.090	−0.128	−0.151
	(−1.99)	(−3.43)	(−4.19)
Prof. (ind.)	0.002	0.030	−0.033
	(0.07)	(1.06)	(−1.04)
Pub. admin.	−0.052	−0.021	0.034
	(−1.60)	(−0.80)	(1.21)
Prof. (occ.)	−0.051	−0.061	−0.119
	(−1.11)	(−1.69)	(−3.06)
Managers	0.009	−0.034	−0.074
	(0.24)	(−1.10)	(−2.31)
Clerical	−0.003	−0.011	−0.061
	(−0.07)	(−0.32)	(−1.58)
Sales	−0.042	−0.094	−0.052
	(−0.83)	(−2.43)	(−1.28)
Craftsmen	0.050	−0.007	0.006
	(1.32)	(−0.22)	(0.19)
Operative	0.087	0.086	0.066
	(2.25)	(2.75)	(2.06)

Table 4   (continued)

Parameter or variable	Health disability (1)	Health compared with others (2)	Health limitation (3)
Srv. and h'hold	0.055	0.067	0.061
	(1.20)	(1.76)	(1.62)
Laborer	0.066	0.141	0.091
	(1.80)	(4.68)	(2.99)
Age	0.070	0.026	0.070
	(48.74)	(19.69)	(53.74)
Married	−0.029	0.001	−0.024
	(−1.68)	(0.09)	(−1.59)
α_1^d	1.327	1.281	0.461
	(133.62)	(204.83)	(89.47)
α_2^d	...	2.196	0.763
	...	(207.98)	(128.46)
α_3^d	...	...	1.608
	...	...	(165.48)
ρ^e	0.442	0.347	0.405
Value of likelihood function	−20,538.17	−33,675.44	−34,187.44

Source: Author's tabulations based on the RHS. Parameter estimates were based on 7,742 male respondents in the RHS. Asymptotic t-statistics appear in parentheses beneath coefficient estimates.
a. Zero to seven years of schooling.
b. Exactly eight years of schooling.
c. Fourteen or more years of schooling.
d. Threshold value of health impairment.
e. Coefficient of correlation (see text).

1906 and 1911 who failed to survive until 1969. (Of men born in those years who survived to age 25, approximately one quarter did not survive to 1969.)

The three columns in table 4 show results based on three different definitions of health status. The first column is based on the following health categories: (1) not handicapped, (2) handicapped or disabled, and (3) deceased. The second column is based on the respondent's assessment of his health compared with that of others his age: (1) better than average, (2) average, (3) worse than average, and (4) deceased. The dependent variable in the last column is the respondent's assessment of the degree of his health limitation: (1) no limitation, (2) some limitation, (3) limited to part-time work, (4) prevented from working altogether, and (5) deceased.

Before discussion of the estimated effects of industry and occupation, it is worth considering the effects of the other variables included. Race does not have a consistent effect on the three measures of health status. Blacks are less likely than whites to have handicaps or disabilities but more likely to report that health limits their ability to work, with other variables controlled. In contrast, educational attainment has a statistically significant and consistent effect on the three health measures examined. The least-educated respondents have significantly greater health impairment, and the most-educated have significantly less. Not surprisingly, the age of a respondent is one of the most important determinants of health status. Older respondents experience greater impairment than younger ones under all three definitions of health status. This is partially, although not entirely, due to the effect of age on mortality, since mortality is included as a category of poor health in all three health measures. The marital status of a respondent has only a modest effect on his health. There is weak evidence that married men may suffer less impairment than unmarried men, with the influence of other factors controlled.

As hypothesized, a respondent's potential earnings have a strong negative effect on the probability of impairment. Men who have typically held better-paid jobs are less likely to be impaired under any of the three definitions of health status. Because potential earnings are measured using a worker's preretirement earning level, the estimated coefficient of earnings is not contaminated by the effects of health-induced early retirement. It is likely, however, that workers in chronically poor health were limited in their earnings even before retirement. The amount of simultaneity bias arising from this relation is unknown. Pension coverage is also an important determinant of health impairment. Men covered on a job by an employer-provided pension plan are significantly less likely to report an impairment than are men who have held jobs not covered by pensions. The negative relation between pension coverage and health impairment suggests that men holding jobs with more generous fringe benefits are more likely to maintain good health in older age. It is reasonable to infer that generous fringe benefits provide the same beneficial effects on health as do higher direct money wages.

The pattern of coefficients on the dummy variables for industry and occupation differs somewhat among the three definitions of health status. Preliminary specification search revealed that five of the industrial categories and two of the occupational categories usually had very similar effects on impairment.[13] These categories are combined and treated as the

13. The five industrial categories are (1) wholesale and retail trade, (2) finance, insurance, and real estate, (3) business repair and service, (4) entertainment and recreation, and (5) no reported industrial attachment. The two occupational categories are farmers and no reported occupational attachment. Only about 2 percent of respondents failed to report the industry or occupation of their longest-lasting job.

excluded category in my specification. In addition, service workers and private household workers were combined into a single category, as were farm and nonfarm laborers. Several of the industrial and occupational categories have a consistent and usually significant effect on all three measures of impairment. Men engaged in agricultural and personal service industries have less likelihood of health impairment, and men in the mining and construction industries have much greater likelihood of impairment, controlling for other influences on health. Among occupations, men in professional and technical jobs have less impairment, and those who work as operatives or as farm and nonfarm laborers have significantly higher chances of impairment. Industrial and occupational attachment usually has a greater effect on the degree of work limitation (column 3) than it does on either disabilities (column 1) or on health compared with that of others (column 2). Moreover, more industries and occupations produce a significant effect on perceived work limitations. The identical distribution of underlying impairment produces a greater variation in the number of men who are capable of working in different industries and occupations, presumably because those industries and occupations impose different health standards determining the ability to continue working.

Table 5 provides some idea of the effects of industry and occupation on the health of an average man 62 years old. Health status is measured by the respondent's report of a health-related work limitation. Slightly more than 37 percent of respondents who had average characteristics reported some limitation to their ability to work at age 62. Column 1 of table 5 shows the direct effect of industry and occupation on a man with average characteristics in all other respects. Thus, a man in the mining industry who otherwise had the same "average" occupation, education, potential earnings, and other characteristics as other men in the RHS sample is 17.3 percent more likely than average to report a work limitation. (That is, he has a 54.7 percent chance of reporting a limitation compared with the 37.4 percent probability faced by an average man.) Column 2 shows the direct plus indirect effects of industry and occupation. I took account of several indirect effects here: the effect of industry on the distribution of occupations, the effect of occupation on the distribution of industries, and the effects of systematic differences in potential earnings and pension entitlements. For example, the mining industry has a systematically different occupational structure than do other industries. It also has a different average level of earnings and pension entitlements. These differences will, in turn, affect the average health status of miners, and they are taken into account in column 2. In a few industries—such as agriculture, manufactur-

Table 5. Effect of Industry and Occupation on Probability of Work Limitation in Men Aged 62
Percentage-point difference from mean

	Probability difference[a]	
	Excluding indirect effects	Including indirect effects
Industry or occupation	(1)	(2)
Agriculture	−5.1	0.3
Mining	17.3	18.8
Construction	5.0	6.7
Manufacturing	0.4	−0.1
Transportation	−0.4	0.1
Personal srv.	−11.2	−6.4
Prof. (ind.)	−1.6	−9.3
Pub. admin.	3.9	−0.2
Trade, finance, business, and entertainment	−1.0	−2.1
Prof. (occ.)	−7.5	−12.0
Managers	−3.9	−5.3
Clerical	−3.4	−4.3
Sales	−5.8	−6.4
Craftsmen	1.1	2.4
Operative	4.0	5.5
Srv. and h'hold	4.3	3.6
Laborer	5.3	7.0
Farmers	0.0	−0.9

Source: Author's estimates based on RHS data and coefficients in column 3 of table 4.
a. The average probability of reporting some work limitation at age 62 was 37.4 percent.

ing, transportation, and public administration—the indirect effects on health are large enough to reverse the direct effects. For a few industries and most occupations, the indirect effects merely reinforce the direct effects.

The differences between the most healthful and least healthful industries and occupations are quite wide. For example, a miner aged 62 is 50 percent more likely to suffer a work limitation than is an average worker (56.2 percent versus 37.4 percent), and he is twice as likely to suffer a work limitation than is a worker in a professional industry (56.2 percent versus 28.1 percent). Similarly, a worker in a professional occupation is one-third less likely to face a work limitation than is an average worker

(25.4 percent versus 37.4 percent), and he is 57 percent less likely to be limited than a laborer (25.4 percent versus 44.4 percent).

The results reported so far are sensitive to the special way in which I have treated mortality. This sensitivity is demonstrated in table 6, which shows the effect of altering the previous treatment of mortality. Column 1 of table 6 ("Health limitation 1") simply repeats the coefficients appearing in column 3 of table 4. Column 2 of table 6 ("Health limitation 2") shows how the estimates are affected if mortality experience is no longer treated as an extreme value of the dependent variable. Under the new definition, the four categories of response are (1) no limit to work, (2) some limit, (3) compelled to work part-time, and (4) health prevents work altogether. The pattern of coefficients remains essentially unchanged under this redefinition (only the coefficient on the transportation industry changes in sign), but the estimated effects of industry and occupation appear stronger and much more significant. For example, manufacturing and public administration are now found to have significant and positive effects on health impairment; clerical and sales occupations are found to cause significantly less impairment of health.

It is natural to ask whether the determinants of self-reported restrictions on work capacity are equally important in affecting more objective measures of health, such as mortality. The simple multiperiod probit model can be applied to answer this question. In each period there are two possibilities—the respondent may be alive or dead. Figure 1 showed the relation between this simple probit model and the ordered-probit models described earlier. The coefficients reported in column 1 of table 6 correspond to the model in the top panel of figure 1; coefficients in column 2 correspond to the model in the middle panel; and coefficients in column 3 correspond to the model represented in the bottom panel.[14]

The mortality function coefficients are listed in column 3 of table 6. Age, education, marital status, and a respondent's potential earning level are important determinants of mortality, and the sign of their effect is the same as for the self-reported measures of health status. In contrast, the effects of industrial and occupational attachment are much smaller than, and sometimes of the opposite sign to, their estimated effects under the more subjective health measures. With the effects of other variables con-

14. Estimates were based on the assumption that the error term in the equation predicting health status was not correlated with the error term in the equation predicting mortality.

Table 6. Multiperiod Ordered-Probit Estimates of Health-Impairment and Mortality Models

Parameter or variable	Health limitation 1 (1)	Health limitation 2 (2)	Mortality experience (3)
Constant	−4.526	−3.477	−4.765
	(−49.35)	(−36.61)	(−18.95)
Race	0.035	0.057	−0.014
	(1.58)	(2.78)	(−0.33)
Education LT8	0.149	0.269	0.034
	(9.05)	(16.82)	(1.14)
Education EQ8	0.043	0.074	. . .
	(2.95)	(4.96)	. . .
Education GT13	−0.077	−0.040	−0.070
	(−3.95)	(−2.02)	(−1.78)
Potential earnings	−0.162	−0.185	−0.124
	(−14.42)	(−15.99)	(−5.13)
Pension	−0.136	−0.193	−0.026
	(−10.53)	(−14.95)	(−0.99)
Agriculture	−0.110	−0.110	−0.211
	(−3.63)	(−3.79)	(−3.57)
Mining	0.242	0.466	0.077
	(5.62)	(11.38)	(1.00)
Construction	0.101	0.158	0.028
	(4.20)	(6.56)	(0.62)
Manufacturing	0.013	0.038	−0.013
	(0.69)	(2.01)	(−0.39)
Transportation	−0.043	0.018	−0.158
	(−1.87)	(0.76)	(−3.36)
Personal srv.	−0.151	−0.289	−0.031
	(−4.19)	(−7.69)	(−0.42)
Prof. (ind.)	−0.033	−0.016	−0.012
	(−1.04)	(−0.48)	(−0.19)
Pub. admin.	0.034	0.129	−0.144
	(1.21)	(4.56)	(−2.49)
Prof. (occ.)	−0.119	−0.204	−0.019
	(−3.06)	(−5.29)	(−0.25)
Managers	−0.074	−0.103	−0.045
	(−2.31)	(−3.31)	(−0.73)
Clerical	−0.061	−0.091	−0.017
	(−1.58)	(−2.35)	(−0.23)
Sales	−0.052	−0.157	0.033
	(−1.28)	(−3.86)	(0.42)
Craftsmen	0.006	0.031	−0.037
	(0.19)	(1.02)	(−0.60)
Operative	0.066	0.106	−0.029
	(2.06)	(3.41)	(−0.47)

Table 6 (continued)

Parameter or variable	Health limitation 1 (1)	Health limitation 2 (2)	Mortality experience (3)
Srv. and h'hold	0.060 (1.62)	0.113 (3.11)	−0.011 (−0.16)
Laborer	0.091 (2.99)	0.138 (4.66)	0.047 (0.78)
Age	0.070 (53.74)	0.054 (39.45)	0.049 (13.97)
Married	−0.024 (−1.59)	−0.033 (−2.19)	−0.069 (−2.30)
α_1	0.461 (89.47)	0.498 (88.36)	...
α_2	0.763 (128.46)	0.844 (126.37)	...
α_3	1.601 (165.48)	...	...
ρ	0.405	0.438	...
Value of likelihood function	−34,187.44	−25,970.37	−2,025.48

Source: Author's tabulations based on the RHS. Parameter estimates were based on 7,742 male respondents in the RHS. Asymptotic t-statistics appear in parentheses beneath coefficient estimates. "Education," α, and ρ are defined in table 4.

trolled, only agriculture, transportation, and public administration continue to have significant effects. Each of these industrial categories has significantly lower mortality rates than other industrial and occupational groups.[15]

The large differences between the coefficients in columns 2 and 3 of table 6 indicate that an objective health measure, such as mortality, is far less affected by industry and occupation than is a subjective health measure, such as the degree of perceived work limitation. This fact does not imply that respondents are inaccurately reporting their true work limitations. As pointed out in the introduction, mortality is not necessarily a good indicator of either health status or work capacity while one is alive. In addition, the pattern of coefficients in columns 1 and 2 of table 6 is consistent with the view that men in different industries and occupations may apply varying criteria when evaluating their capacity to continue

15. One can speculate that the low mortality rates reported in these industries are attributable to limitations in the social security mortality data used here. Some respondents who spent much or all of their careers in uncovered employment might not have had their deaths reported to the Social Security Administration.

working. These criteria may reflect objective assessments of the level of impairment that would prevent continued employment in different lines of work. In the next section, I consider the effect of perceived impairment on the actual work status of RHS respondents.

Self-reported Health Impairment and Work Status

A variety of job-related factors, including earnings, pension coverage, and industrial and occupational attachment, have been shown to be related to perceived health status. Past research studies have concluded that health status in turn exercises a major influence on the employment behavior of older workers. The net effect of industrial and occupational factors on the work behavior of older men therefore arises from both direct and indirect effects. Retirement patterns may differ because of the direct influence of industry and occupation. For example, pension plans and mandatory retirement rules differ systematically among industries and occupations, as do the tastes of workers and their employers. In addition, as already shown, industrial and occupational factors exercise an indirect influence through their effect on health and self-reported work capacity.

These direct and indirect effects can be summarized in a simple recursive model of health impairment and work status:

$$(5) \qquad I_{it}^* = X_{it}\beta + \epsilon_{it}$$
$$H_{it} = 0 \quad if \quad I_{it}^* \leq \alpha_1$$
$$= 1 \quad if \quad I_{it}^* > \alpha_1$$

$$(6) \qquad E_{it}^* = Z_{it}\gamma + \delta H_{it} + u_i + v_{it}$$
$$= Z_{it}\gamma + \delta H_{it} + e_{it}$$
$$W_{it} = 0 \quad if \quad E_{it}^* \leq \theta_1$$
$$= 1 \quad if \quad \theta_1 < E_{it}^* \leq \theta_2$$
$$= 2 \quad if \quad E_{it}^* > \theta_2.$$

Equation 5 is a simplified restatement of equation 2, and equation 6, which has an identical structure, determines the work status of older men. E_{it}^* is an unobserved variable that indexes the employment propensity of individual i in period t; Z is a vector of variables affecting employment and γ an associated vector of coefficients; δH_{it} is the effect of health status on the individual's employment propensity; and u_i and v_{it} are the individual-specific and time-varying disturbance terms, respectively. As in the models of health status, $e_{it} = u_i + v_{it}$ with $e \sim N(0,1)$. W_{it} denotes the work status of individual i in the tth period. I define three work states: full-time work ($W = 0$), part-time work ($W = 1$), and nonemployment ($W = 2$). Part-time work is defined as employment of greater than zero but less than thirty hours of work per week; θ_1 and θ_2 are threshold values of E^* equivalent to the αs in the previous models (for convenience, I use the normalization $\theta_1 = 0$). The likelihood function for equation 6 is identical in structure to equations 3 and 4.

The RHS provides detailed information with which to measure the work status of respondents over the period 1968–79. I measured the work status of respondents during each of the six survey weeks. Respondents who failed to complete the six surveys would, of course, have fewer than six periods of data. The definition of work status used here does not necessarily correspond to the definition of retirement used in the second section. Some respondents who were not employed during a particular survey week are not considered to have retired; they were temporarily unemployed. In contrast, some who were employed full-time might be defined as retired under the previous definition because there was evidence on some earlier survey that the worker had retired.

The variables included in Z to explain employment status are factors commonly believed to affect the work effort of older men. In addition to health status and the industrial and occupational variables described earlier, Z includes each worker's current age, educational attainment, potential 1968 earning level, and coverage by a pension plan either on his 1969 job or his longest-lasting job. Race was originally included in Z but was excluded in the final specification because it was found to have a negligible and statistically insignificant effect in preliminary work.

In addition, Z includes variables to capture the effects of social security on retirement. The first of these, corresponding to the level of social security entitlement, is the primary insurance amount (PIA) for which the respondent was eligible on his 56th birthday.[16] The early age was chosen so that the measure of social security entitlement would not be affected by the respondent's actual retirement (and employment) behavior over the 1969–79 period. The second social security variable, ΔPIA, measures the

16. The PIA is equivalent to a retiree's basic social security benefit if he begins collecting benefits at age 65 and is single. A worker's age of first collecting benefits and his number of dependents will affect the actual benefit for which he is eligible.

change in a worker's *PIA* entitlement (based on the 1968–69 social security formula) between ages 56 and 62 under the assumption that his annual earnings between those two ages would correspond to the potential earning level discussed earlier.[17] ΔPIA thus provides an index of the rate of gain in benefits a worker could expect to obtain if he continued working full-time. The level of benefits and the rate of change in benefits should affect the timing of retirement in a carefully specified model of retirement. To capture the special effects of social security on retirement around the ages of 62 and 65, when early benefits and normal benefits, respectively, are first payable, I have also included two additional variables. *AGE62* is equal to zero or the respondent's age minus 61.5 years, whichever is greater; *AGE65* is equal to zero or the respondent's age minus 64.5 years, whichever is greater.[18]

Finally, changes in the basic social security formula must be taken into account. Between the RHS interviews of 1969 and 1973, real social security benefits were raised approximately 20 percent. Hence younger workers in the RHS sample faced considerably different social security retirement incentives from those faced by older workers. I have tried to capture this effect by including dummy variables that designate two different age cohorts: *COH58–59* takes the value of unity for respondents aged 59 or less in the 1969 survey; *COH62–63* takes the value of unity for respondents aged 62 or more in the 1969 survey.[19] Note that these cohort variables will capture the effects of secular and cyclical influences in addition to the change in the social security formula. Between 1969 and 1975 cyclical unemployment rose from one of the lowest rates of the postwar period to one of the highest. Hence younger workers faced considerably worse employment prospects in their early to mid-60s than did workers in the oldest RHS cohort. The estimated coefficients on the cohort variables will capture this effect.

Column 1 in table 7 contains estimated coefficients for the model just described. Note that negative coefficients correspond to a greater propen-

17. Potential earnings were assumed to grow in real terms at 2.5 percent per year—the average observed in the sample.

18. For a graphical exposition of the economic theory of retirement, see Gary Burtless and Robert A. Moffitt, "Social Security, Earnings Tests, and Age at Retirement," *Public Finance Quarterly*, vol. 14 (January 1986), pp. 3–27.

19. For a much more careful structural specification of the effects of social security on retirement, see Burtless and Moffitt, "The Effect of Social Security Benefits"; and Gary Burtless, "Social Security, Unanticipated Benefit Increases, and the Timing of Retirement," *Review of Economic Studies* (forthcoming).

sity to work, positive coefficients to a greater propensity to retire. Educational attainment has a pronounced and statistically significant effect on employment. Men with low educational attainment are more likely to retire, and those with high attainments more likely to work full-time at any given age. Age itself has a very strong effect on employment, and the pattern of age coefficients is reasonable. The coefficient on the main age term is significant and positive, implying that the probability of working declines with age through age 61.5. After age 61.5 the probability of working drops even more sharply with age, and past age 64.5 the probability continues to fall but at a more gradual rate than over the age range from 61.5 to 64.5. The age-cohort effects are highly significant and of the expected pattern. Members of the older cohorts remain employed until ages later than those of men in the youngest cohort, presumably because of the social security benefit changes and unemployment trends alluded to above.

Two variables specifically reflect the generosity of social security. Both have the anticipated signs, but only one—ΔPIA—is statistically significant. The coefficient on that variable implies that workers expecting a faster rate of growth in their social security entitlements work longer than men expecting slow benefit growth. Not surprisingly, a worker's coverage by a pension plan is associated with a smaller probability of working at older ages. Not all men who are covered can expect to receive a pension at retirement because some men may be covered but not vested. For men who are vested and eligible to receive a pension, however, the potential pension usually constitutes an unambiguous incentive for aged workers to retire earlier. It is interesting that the potential earning level of an older worker has a small and statistically insignificant effect on employment status. The theoretical influence of this variable on employment is of course indeterminate at older ages. Men with high wages pay a relatively high price for retiring early and so might postpone their retirement. Yet high-wage workers usually have the resources to finance a more comfortable retirement starting at an early age. Which of these two effects will predominate is an empirical question.

The effect of health limitations on work effort is quite strong and statistically significant. The measure of health limits used is the response to the question "Does health limit the kind or amount of work you can do?" Workers who responded affirmatively were far less likely to be working full-time than workers with no self-reported health limits. For example, at age 62 the average probability of working full-time for a man

Table 7. Multiperiod Ordered-Probit Estimates of Employment-Status Model

Parameter or variable	Employment status 1 (1)	Employment status 2 (2)
Constant	−7.680	−5.180
	(−9.72)	(−1.96)
Education $LT8$	0.142	0.156
	(7.03)	(6.05)
Education $EQ8$	0.074	0.050
	(3.85)	(2.06)
Education $GT13$	−0.166	−0.213
	(−7.52)	(−7.84)
Potential earnings	−0.007	−0.059
	(−0.49)	(−3.46)
Pension	0.124	0.279
	(7.42)	(13.64)
Social security PIA[a]	0.000	0.001
	(0.65)	(2.28)
ΔPIA[b]	−0.005	−0.001
	(−11.72)	(−1.40)
$COH58$–59[c]	0.130	0.202
	(7.35)	(9.52)
$COH62$–63[d]	−0.245	−0.308
	(−14.16)	(−13.76)
Agriculture	−0.731	−0.430
	(−23.36)	(−8.38)
Mining	0.345	0.231
	(6.89)	(3.56)
Construction	0.058	0.117
	(1.97)	(3.14)
Manufacturing	0.125	0.152
	(5.68)	(5.52)
Transportation	0.144	0.202
	(4.53)	(5.04)
Personal srv.	−0.254	−0.217
	(−5.66)	(−3.61)
Prof. (ind.)	−0.164	−0.113
	(−4.12)	(−2.71)
Pub. admin.	0.189	0.171
	(5.59)	(3.91)
Prof. (occ.)	−0.402	−0.189[e]
	(−10.53)	(−3.42)
Managers	−0.444	−0.189[e]
	(−15.45)	(−3.42)
Clerical	−0.381	−0.204
	(−9.86)	(−3.06)
Sales	−0.542	−0.246
	(−12.15)	(−3.64)

Table 7 (continued)

Parameter or variable	Employment status 1 (1)	Employment status 2 (2)
Cfts. and opr.	−0.237	−0.041
	(−9.19)	(−0.75)
Srv. and h'hold	−0.232	−0.170
	(−6.43)	(−2.61)
Laborer	. . .	0.078
	. . .	(1.64)
Self-employed	0.191	0.078
	(9.40)	(2.93)
Health limit	0.578	0.279
	(41.76)	(14.80)
Age	0.112	0.061
	(8.64)	(1.42)
AGE62	0.304	0.406
	(15.94)	(8.08)
AGE65	−0.243	−0.273
	(−23.90)	(−21.12)
α_1	0.265	0.306
	(70.76)	(62.97)
ρ	0.437	0.432
Value of likelihood function	−16,528.29	−12,000.33
Number of observations	7,742	5,769

Source: Author's tabulations based on the RHS. Asymptotic t-statistics appear in parentheses beneath coefficient estimates. "Education," α, and ρ are defined in table 4.
a. Primary insurance amount of social security entitlement at age 56.
b. Change in *PIA* between ages 56 and 62.
c. Cohort variable for men aged 59 or under in 1969.
d. Cohort variable for men aged 62 or over in 1969.
e. Coefficients are constrained to be equal.

in good health is 82 percent. For a man with a health limitation the probability is only 63 percent, or nearly one quarter less.

Industrial and occupational attachment plays an important role in the employment patterns of older men, even when all the health, demographic, and financial variables just mentioned are controlled. Men engaged in mining, manufacturing, construction, transportation, and public administration leave employment significantly earlier than men in other industries; workers in agricultural, personal service, and professional industries leave significantly later. Occupations appear to fall into three distinct groups with respect to employment behavior. Men in professional, managerial, clerical, and sales occupations tend to work the longest, with other variables controlled. Men in crafts, operative, and service occupations retire at an intermediate age. Finally, men in the remaining occupational categories (farmers, farm and nonfarm laborers, and those with no occupation listed) tend to leave work at the youngest ages. (Note, however, that all farmers work in the agricultural industry, where full-time work continues until much later ages than in other industries.) The differences in employment patterns of these three occupational groups are statistically significant.

There is a strong correspondence between the pattern of industrial and occupational effects on employment status and the pattern of these effects on the health status of surviving men (see column 2 in table 6). Workers appear to leave work earlier in industries and occupations with generally poorer self-reported health and to remain at work longer in industries and occupations in which health status is better. This would appear more reasonable if the employment equation did not already control directly for the effect of health limitations. The implication of the employment-equation results is that *even with the effects of self-reported health on employment status controlled,* workers in industries and occupations in which health is generally poor tend to leave employment at younger ages.

This finding could be explained by unobserved variations in mandatory retirement rules, by pension plan generosity, or by other differences among industries and occupations. But differences in health requirements among industries and occupations probably explain part of the pattern of retirement differences. In the previous section, I emphasized that observed industrial and occupational differences in reported health status might overstate the systematic differences in true average health. Nonetheless, those observed differences might understate the overall effects of health on work capacity. A worker with a particular level of self-reported health might be perfectly able to continue work in one occupation—say, as a manager—but less able to continue in another—say, as a laborer. The pattern of industrial and occupational coefficients in table 7 reflects, at least in part, this effect of health on employment capacity in different lines of work.

Table 8 shows the effects of industry and occupation on the full-time work status of men 62 years old. Approximately 76 percent of men with average characteristics—including average health status—worked full-time at age 62. Column 1 in the table shows the direct effect of an industry or occupation on the probability of working full-time, with all other variables that directly or indirectly affect health and work status held constant.

Table 8. Effect of Industry and Occupation on Probability of Men Working Full-Time at Age 62
Percentage-point difference from mean

Industry or occupation	Probability difference[a]		
	Excluding indirect effects (1)	Including indirect health effects (2)	Including all indirect effects (3)
Agriculture	13.8	14.3	10.3
Mining	−18.6	−22.6	−22.9
Construction	−7.8	−8.8	−8.7
Manufacturing	−10.2	−10.3	−10.1
Transportation	−10.9	−10.8	−10.5
Personal srv.	2.4	4.3	5.2
Prof. (ind.)	−0.3	−0.0	4.4
Pub. admin.	−12.6	−13.5	−12.9
Trade, finance, business, and entertainment	−5.8	−5.6	−0.0
Prof. (occ.)	7.7	8.7	1.8
Managers	8.7	9.2	1.1
Clerical	7.1	7.6	−4.4
Sales	10.9	11.6	4.8
Craftsmen	3.2	3.0	−9.9
Operative	3.2	2.5	−11.4
Srv. and h'hold	3.1	2.3	−6.6
Laborer	−4.3	−5.3	−11.6
Farmers	−4.3	−4.3	10.2

Source: Author's estimates based on RHS data and coefficients in column 1 of table 7.
a. The average probability of working full time at age 62 was 75.7 percent.

Column 2 includes the direct effects of the industry or occupation, as well as the indirect effect through health status. For example, a miner is 18.6 percent less likely to work than an average man aged 62 with identical characteristics. But a miner is 22.6 percent less likely to work taking into account the fact that he is more likely to suffer from a health limitation. Column 3 shows all direct and indirect effects of industry and occupation. In the case of a particular industry, it shows the direct plus indirect effects of that industry on the occupational distribution, potential earnings, pension entitlement, social security benefits, self-employment status, and health status. (In the case of health status, both the direct and indirect effects of the industry on health status are included.) Table 8 shows that the direct effect of a particular industry or occupation is quite strong compared with the indirect effect through health status. Thus miners are far less likely than average to be working at age 62, but the difference in their reported health plays only a small part in explaining this large difference. For an individual miner, health status is an extremely important determinant of employment status. But the average difference in the reported health status of miners and workers in other industries is small enough so that only 4 percentage points of the difference in work probabilities is due to the difference in average health.

The health measure used as an independent variable in column 1 of table 7 has been criticized because of the strong presumptive association between self-reported health limits and contemporaneous employment status. Bazzoli and others criticize the health measure because it is in many cases tantamount to a description of the individual's current work status. This simultaneity can be reduced, although not eliminated, by using a predetermined index of health limitation.[20] It can be further reduced by concentrating on the work patterns of a group that was employed in some initial year. By definition, that group is not prevented from working as a result of poor health status in that year.

Column 2 in table 7 gives results based on a predetermined index of health and a sample restricted to respondents who were employed in 1969. The dependent variable is defined as in equation 6, but observations of the dependent variable come only from the five RHS surveys occurring in 1971 or later. In explaining 1971 employment status, the self-reported health limit in 1969 was used as an explanatory variable; in explaining 1973 work status, 1971 health status was used; and so on for subsequent surveys. The estimates are based on only 5,769 observations because of the aforementioned exclusion of nonworkers in 1969 and because of sample attrition by 1971.

The results in column 2 of table 7 are quite consistent with those in column 1, notwithstanding the sample exclusions and the lagged-value definition of health limitations. A respondent's self-reported health limitation continues to be an important and highly significant predictor of work status. The effect of health is less pronounced in column 2 than in column 1 in part because of the reduced simultaneity of employment and health. But probably of greater importance is the effect of the sample exclusions. Excluding nonworkers in 1969 from the sample ignores the portion of the sample that is most affected by health limitations—that is, those men

20. Simultaneity cannot be eliminated because self-reported health status is highly correlated in successive surveys. See the estimates of ρ in table 4.

forced to retire even before the early retirement age of 62. If these men are excluded, there is much less scope for health to affect drastically the retirement pattern of less healthy workers.

Aside from the estimated effect of health limits on work, most of the remaining coefficients in column 2 of table 7 conform quite well with those in column 1. Where differences occur, they can be explained at least in part by the differences in the samples used in estimation. In the case of four variables, there are sizable differences between coefficients in the first and second columns. The estimated effect of the rate of change in social security benefits is much smaller in column 2 than in column 1. The estimated effects of potential earnings, pension entitlement, and the social security benefit level (*PIA*) are much greater in column 2 than in column 1. In part the smaller coefficient in column 1 is due to simultaneity bias. For example, potential earnings are strongly and negatively related to poor health (see table 4). If contemporaneous health status is included in the equation that predicts employment status, the coefficient of health status may capture part of the effect that is properly due to low potential earnings. The difference in coefficient estimates is also attributable, however, in part to the difference in the samples used in estimation. The pattern of coefficients on the industrial and occupational categories is virtually identical in the two columns. This congruence strongly confirms the earlier finding that once the effects of reported health status are controlled for, workers in industries and occupations in which health is generally poor tend to retire earlier than workers engaged in more healthful industries and occupations.

Summary

In this paper I have analyzed the health status and employment patterns of approximately 7,700 older men interviewed in the Retirement History Survey. The analysis has focused on two issues related to health and work capacity. First, I investigated the economic and demographic determinants of health impairments, giving special attention to the role of industrial and occupational attachment on the work capacity of older men. Second, I estimated the effects of health and industrial and occupational attachment, as well as of other factors, on the employment patterns of these men.

The results in this study confirm that the industrial and occupational classification of a worker's lifetime job plays a significant role in determining his self-reported work capacity as he enters old age. Men who were engaged in mining and construction or who worked as operatives or farm and nonfarm laborers reported significantly worse health and more work limitations than did men from other lines of work. In contrast, workers in professional, technical, and related occupations consistently had less impairment according to a variety of health measures. Two additional job-related variables play an important role in determining health—annual earning levels and coverage by a private pension plan. Workers in lower-paying jobs and in jobs not covered by employer-provided pensions tended to report far more health problems than did other men. In addition, a worker's average earning level played a significant role in determining mortality rates. More highly paid men had a better chance of surviving to age 70 than did men whose potential earnings were low.

Although there were significant differences in self-reported health by industry and occupation, the differences in mortality appear to be much less important. Since mortality rates provide an objective measure of poor health, this finding might suggest that the self-reported health indexes are suspect. This interpretation should be rejected for two reasons. First, self-reported health status turns out to be highly correlated with mortality experience, implying that the self-reports from respondents contain at least some objective information about true health. Mortality is itself a very crude, albeit objective, measure of poor health. A respondent's assessment of health while he is alive contains some information about impairment that is not conveyed by knowing the respondent's age of death. Second, a respondent's self-described health status may convey information about the quality of health required for continued work in his usual industry or occupation as well as information about his "true" level of impairment. Thus his subjective response may be providing an essentially accurate assessment of how health affects capacity to work in his customary job, even though that assessment might not be valid in another industry or occupation.

The observed employment pattern in the RHS sample is quite consistent with respondents' self-assessment of health status. Respondents who reported at least some health limit to their work capacity were employed far less frequently than similar men who reported no health limitation. Although this result should hardly be surprising, it confirms that industrial and occupational effects on self-reported health status can play a role in causing men to leave employment. In addition to this indirect effect of industry and occupation through effects on health, a much larger direct effect of industrial and occupational attachment on employment was also found. Because of custom, pension and mandatory retirement rules, or systematic variations in worker and employer tastes, there are important differences among industries and occupations in the timing of worker retirement. It is interesting that these differences correspond quite closely to differences among industries and occupations in worker-reported health. Some unknown part of this difference in retirement patterns no doubt arises from differences in the health requirements for continuing to work. Several industries and occupations in which retirement occurs early, even when self-reported health limits are controlled, impose above-average physical demands on workers. Among industries these include mining, manufacturing, construction, and transportation; among occupations they include craftsmen, operatives, service workers, and farm and nonfarm laborers. Men who work as managers and professionals and in clerical and sales occupations leave work at ages older than average, and these occupations would seem to place below-average demands on the physical abilities of workers.

With much better measures of objective health status and more detailed information about the industrial and occupational attachment of workers it would be possible to improve greatly this analysis of the effect of industry and occupation on health limitations and retirement. Such an analysis is required to determine how the pension and social security retirement system could be modified to accommodate the varying health requirements and health consequences of different industries and occupations. Even though this kind of determination cannot be made solely on the basis of the results reported here, the findings confirm that industrial and occupational differences are extremely significant. Workers employed in the most healthful and least physically demanding industries and occupations are far less likely to report a work disability, and up to 25 percent more likely to continue working to age 65, than workers in the least healthful and most demanding industries and occupations. These differences will not disappear when the social security retirement age has been raised by two years.

Table A-1. Average Characteristics in the Estimation Samples

Variable	Valid 1969 observations	Workers in 1969
Industry		
Agriculture	0.102	0.116
Mining	0.023	0.019
Construction	0.092	0.090
Manufacturing	0.316	0.315
Transportation	0.096	0.094
Personal service	0.023	0.024
Professional	0.061	0.067
Public administration	0.061	0.057
Occupation		
Professional	0.086	. . .
Managers	0.166	. . .
Professional and managers	. . .	0.263
Clerical	0.051	0.050
Sales	0.036	0.038
Craftsmen	0.220	. . .
Operative	0.198	. . .
Craftsmen and operative	. . .	0.413
Service and household	0.054	0.054
Laborer	0.087	0.082
Demographic and financial		
Race	0.081	. . .
Education less than 8 years	0.185	0.174
Education 8 years	0.215	0.210
Education more than 13 years	0.148	0.155
Age in 1969	60.971	60.845
Married (in 1969)	0.883	. . .
Self-employed	0.121	0.121
Potential earnings ($10,000)	0.752	0.763
Pension	0.511	0.521
Social Security PIA (dollars per month)	95.239	96.269
Change in PIA (dollars per month)	31.469	32.789
Cohort 58–59	0.350	0.375
Cohort 62–63	0.317	0.286

Source: Author's tabulations based on the RHS.

Comment by Richard V. Burkhauser

This is an ambitious piece of work. Using data from the Retirement History Survey (RHS), Gary Burtless develops five different measures of health for men aged 58 to 63 in 1969. Three combinations of these health measures are used to show the relation between levels of health within a cohort of older men and their earlier work history. An employment-status model is developed to explain the retirement decision and the influence of health on that decision for these men over the period 1969 to 1979. The results are then linked to a discussion of the increase in normal retirement age for social security benefits scheduled to take place after the turn of the century.

My criticisms originate in the—perhaps inevitable—deficiencies of the various measurements used: income, education, and health itself. Following the contours of the paper, I divide my comments into three parts. First, I consider the discussion of the effect of past employment on current health, especially that centering around tables 4 and 6 in Burtless's paper. Second, I discuss the estimated effect of current health on future work, especially with respect to table 7. Finally, I suggest some policy implications of the evidence presented.

Job History and Current Health

The author provides a service to his readers with his explicit recognition of several of the problems inherent in attempts to quantify the effects of past work experience on current health status. One such problem is establishing causation. It is recognized that correlations between either poor health in old age or higher mortality rates over the years of the study and job history do not prove causality. Rather than showing that certain industries and occupations increase the risk of a worker's falling into poor health at older ages, causality may run in the opposite direction if those with initially lower levels of health choose a particular mix of industries and occupations. Only if initial health conditions as well as subsequent health are known can the direction of causality be determined. Such problems plague most empirical attempts to measure the effects of investment in human capital or, in this case, disinvestment.

Other general data problems must also be raised. Serious discrete health hazards linked to industry or occupation will be missed because the RHS excluded anyone who died before age 58. In addition, because only the worker's longest-lasting job is considered here, those seriously injured but not killed on a job at an early age could be misclassified with respect to the origin of their change in health.

Furthermore, the model of health developed in the paper is of a world in which deterioration of health is slow and continuous over all workers in a given industry and occupation mix rather than quick or specific to a given worker in that industry or occupation. This is a world of asbestos workers rather than of Seven-Eleven store employees, who may be shot or stabbed on the night shift. The empirical specifications will systematically understate the health hazards associated with these kinds of fatal or career-changing work accidents. This is a general problem associated with using data concerning employment near the end of work life to make inferences about lifetime employment effects.

Despite these caveats, the RHS does provide useful information on work and health, and, although far from perfect, the RHS is an appropriate data source for exploring the issues raised in this paper.

Of more concern, because alternatives are available, is the empirical specification of potential earnings in table 4. This measure seems out of place in a model in which current health is a function of past experience. The inclusion of potential earnings is likely to yield a problem of inferred causality between health and wealth that is more serious than that raised regarding industry or occupation. At a minimum, a more permanent mea-sure of lifetime earnings or wealth would be appropriate here. The issue of the importance of income as a determinant of morbidity or mortality is an unsettled one in the health literature. A more careful treatment of this variable that still found the same strong negative relation between initial earning potential and subsequent poor health would be noteworthy.

The choice of educational categories in table 4 is puzzling. Is health monotonically related to levels of educational attainment? It seems odd to group those with one year of college with high school students. Is it possible that more natural educational groupings yield unexpected results? Orcutt Duleep, for instance, finds that high school graduates who did not go to college had lower mortality rates over a five-year period in the 1970s than did college dropouts.[21] Is this result confirmed in the RHS data?

Burtless conceptualizes an "index of health impairment" in his theory section. This is a useful concept, but it could be more fully tested in his empirical model. Although I am prepared to believe work on a specific job affects a worker's index of health impairment, I would like to know more about how workers reacted to increases in this index. Does reinvestment in health occur? Will it vary systematically by industry or occupation?

21. Harriet Orcutt Duleep, "Measuring the Effect of Income on Adult Mortality Using Longitudinal Administrative Record Data," *Journal of Human Resources*, vol. 21 (Spring 1986), pp. 238–51.

Answering these questions would require a fuller model than is provided here and may not be central to the paper.

One addition that does seem central, however, is duration in longest-lasting job. If one is to believe that health decay is smooth, continuous, and long-standing, it would be useful to see if the share of lifetime work in a hazardous job was related to poorer subsequent health. RHS data are available to answer this question. With regard to industry and occupation, why limit the investigation to two-digit RHS groups? The RHS had three-digit codes that would allow a more interesting aggregation of categories. One possible offshoot would be to see whether the dangerous occupations cited by Thaler and Rosen in their study of wage differences are also found to be associated with the long-term health problems that Burtless's study postulates.[22]

In table 6 the author shows that there is little difference in his multi-period ordered-probit estimates of health limitation when mortality is added as an extreme measure of poor health. I believe that the important distinction in table 6 is the substantial difference between the conventional self-reported measure of health and the mortality measure. Only potential earnings, age, and marital status significantly affect mortality. Only agriculture among all the industries and occupations considered is of the same sign and significance. Clearly these are two different equations.

I suspect that the differences between equations 2 and 3 will not be substantially affected by a much simpler specification that ignores the longitudinal nature of the data and simply looks at 1969 data and a subsequent mortality measure of health. If this is the case, a more detailed specification of education, industry, and occupation becomes more feasible.

Current Health and Future Employment

The literature on retirement choice has grown enormously in both size and sophistication over the past decade. Burtless has been a major contributor to both aspects of this change. Table 7 offers two reduced-form models of the decision to work full-time, part-time, or not at all. Here

22. Richard Thaler and Sherwin Rosen, "The Value of Saving a Life: Evidence from the Labor Market," in Nestor E. Terleckyj, ed., *Household Production and Consumption* (Columbia University Press, 1975), pp. 265–98.

potential earnings is an appropriate measure, but it is insignificant in equation 1, as is a measure of social security wealth. Health limitation is highly significant and negatively related to work.

This is a typical finding in the literature. Use of a self-reported measure of health, however, is controversial. In recognition of this, equation 2 uses health limitations in the previous period rather than in the current period and reduces the sample to those working in 1969. Industry and occupation variables are not much affected by this change in specification, but two key policy variables are. The coefficient on potential earnings is eight times larger and significant, and the social security wealth measure is three times larger and significant, when the specification is changed. Pension wealth is twice its former size and continues to be significant, whereas the health-limit measure is significant but at less than half its former size. These results are quite similar to those found in Anderson and Burkhauser, where subsequent mortality is substituted for self-reported health as a proxy for true health in a simple reduced-form labor supply equation.[23] Here Burtless provides additional evidence of the sensitivity of policy and health variables to the health measure chosen.

The specification of the overall model in table 7 is reasonable, but more sophisticated versions of some of the variables are possible. For instance, the actual measure of social security wealth and of changes in that wealth over each year of the data can be estimated from the RHS. In addition, because by 1979 private pension benefits were accepted by the great majority of those eligible to receive them in these data, a relatively good measure of actual benefit amounts could be derived.

Burtless does add an important dimension in his retirement model. Unlike most empirical estimates of the labor supply of older men that use data from these years, he rightly worries about unexpected changes in social security wealth.[24]

Real social security wealth increased dramatically between April 1969, when the first RHS questions were answered, and April 1973. The primary insurance amount (*PIA*) formula used to set benefits increased by 15 percent in January 1970, by 10 percent in January 1971, and by 20 percent in September 1972—an increase of 52 percent in nominal dollars over the

23. Anderson and Burkhauser, "The Retirement-Health Nexus."

24. Exceptions are Gary Burtless, "Social Security, Unanticipated Benefit Increases," and Kathryn H. Anderson, Richard V. Burkhauser, and Joseph F. Quinn, "Do Retirement Dreams Come True? The Effect of Unanticipated Events on Retirement Plans," *Industrial and Labor Relations Review*, vol. 39 (July 1986), pp. 518–26.

period. Inflation over the same period was only 14 percent. Beginning in 1974 increases in benefits were automatically tied to the cost-of-living index. However, a mistake in the index formula overcompensated for inflation for the rest of the decade. One final increase in benefits during this period that is often overlooked was the change in the survivor benefit from 82.5 percent of *PIA* to 100 percent in 1972. This change substantially increased the overall value of lifetime family benefits for married men.

Burtless finds some evidence that unanticipated changes in the social security law did affect labor supply. It would be interesting to see if a more specific measure of this change in wealth continued to show such an effect.

I am in general agreement with the conclusions Burtless bases on his findings in table 7. I believe, however, that much more analysis is necessary to separate the health component of industry and occupation from the institutional relations unique to these categories. For instance, is it generous black-lung disability benefits or the reduced health of miners that is the reason the mining coefficient is significant?

Despite these caveats, improvements in the empirical specifications of the sort discussed above are unlikely to change the basic results. The most important finding from table 7 is that a retirement model that uses a self-reported health variable collected after a change in work behavior as its "index of health" yields considerably different results from one using either mortality, as Anderson and Burkhauser did, or the same self-reported health variable measured in the period before the change in work effort, as used by Bazzoli.[25] Burtless, using a different overall specification, ends up with results with regard to measured health that are consistent with these earlier findings.

Burtless is on target in calling for better data on health. I wish, however, that he had tried the Fillenbaum-Maddox health index.[26] This measure was developed to be used with RHS data. It is a crude impairment index, but it does offer an alternative to either a simple one-dimensional self-reported health measure or a subsequent-mortality measure. Bazzoli used this measure both in the period just before and just after the change in

25. Anderson and Burkhauser, "The Retirement-Health Nexus," and Bazzoli, "The Early Retirement Decision."

26. G. G. Fillenbaum and George L. Maddox, "Assessing the Functional Status of LRHS Participants: Technique, Findings, Implications," Technical Report 2 (Duke University, Center for the Study of Aging and Human Development, September 1977).

work effort in two separate retirement equations. Similar significant health effects on retirement were found using this health index.[27]

One final point on the strong correlation between health measures that Burtless reports in table 7. The real issue is whether these measures are correlated with other variables. Sammartino provided a careful review of the literature on this point with regard to retirement models.[28] Burkhauser and others looked at a specific health condition, arthritis, and compared a self-reported measure with a joint-count measure.[29] Rheumatologists count the number of inflamed joints in this manner to diagnose arthritis. Using a tetrachoric correlation, Burkhauser and his coauthors showed that the two measures were highly correlated. Some measurement error, however, still existed. Regression analysis demonstrated that the measurement error varied systematically among different socioeconomic groups. In particular, individuals who were not working tended to err in reporting their health. This finding suggests that measurement error may be an important source of bias in studies using self-reported health indicators of the type used in the first column of table 7 to explain work behavior.

Policy Implications

It is likely that both health and economic policy variables affect the labor supply of older workers. Burtless is right to point out that the level of health in the older population is not uniform and that it may have been affected by previous work experience. In addition, current jobs may require different levels of healthiness, leading to different retirement ages among them. Moving the normal retirement age up to age 67 will systematically hurt those in poor health or in jobs that require healthier workers. But this must also be true of the current system. It is possible that private market forces have already reacted to these systematic differences and that this effect is what industry or occupation variables are picking up. For instance, early retirement provisions of private pension plans may be more likely in industries or for occupations where health depreciation is great-

---

27. Bazzoli, "The Early Retirement Decision."

28. Frank Sammartino, "The Effect of Health on Retirement," working paper prepared for the Retirement Age Study (Social Security Administration, 1985).

29. Richard V. Burkhauser and others, "The Importance of Measurement Error in Dichotomous Self-Reported Health Variables: A Tetrachoric Correlation Approach," Working Paper 1984-W24 (Nashville: Vanderbilt University, 1984).

est. If this is the case, general market forces may rectify some of the concerns that Burtless raises about advancing the social security retirement age uniformly to 67.

It is important to frame any calls for change in the 1983 social security compromise in the context of that debate. In anticipation of the graying of the baby boom and the increase in life expectancy over the history of the social security system, a consensus was reached that a reduction in the liabilities of the system was necessary. How will those who oppose raising the retirement age manage the liability issue? Alternatives that raise taxes or reduce benefits will hurt some different mix of people. Is it obvious that these others are better able to absorb those losses? One study of alternatives, by Warlick and Burkhauser, shows that, for a given saving in social security liability, it is more equitable to reduce yearly benefits than to raise the age of normal retirement.[30]

Equity issues of this sort should figure prominently in determining who bears the burden of benefit reductions, but efficiency issues are also important. The enormous surpluses projected for the social security trust fund in the 1990s may give the illusion that the long-term demographic problems of the system have been solved and that no one will have to bear the burden. Calls for postponing the change in retirement age are likely to grow stronger. A real danger is that such untenable arguments will increase speculation over the will of the government to go through with the proposed changes in the normal retirement age. This uncertainty will make it more difficult for current younger workers to plan accurately for change. This uncertainty is a real loss to them, a loss from which no one benefits.

This is not to say that some changes in social security policy should not occur. The architects of the 1983 Social Security Amendments did not consider the full set of responses to this policy change. For instance, if no other changes occur before the turn of the century, the increase in normal retirement age will certainly mean additional applications for social security disability benefits. For those currently aged 62, benefits are 25 percent higher if they are eligible for disability than if they simply take early social security benefits. This percentage will increase to nearly 43 percent when the actuarial reduction for early benefits at age 62 increases from 0.2 to

30. Jennifer L. Warlick and Richard V. Burkhauser, "Raising the Normal Retirement Age under Social Security: A Life-Cycle Analysis," in Marilyn Moon, ed., *Economic Transfers in the United States* (University of Chicago Press, 1984), pp. 359–79.

0.3 of *PIA* after the turn of the century. The age group 55–64 is already the highest per capita age cohort among disability recipients. The increase in the normal retirement age will certainly increase this ratio.

This paper has raised several provocative points regarding the health of older workers. Clearly, better data and more careful modeling of the interaction of health and work should be major priorities for those interested in the effects of the 1983 Social Security Amendments on the work effort and well-being of the future aged.

Jerry A. Hausman and Lynn Paquette

Involuntary Early Retirement and Consumption

Until 1961 social security benefits from the retirement fund could not begin for men until they reached age 65. In 1961 the age for initial receipt of benefits was decreased from 65 to 62. However, 65 was still taken to be the age of normal retirement, and early retirees between the ages of 62 and 64 had their benefits reduced by what was supposed to be an actuarially fair amount. While some debate has arisen over whether the reduction was actuarially fair or whether the social security retirement benefit formula gave a large incentive for continued work over the 62–64 age range,[1] the data on labor force participation among males do demonstrate a clear decrease after 1963 (table 1).

Table 1 shows that the labor force participation rates for 63-year-old men decreased from 75.5 to 52.8 percent over the seventeen-year period from 1963 through 1979. Additional evidence is provided by Diamond and Hausman, who estimated a model of retirement behavior.[2] Their empirical results indicate that approximately 50 percent of retirements of men aged 62 through 64 would not have occurred in 1966–74 if early retirement benefits had not been available.

In spite of the trend toward early retirement, low income and low wealth are common among retired workers. Diamond and Hausman, using data from the National Longitudinal Survey of Older Men (NLS), found that a significant proportion of newly retired or soon-to-retire men had

We thank Beverly Hirtle for her research assistance.

1. Alan S. Blinder, Roger H. Gordon, and Donald E. Wise, "Reconsidering the Work Disincentive Effects of Social Security," *National Tax Journal*, vol. 33 (December 1980), pp. 431–42; and James A. Kahn, "Social Security, Liquidity, and Early Retirement" (MIT, 1985).

2. Peter A. Diamond and Jerry A. Hausman, "The Retirement and Unemployment Behavior of Older Men," in Henry J. Aaron and Gary Burtless, eds., *Retirement and Economic Behavior* (Brookings, 1984), pp. 97–132.

Table 1. U.S. Male Labor Force Participation Rates, Selected Years, 1963–79
Percent

	Age			
Year	60	63	66	70
1963	88.1	75.5	43.4	27.0
1965	86.0	72.5	45.5	26.7
1967	85.5	73.2	47.1	30.3
1969	85.0	68.4	45.6	30.2
1971	83.6	68.5	41.6	28.9
1973	79.2	62.1	37.1	25.4
1975	76.9	58.3	33.7	23.7
1977	77.2	53.1	30.3	24.8
1979	75.0	52.8	31.1	24.4

Source: Philip L. Rones, "Using the CPS to Track Retirement Trends among Older Men," *Monthly Labor Review*, vol. 108 (February 1985), pp. 46–49.

little financial wealth in absolute terms or in relation to their permanent income.[3] In 1966 they found that 20 percent of the survey respondents, who were men between 45 and 59, had wealth of less than $1,000. This percentage rises to 50 percent when financial wealth in houses is eliminated from the measure of total financial wealth. An alternative measure that estimates the ratio of financial wealth to permanent income demonstrates this same low level of wealth. More than 30 percent of the sample reported wealth-to-income ratios below 0.75, and 50 percent below 1.6. Thus a large percent of the population plans to finance its retirement consumption largely from social security and pension benefits.

This finding of low levels of financial wealth among a significant number of men is not necessarily at odds with a life-cycle model of savings behavior under conditions of economic certainty. These men may be at a corner condition with respect to savings. That is, they may have decided that their social security benefits and pension benefits will be high enough to finance postretirement consumption and that no additional accumulation of wealth is needed. But in a world of economic uncertainty there are reasons to accumulate financial wealth apart from social security and pension wealth. Precautionary savings would be expected to exist to cover unanticipated reductions in earnings that arise because of unexpected job loss or health problems. Nonprecautionary savings would also be expected to exist for people who anticipated that problems, such as deteriorating health, would occur, though the line between unanticipated and anticipated

3. Peter A. Diamond and Jerry A. Hausman, "Individual Retirement and Savings Behavior," *Journal of Public Economics*, vol. 23 (February–March, 1984), pp. 81–114.

events is difficult to draw here. Thus the finding of the Diamond-Hausman research seems to indicate that the economic life-cycle model of savings behavior is implausible for an important minority of workers. The retirement savings of these workers are too low.

In this paper we consider the economic status of men who retire early, in particular men who retire before they are eligible for social security or pension benefits. Given the large proportion of the population that does not have significant amounts of financial wealth, we would expect an important effect on their economic status from early retirement. Do the majority of people who retire before age 62 do so because of the desire for increased leisure? Previous research has suggested this reason to be of primary importance in the decreasing male labor force participation rates.[4] Our empirical results indicate to the contrary that a significant proportion of men retire "involuntarily." In our definition, involuntary retirement occurred if a man left his last job because he was laid off or fired or because his physician or employer suggested he leave for reasons of age or health. We find that most men who retired before 60 did so involuntarily.

An examination of the economic status of these early retirees is needed, however. Several analysts have claimed that "poor health" is given as a socially acceptable reason for early retirement or that employers generously fire their employees who plan to retire early so that the employees can qualify for unemployment benefits.[5] Evidence contrary to these objections to the involuntary retirement finding has previously appeared in the literature.

Diamond and Hausman, again using the NLS data, found that a significant proportion of the men who retire before they are eligible for retirement income have low permanent income and wealth relative to nonretirees.[6] Also, a significant proportion of the early retirees indicated the presence of health problems that greatly affected their labor force participation choices. Kingson independently examined young retirees who described themselves as unhealthy and found a sizable group likely to

4. See Michael J. Boskin, "Social Security and Retirement Decisions," *Economic Inquiry*, vol. 15 (January 1977), pp. 1–25; Kathryn H. Anderson and Richard V. Burkhauser, "The Retirement-Health Nexus: A New Measure of an Old Puzzle," *Journal of Human Resources*, vol. 20 (Summer 1985), pp. 315–30; and Gloria J. Bazzoli, "The Early Retirement Decision: New Empirical Evidence on the Influence of Health," *Journal of Human Resources*, vol. 20 (Spring 1985), pp. 214–34.

5. See, for example, Bazzoli, "The Early Retirement Decision."

6. Diamond and Hausman, "Retirement and Unemployment Behavior of Older Men," p. 104.

be suffering economic distress.[7] That these early retirees do not have enough financial assets to maintain their consumption pattern until they turn 62 or qualify for receipt of private pension benefits indicates that the desire for increased leisure was probably not the primary reason for their early retirement.

Another possible objection to the involuntary retirement finding is that people can find another job after leaving their previous jobs for health reasons or because of layoffs. But older people who are fired may find it difficult to find new employment. A firm may be reluctant to hire older people because of the limited years in which it can receive a return on its training costs, because of the perceived difficulty of older people adapting to a new job environment, and because of the higher probability of bad health. Diamond and Hausman found that about 20 percent of the men aged 55 to 62 who were fired did not take another job.[8] Again a large proportion of these men had low financial wealth. In research using the Retirement History Survey (RHS) data Hausman and Paquette found that 86 percent of the men between the ages of 58 and 62 who lost their previous job retired from the labor force without finding another job despite often long periods of searching for employment.[9]

As a partial test of the competing "voluntary" versus "involuntary" behavioral hypotheses for early retirees, we consider their consumption behavior in relation to their preretirement consumption. Since the main implication of the life-cycle hypothesis of economic savings is a smoothing of lifetime consumption, we would not expect to find a substantial decrease in consumption after retirement if the retirement is voluntary. Some decrease in consumption might be expected, and this decrease can be used as a benchmark when assessing the consumption decline that occurs among workers who are forced to retire involuntarily. A significant decrease in consumption of the involuntary retirees relative to that of the voluntary retirees would cast significant doubt on the argument that all retirements are for the most part voluntary and under the control of the worker.

7. Eric R. Kingson, "The Early Retirement Myth: Why Men Retire before Age 62," Report by the House Select Committee on Aging, 97 Cong. 1 sess. (Government Printing Office, 1981).

8. "Retirement and Unemployment Behavior of Older Men," p. 119.

9. Jerry A. Hausman and Lynn Paquette, "The Labor Force Behavior of Older Men Following Involuntary Job Losses" (MIT, 1985).

In this paper we use the RHS to estimate the change in consumption of individuals who suffer involuntary retirement.[10] Because of data limitation in the RHS, we cannot measure total consumption. Instead, we estimate the effect of involuntary retirement on food consumption. Hammermesh provides evidence that food consumption and the other limited categories of consumption from the RHS provide a reliable indicator for total consumption.[11] He has compared data for these consumption categories reported in the RHS to similar consumption categories in the Consumer Expenditure Survey, which provides detailed data on all categories of consumption. Nevertheless, the limitation to food consumption in the RHS should be noted.

We find that food consumption declines by about 30 percent for men who suffer involuntary retirement. Their decline in food consumption is 20 percent greater than that of men who retire voluntarily, since that group reduces food consumption by about 10 percent. We estimate this decrease of 30 percent in a regression model that controls for individual consumption before involuntary retirement. Thus we do not find the possibly spurious result that men who suffer involuntary retirement consume less than the population because of their lower permanent income before their job loss. Our model also controls for the decrease in consumption that occurs with voluntary retirement. We interpret our results to indicate a large and significant decrease in food consumption among involuntary retirees, both in relation to their previous consumption and in relation to the change in consumption for voluntary retirees. Our evidence therefore casts serious doubt on the argument that the desire for more leisure explains retirement behavior for men who report serious health problems or job loss as the reason for their retirement. Instead, the clear indication exists that men's "involuntary" retirement is accompanied by a significant decrease in consumption.

The policy question now arises whether the safety net of public welfare programs should be further extended to cover these involuntary early retirees. Jorgenson, Lau, and Stoker estimate the income elasticity for the

10. The RHS data are available on tapes. The data are described in Lola M. Irelan and others, *Almost 65: Baseline Data from the Retirement History Study,* U.S. Department of Health, Education and Welfare, Social Security Administration, Office of Research and Statistics, Research Report 49 (GPO, 1976).

11. Daniel S. Hammermesh, "Consumption during Retirement: The Missing Link in the Life Cycle," *Review of Economics and Statistics,* vol. 66 (February 1984), pp. 1–7.

category food and clothing to be approximately 0.75.[12] The change in utility or real income cannot be calculated without reference to a specific utility or expenditure function specification, but an approximate income decline of 30 to 50 percent would seem to have occurred for this group of involuntary retirees. Is a change of this size acceptable under the current institutional arrangements for retirement in view of the fact that the men under consideration have been especially unlucky with respect to their health or employment opportunities? If the change is considered to be large enough to merit a response, then either a means-tested benefit program may be appropriate or a means-conditioned change in the early retirement age for social security could be considered.

The specific change in the social security retirement age that might be considered would allow people to withdraw part of their social security contributions before the current early retirement age of 62 if they become involuntarily unemployed after a certain age, such as 55. Similar provisions for early withdrawal of savings currently exist in private retirement plans that receive tax-favored status. Since for most people social security provides an important part of retirement income and also of lifetime savings, the provision that does not allow retirement before age 62, coupled with the inability to borrow against future social security benefits, can have a significant effect on the economic welfare of the early involuntary retirees.[13] Our results indicate that non–social security and nonpension savings are not high enough to enable a large proportion of the early retirees to finance consumption from other forms of savings. Permitting retirement before 62 may well conflict with the essentially paternalistic rationale for social security, that its primary feature is a forced savings system for retirement. Also, fear of "excessively" early retirement or adverse selection effects would have to be kept in mind.[14] These distortions would need to be considered in relation to the size of the economic hardship that occurs among the involuntary early retirees. Given that they have contributed to the social security system, their inability to use their

12. Dale W. Jorgenson, Lawrence J. Lau, and Thomas M. Stoker, "The Transcendental Logarithmic Model of Aggregate Consumer Behavior," in R. L. Basmann and George F. Rhodes, Jr., eds., *Advances in Econometrics*, vol. 1 (Greenwich, Conn.: JAI Press, 1982), p. 225.

13. In 1961 Congress seemingly granted early retirement for men at age 62 because it had granted early retirement for women at age 62 in 1956.

14. Adverse selection occurs when people who know they are likely to die sooner than others of the same age retire earlier or, say, buy insurance policies. These actions lead to a greater financial burden on the social security or insurance system.

social security savings before age 62 may impose an important constraint on their economic well-being.

The plan of the paper is as follows. In the first section we describe the RHS data set. We also give our data definitions, including a detailed definition of involuntary retirement and of food consumption. In the second section we consider sample data on the causes of retirement before age 62. We also compare the ratios of consumption before and after leaving a job for men who left involuntarily with the ratios for men who left voluntarily. Next we specify and estimate regression models for food consumption. A more complete characterization of the effects of involuntary retirement can be estimated in a regression model, since such factors as the effect of financial wealth can be controlled for. In the last section we return to the question of the effect of the current social security law on the economic well-being of the involuntary early retirees.

The Data Set

In 1969 the Social Security Administration began the Retirement History Survey and until 1979 continued to collect data on a biennial basis. We use survey data from 1969, 1971, 1973, 1975, 1977, and 1979. The initial 1969 survey collected data from approximately 11,000 respondents between the ages of 58 and 63. Its rather narrow age range restricts the ability to measure the experience of very early retirees or the job market experience of individuals apart from their social security earnings histories.

We constructed a measure of permanent income from the social security earnings histories that are included in the RHS public use file. Permanent income is defined as the average of annual real earnings during the five years before retirement.[15] For years in which the limits on social security contributions were reached, a truncated regression (Tobit) model was estimated on the log of earnings. Predicted values of earnings were then used in the permanent income calculation.

We also constructed a financial wealth variable (that is, wealth excluding home equity) from the detailed questions on wealth asked in the RHS. People had reported on the value of their stocks, bonds, checking accounts, savings accounts, life insurance, annuities, loans to other per-

---

15. Wives' income as well as husbands' income is included in the calculation of permanent income, but other nonwage income is excluded.

sons, and mortgages held. However, a substantial amount of data on wealth is missing. Therefore, we estimated models explaining the probability of holding an asset and the amount of the asset held for each of the categories of financial wealth and for each survey year. These models were then used to impute assets for the categories in which data were missing. Two potentially important components of wealth are absent from our measure of financial wealth: the value of consumer durables and the cash value of life insurance. But insofar as the resale of most consumer durables except cars is likely to be low, this omission may not be too serious.

We constructed a health status variable from the answer to the questions on whether health limits work or whether a person is unable to work at a given date. The self-reported nature of this variable is a potential cause for concern. However, since it plays only a minor role in most of our analysis, it should not have an undue effect.

Our sample consisted of 4,009 observations. We concentrated on male-headed households and considered food consumption on a per person basis within the family. Because 630 observations had only one food observation in the ten-year period, they were eliminated from our regression estimates. We eliminated from our sample farmers, persons who were self-employed, or those who worked for the federal government. The self-employed and farmers are difficult to divide into voluntary or involuntary retirees, and their preretirement labor patterns are very different from those of other workers. Because federal employees are not covered by the social security retirement program, they are not affected by the age 62 restriction. In fact, they are eligible to receive their pension at age 55 if they have worked for the federal government for thirty years by that age. Significant attrition exists in our sample, with only 73 percent of the original observations remaining in the last year. Presumably, most of this attrition has occurred because of death. But no formal analysis has been conducted along the lines of Hausman and Wise to test for the presence of nonrandom attrition.[16]

16. See Jerry A. Hausman and David A. Wise, "Attrition Bias in Experimental and Panel Data: The Gary Income Maintenance Experiment," *Econometrica*, vol. 47 (March 1979), pp. 455–73. Nonrandom attrition could affect our results if retirement and consumption patterns differed significantly among the group that dropped out of the sample for reasons other than death. But under plausible assumptions we would expect the group that dropped out to demonstrate greater adverse effects from involuntary retirement than those in our sample.

Our definition of retirement for a man is that he is not working and not looking for work or that he is currently working fewer than thirty-five hours a week.[17] The date of retirement is set at the date that the man left his last full-time job. Involuntary retirement after the survey began in 1969 was defined in the following way. If the answer to the question of "why you left your last job" for a man now retired was either "laid off" or "health" or "old age" and the man left his job at a physician's or employer's suggestion, then we define him as being involuntarily retired. For persons who retired before the sample began in 1969, we consider that involuntary retirement occurred if the response to the question of "why you left your last job" was "slack work conditions," or if it was "health" or "old age" and the man reported that "health limits the ability to work."

Our definition of food consumption is as follows. We take the usual expenditures in food stores and for food deliveries, and other similar food expenditure categories that are reported weekly, and multiply by fifty-two weeks. We then divide by the number of persons usually eating at home to place expenditures on a per person basis. We then add expenditures for food at work by the respondent and spouse and put the expenditures on a yearly and a per person basis. Finally, we add in the usual monthly expenditures by respondent and spouse for food away from home, after putting these expenditures on a yearly and a per person basis. We take these food expenditures in annual dollars and deflate them by the average of the monthly consumer price index for food during the first four months of the survey year, since most surveys were completed during April of that year. Thus all food expenditures are in 1967 dollars.

The data on food consumption in the RHS are quite "noisy," in the sense that both the across-family variation and over-time variation within a family are fairly large. We deleted obvious nonsensical responses and tested our results for sensitivity to extreme observations. Nevertheless, two cautions are in order. Shapiro found large amounts of noise in his analysis of the Panel Study of Income Dynamics (PSID) data set, which asked similar questions on food consumption.[18] Our analysis of the RHS indicates less noise than is found in the PSID. Also, we tried to use econometric techniques that are not extremely sensitive to errors in depen-

17. We also reanalyzed the data defining retirement to be zero hours of work a week. The results are quite similar to the results reported in the paper.

18. Matthew D. Shapiro, "The Permanent Income Hypothesis and the Real Interest Rate," *Economics Letters,* vol. 14, no. 1 (1984), pp. 93–100.

dent variable types of problems.[19] The second caution concerns the use of food consumption to make inferences about the level of economic welfare. The expenditure on food is certainly one of the necessities of economic well-being, but expenditure on restaurant meals may be considered a luxury good by some. Insofar as we find a significant reduction in food expenditure after involuntary retirement, some decrease in economic welfare seems to be the correct inference. But the exact percentage fall in economic welfare, as opposed to food consumption, cannot be calculated without reference to an explicit utility function or expenditure function.

Characteristics of Retirement and Food Consumption

We first consider the causes of retirement among the men in our sample from the RHS. In particular, we want to see what proportion of the sample retired involuntarily. Recall that we define involuntary retirement as occurring if a person left his last job because he was laid off or because of old age or bad health at his physician's or employer's suggestion. In table 2 we examine the proportion of involuntary retirees by age group; our data set of 3,416 men is 85 percent of our total sample of 4,009 men. Of the 3,416 retirees 37 percent retired involuntarily. However, note that the proportion of involuntary retirements is considerably higher for retirements that occur at younger ages.

For the youngest group of retirees—those who retired at age 55 or younger—almost 75 percent retired involuntarily. In the next age bracket the percentage falls to 61 percent. But the percentage of involuntary retirees remains quite high until age 62, when the men qualify for early retirement social security benefits. The percentage of involuntary retirees then falls to 27 percent. The percentage remains at approximately this level up through age 65, when it decreases further to 21 percent. The percentages in table 2 clearly demonstrate that a significant proportion of retirements are involuntary. Furthermore, a significantly higher proportion of involuntary retirements occur at an age when the man cannot yet collect social security early retirement benefits. In our sample 639 of the retirements before age 62 are involuntary; thus approximately 19 percent of all

19. In particular, we used fixed effects estimation with food consumption used only as a dependent variable. Use of food consumption as a (lagged) right-hand side variable could lead to very large biases in estimated coefficients. See Zvi Griliches and Jerry A. Hausman, "Errors in Variables in Panel Data," *Journal of Econometrics*, vol. 31, no. 1 (1986), pp. 93–118.

Table 2. Age of Retirement, by Type of Retirement

Age last worked	Number	Percent retired involuntarily
Under 56	302	74.8
56–59	358	60.9
60	183	41.0
61	296	40.5
62	420	26.9
63	360	28.1
64	506	31.8
65	559	30.2
66–68	291	21.0
Over 68	52	25.0
Data missing	89	. . .
Total retirees	3,416	36.8

Source: Authors' calculations based on the Retirement History Survey.

of our retirees retired involuntarily and did not qualify for social security benefits at the time of their retirement.

We next consider the possible sources of income during retirement that people can use to finance their consumption. Private pensions provide a source of retirement income in addition to social security benefits. In table 3 we consider the age at which a man is eligible to receive either social security benefits or pension benefits and the age of his retirement. We calculated the age of eligibility by taking the minimum of the following: age in the year in which pension or social security income is first reported; age reported in the surveys as the age in which a man is eligible for a reduced or a full pension from his current, last, or longest job; 62 if the

Table 3. Age of Retirement and Age of Retirement Income Eligibility
Percent

Age of eligibility minus age of retirement	Age			
	Under 55	55–61	62–64	Over 64
Less than −4 years	0.4	4.0	14.9	29.6
−4 to −3 years	0.0	4.1	7.4	36.9
−2 to −1 years	0.0	4.7	41.3	30.4
0 years	2.8	40.7	34.8	2.0
1 to 2 years	7.5	27.1	1.2	0.9
3 to 4 years	6.3	12.5	0.0	0.1
More than 4 years	78.3	5.9	0.0	0.0
Not eligible	4.7	1.0	0.3	0.1
Number of observations	254	885	1,286	902

Source: See table 2.

man is eligible for social security given the number of quarters of coverage from his social security earnings history. A potential problem arises here if a person had to work between age 62 and 64 to qualify for social security benefits, since our calculations will make it appear that he qualified for benefits before he retired. However, this problem should be quite small.

The interpretation of this somewhat complicated table is as follows. In the first row, 14.9 percent of the men who retired at ages 62 through 64 could have retired four or more years earlier and still received a private pension (since they would not have been eligible for social security benefits). Almost all, 98.5 percent, of those men were eligible for either a private pension or social security at the time of their retirement. However, the situation is quite different for early retirees, those younger than 62. For the youngest age group, retirees under 55, only 3.2 percent (0.4 percent + 2.8 percent) qualified for pension or social security benefits at the time of their retirement. Of course, if they had enough financial wealth, they could finance their retirement consumption from that. But note that 78 percent would have to wait more than four years before they would begin to receive any retirement benefits. For the other group of early retirees, men aged 55 through 61, 54 percent had qualified for retirement benefits at the time of their retirement. But 18 percent still had to wait more than two years before they would begin to receive retirement benefits. Therefore, as far as these men did not have significant amounts of financial wealth at the time of retirement, they might suffer financial distress because of their inability to maintain their postretirement consumption levels.

We next consider the relationship between job loss and financial wealth. The possibility exists that retirees who are not yet eligible for social security or pensions may have substantial amounts of financial wealth that would allow them to finance their postretirement consumption until they begin to receive retirement benefits. We could then interpret the retirement decision as a labor-leisure choice by the persons. However, a significant proportion of low-wealth men among the retirees are those who retired involuntarily (table 4). These men are unlikely to have financial resources or to be eligible for sufficient social welfare benefits to maintain their consumption patterns. Furthermore, the levels of wealth, excluding house value, are sufficiently low with respect to permanent income to make it unlikely that preretirement consumption can be maintained. It is important to note here that the wealth data we use here are of questionable reliability, given their self-reported nature. In fact, the ratios reported here

Table 4. Ratio of Wealth to Permanent Earnings, 1971[a]

Quartile	W/PE ratio	Number of observations	Lost job (percent)
1	W/PE < .107	801	38
2	.107 < W/PE < .455	930	32
3	.455 < W/PE < 1.17	950	31
4	W/PE > 1.17	952	25
Wealth missing		3	
Total		3,636	31

Source: See table 2.
a. Wealth excludes value of home.

are distinctly lower than those that Diamond and Hausman found.[20] Nevertheless, both the Diamond-Hausman data and the current data lead to the conclusion that wealth is quite low relative to permanent earnings. In our subsequent econometric work we use only the quartile rankings of table 4, rather than the exact ratios, to minimize possible econometric problems that can arise from this type of noisy data.

We now turn to a comparison of food consumption before and after leaving a job, to see if those who left their job involuntarily are affected by their job loss more than those who left their job voluntarily. In table 5 we consider the ratio of food consumption reported in the survey before the job loss to the consumption reported in the survey after the job loss (for job losses occurring between 1969 and 1979), where all consumption has been deflated by the CPI.

If we first compare men who left a job before the age of 62, we see that 48 percent of those who left involuntarily had a ratio of postretirement to preretirement food consumption of 0.7 or less. Only 33 percent of those who left voluntarily at an age less than 62 had a similar ratio. The percentage of persons whose consumption decreased after leaving a job is 76 percent for those who left involuntarily at age less than 62, and 63 percent for those who left voluntarily. A Pearson chi-square test of the hypothesis that the multinomial distribution of consumption for those who left involuntarily is the same as for those who left voluntarily is calculated to be 10.02 with 4 degrees of freedom, which is significant at the 5 percent level. Therefore, we conclude that for men aged less than 62, the distribution of food consumption differs by cause of the job loss.

When we look at persons who left their jobs when they were older than

20. "Individual Retirement and Savings Behavior."

Table 5. Changes in Food Consumption before and after Leaving a Job
Percent

Ratio of food consumption before leaving job to after leaving it	Left involuntarily			Left voluntarily		
	Under 62	62 and over	Total	Under 62	62 and over	Total
Less than 0.5	14	19	18	10	14	13
0.5 to 0.7	34	26	27	23	26	25
0.7 to 1.0	28	32	32	30	33	32
1.0 to 2.0	22	20	20	33	23	26
More than 2.0	2	3	3	4	5	5

Source: See table 2.

62, the difference is somewhat less between those who left involuntarily and those who left voluntarily. For those who left involuntarily, the percentage whose consumption ratio is less than 0.7 is 45 percent, while for those who left voluntarily, it is 40 percent. If we consider ratios of food consumption of less than 1.0, we find that 77 percent of those who left jobs involuntarily have consumption decreases, while the corresponding percentage is 73 percent for those who left jobs voluntarily. The chi-square test for the same multinomial distribution is again rejected, since it takes on a value of 10.6, with 4 degrees of freedom. But most of the difference occurs in the lowest category of the consumption ratio, less than 0.5.

To summarize, our examination of the data demonstrated that most retirements before the age of 60 are involuntary retirements. Even at ages 60 and 61, more than 40 percent of the retirements are involuntary. Only a small fraction of these early retirees qualify for retirement benefits at the time of their retirement—3.2 percent of the retirees under 55 and 53.5 percent of the retirees aged 55 to 61. Furthermore, most of the involuntary retirees do not appear to have sufficient financial wealth to maintain their consumption patterns until they begin to receive retirement benefits. Their level of financial wealth is not high, and they cannot borrow against their retirement benefits. Finally, when we consider food consumption after a job loss, we observe that a significant proportion of those leaving jobs involuntarily have a large drop in their food consumption. Furthermore, the proportion of those who leave involuntarily who have a decrease in their food consumption is statistically significantly greater than the corresponding proportion for those who leave their jobs voluntarily. We also find that involuntary retirees' food consumption decreases significantly more than voluntary retirees before age 62: 48 percent of involuntary retirees are below 0.7 of preretirement consumption while only 33 percent of voluntary retirees are below the same threshold. However, for retirement after age 62, when social security begins, the percentage changes are much closer between the involuntary and voluntary retirees.

A tabular comparison of the type we have done, however, cannot control for other potentially important factors, nor can we easily quantify the difference in food consumption. In the next section we turn to a regression model of food consumption so that we can obtain a more precise estimate of the effect of involuntary retirement.

Food Consumption over Time

The life cycle–permanent income hypothesis of consumption basically states that a person will smooth his consumption over time. That is, consumption at time t is determined primarily by lifetime wealth, which forms the appropriate budget constraint. The standard formulation of the problem is to assume an additively separable utility function over time in which the individual maximizes subject to the constraint that private wealth holdings in each period are nonnegative. In general, no closed form solution to the utility maximization problem exists. But for specific forms of the utility function, closed form solutions can be found in either the change in consumption or in the percentage change in consumption. For individual i in period t, assume that the single-period utility function is determined by consumption of food, C_{1it}, consumption of other commodities, C_{1it}, and by leisure, L_{it}:

$$(1) \qquad U_{it}(C_{1it}, C_{2it}, L_{it}) = f_1(C_{1it}) \times e^{W_{it} + bL_{it}} + f_2(C_{2it}, L_{it}),$$

where the term $\exp(W_{it} + bL_{it})$ reflects individual i's taste for the food consumption categories relative to consumption of other goods at time t. Note that the trade-off between the two categories of consumption depends on leisure at time t. The taste terms reflect both observed individual characteristics as well as unobserved tastes, which are assumed to be distributed independently.

Solving the maximization problem leads to an Euler equation that can be solved in closed form given an assumption on the $f_1(C_{1it})$ function. If we assume the constant absolute risk-aversion form

$$(2) \qquad f_1(C_{1it}) = \exp(-a \times C_{1it}),$$

where a is the coefficient of absolute risk aversion, we derive an equation that involves the change in food consumption:

$$(3) \qquad C_{1it+1} - C_{1it} = d_{t+1} + X_{it+1}\beta + e_{it+1},$$

where the d_{t+1}'s are time dummies that reflect the effect of the interest rate on intertemporal consumption, the X_{it}'s represent the expected change in age, health, and labor supply, and the e_{it}'s contain both the unexpected changes in tastes over time and the changes in information. The most important new information that we concentrate on in our empirical work is that a person involuntarily loses his job. That change will cause a change in his expected lifetime wealth and will therefore cause his consumption pattern to change also. The other utility function we investigate is the constant relative risk-aversion utility function:

$$(4) \qquad f_1(C_{1it}) = C_{1it}^{1-a}/(1 - a),$$

where a is the coefficient of relative risk aversion. For this utility function the Euler equation leads to a regression specification in the percentage change of food consumption

$$(5) \qquad \log(C_{1it+1} / C_{1it}) = d_{t+1} + X_{it+1}\beta + e_{it+1},$$

where e_{it} has the same interpretation as before. Constant absolute risk aversion implies that a person applies the same risk premium to an uncertain outcome regardless of wealth, whereas relative risk aversion is affected by the level of wealth. The constant relative risk-aversion hypothesis is the most often used of the two hypotheses.[21] We now proceed to estimate regression models in first-difference that correspond to these two formulations. Note that the first-difference specification corresponds to a fixed-effects specification for the level of consumption specification which eliminates potential bias caused by unobserved individual effects.[22]

We estimate the two formulations of the changes in consumption by

21. Kenneth J. Arrow, *Essays in the Theory of Risk-Bearing* (Chicago: Markham, 1971), chap. 3.

22. See Yair Mundlak, "On the Pooling of Time Series and Cross Section Data," *Econometrica*, vol. 46 (January 1978), pp. 69–85; and Jerry A. Hausman and William E. Taylor, "Panel Data and Unobservable Individual Effects," *Econometrica*, vol. 49 (November 1981), pp. 1377–98.

Table 6. Coefficient Estimates for Food Consumption Differences

Variable	Difference (1)	Difference (2)	Log difference (3)	Log difference (4)
Household size	−76.6	−76.5	−0.124	−0.123
	(−3.95)	(−3.95)	(−0.005)	(−0.005)
Married	−472.2	−472.2	−.540	−.540
	(−13.2)	(−13.2)	(−0.016)	(−0.016)
Health limits work	7.60	7.68	0.013	0.013
	(6.83)	(6.83)	(0.009)	(0.009)
Age squared	0.452	0.459	0.00017	0.00019
	(0.412)	(0.412)	(0.00051)	(0.00051)
Retired	−107.0	−106.9	−0.136	−0.136
	(−9.95)	(−9.95)	(−0.011)	(−0.011)
Involuntary job loss	440.1	−120.4	0.552	−0.105
	(179.5)	(−38.9)	(0.201)	(−0.044)
Retired × loss	−13.5	−14.6	−0.025	−0.026
	(−25.8)	(−25.8)	(−0.030)	(−0.030)
Loss age < 62	−71.4	−70.2	−0.093	−0.093
	(−35.9)	(−36.1)	(−0.039)	(−0.040)
Loss log (PEH)	−56.7	. . .	−0.068	. . .
	(−19.5)	. . .	(−0.022)	. . .
Loss first quartile of PEH	. . .	90.9	. . .	0.096
	. . .	(43.0)	. . .	(0.048)
Loss second quartile of PEH	. . .	47.6	. . .	0.041
	. . .	(39.2)	. . .	(0.042)
Loss third quartile of PEH	. . .	13.6	. . .	0.0065
	. . .	(37.8)	. . .	(0.042)
Loss low total wealth	−61.3	−63.3	−0.081	−0.089
	(−45.0)	(−45.1)	(−0.050)	(−0.050)
Loss low wealth × eligible for social security	44.8	47.6	0.079	0.085
	(39.0)	(39.2)	(0.043)	(0.043)
Additional variables—5 time dummies for each year				

Source: See table 2. Numbers in parentheses are *t*- statistics.

using multivariate least squares (seemingly unrelated regression) on the biennial data from 1969 to 1979.[23] For any person the maximum number of first-difference observations is five. However, because of missing data and sample attrition the actual number of first-difference observations varied from 1,311 up to 2,397, depending on the pair of years used to form the first difference. In table 6 we present the coefficient estimates for equation 3 and equation 5, which correspond to the alternative utility

23. Note that our econometric specification includes both an individual dummy variable plus a dummy variable for each year. The stochastic specification allows for arbitrary serial correlation across individual observations.

function formulations. Note that the elasticity of the utility of consumption with respect to changes in consumption in equation 2 depends on the level of consumption, while in equation 4 it is constant. Therefore, equation 3 should be interpreted in relation to changes away from the level of initial food consumption, while equation 5 should be interpreted in relation to percentage changes in food consumption.

The best way to interpret the first two columns, which arise from equation 3, is against average food consumption of $688 per person in our sample. The second two columns for log change (based on equation 5) correspond to the percentage change in food consumption. Therefore, each additional person in the household raises food consumption less than the first person, that is, there are economies of scale, and the percentage difference is about − 12 percent for each person. Likewise, consumption per person is significantly less if the person is married rather than single. Retirement leads to a decline in food consumption of $106 per year, or about 13.6 percent of consumption. We now turn to the estimated coefficients showing effects of involuntary job loss. Since the relevant independent variables are interacted with both permanent earnings of the husband (PEH) and wealth, the coefficients are somewhat difficult to interpret. Column 4 is perhaps the easiest to understand. For a person in the highest income quartile, involuntary job loss leads to a decline in per person food consumption of 10.5 percent. The estimated effect is highly significant. If the person is less than 62, his consumption falls by an additional 9.3 percent. If he is in a lower permanent income quartile, the decrease in consumption is less, which might be expected given the inverse relationship found in econometric studies between income and the income elasticity of food consumption. Also, people in the lower quartiles may qualify for food stamp assistance. The effect, however, is always to decrease consumption. Finally, if the ratio of the person's total wealth (including the value of his house) lies below the median of 1.5, his consumption falls by an additional 8.9 percent. But a person with low wealth who is eligible for either social security or retirement benefits will have this last effect negated, since his consumption will fall by only 0.4 percent.

In terms of the life-cycle model two findings emerge. First, involuntary job loss leads to a sizable decrease in food consumption. The life-cycle model would predict a decline in consumption, since lifetime wealth has been decreased by the loss of job; however, the size of the decrease is estimated to be quite large. Second, eligibility for retirement benefits is important for low-wealth men. For a man in the lowest wealth quartile,

Table 7. Change in Expenditure on Food Consumption from Involuntary Job Loss[a]
Dollars

Age and wealth	Permanent earnings quartile			
	1	2	3	4
Under 62, no social security				
Low wealth	−177	−221	−255	−269
High wealth	−114	−157	−192	−205
62 and over, social security				
Low wealth	−59	−103	−137	−151
High wealth	−44	−87	−121	−135

Source: See table 2.
a. Average yearly food consumption is $688.

involuntary job loss before age 62 lowers consumption by about 19 percent. However, when he becomes eligible to receive his retirement benefits, food consumption increases by 8.5 percent, which brings his consumption into line with men in positions of higher wealth. Therefore, men with below-median wealth appear to be constrained by their inability to receive their retirement benefits. Their food consumption increases significantly when they begin to receive the benefits.[24]

Because the interpretation of the coefficients is complicated by the interactions of other variables with job loss, we present in table 7 the net effects of involuntary job loss, which correspond to column 2 in table 6.

The consumption of people who lose their jobs before age 62 falls significantly, with low-wealth men experiencing a greater decrease as expected. The size of the decrease grows with the permanent earnings loss as we would also expect. Note that for people who suffer involuntary job loss at an age where they qualify for social security benefits, whether they have low wealth or high wealth, the decrease in consumption is also considerably less. More important, the difference between low-wealth and high-wealth people is much less. This smaller difference is in part the result of the ability to receive social security retirement benefits.

In table 8 we do similar calculations for the percentage change in food consumption, from the estimates in column 4 of table 6. The results are similar to those in table 7. The decrease in food consumption is quite large for people who lose their jobs before age 62, with low-wealth people affected more. For low-wealth men the percentage decrease from their

24. Paquette also found evidence in the RHS of constrained food consumption behavior among low-wealth men. However, here we are concentrating on the effect of consumption after involuntary job loss, which she did not consider. Lynn Paquette, "Liquidity Constraints and the Consumption Patterns of the Elderly" (MIT, 1984).

Table 8. Percentage Change in Food Consumption from Involuntary Job Loss

Age and wealth	Permanent earnings quartile			
	1	2	3	4
Under 62, no social security				
Low wealth	−22	−27	−31	−31
High wealth	−13	−18	−22	−22
62 and over, social security				
Low wealth	−4	−9	−13	−13
High wealth	−4	−9	−13	−13

Source: See table 2.

preretirement consumption is 29 percent; for high-wealth people it is 19 percent. However, for involuntary job loss after age 62 the decrease in food consumption is considerably less. Furthermore, wealth no longer has any effect on the decline in consumption. Both low-wealth and high-wealth people change their food consumption by identical percentage amounts. Note that this finding of an approximately 30 percent drop in consumption for involuntary retirees will be an *underestimate* for people who did not anticipate the onset of bad health or their job loss. People who anticipated their involuntary retirement would have adjusted their savings to some extent before their job loss. We cannot measure the difference created by anticipated and unanticipated job loss, and appropriate definitions to distinguish the two groups are not clear. Nevertheless, our finding of a 30 percent decrease in food consumption can be seen as a lower bound for people whose previous health or job history did not indicate the likelihood of involuntary retirement.

A potential problem with the above results is their neglect of the possible endogeneity of the retirement and wealth variable in the consumption equations. That is, people who plan to retire earlier will save more to amass greater levels of wealth to finance their retirement. If their health subsequently deteriorates or they lose their jobs, they will be more likely to retire than other people, since the higher level of accumulated wealth may allow them to do so. Therefore, the change in food consumption may depend on unobservable taste variables that also affect the retirement decision and the level of wealth, which are used as right-hand-side variables in the regression specification. This possible joint endogeneity could then lead to biased coefficient estimates. To see the possible effect of this joint endogeneity, we used the retirement model of Diamond and Hausman, which was estimated on the RHS data by Hausman and Wise, to predict the cumulative probability of retirement in each year for a given

Table 9. Instrumental Variable Estimates of Consumption

Variable	Difference (2)	Log difference (4)
Household size	−77.5	−0.122
	(−4.4)	(−0.005)
Married	−0.499	−0.559
	(−14.8)	(−0.018)
Health limits work	10.4	0.013
	(8.3)	(0.010)
Age squared	0.239	0.00011
	(0.473)	(0.00058)
Retired	−148.7	−0.158
	(−55.2)	(−0.062)
Involuntary job loss	−197.6	−0.081
	(−79.7)	(−0.090)
Retired × loss	123.1	0.005
	(90.2)	(0.100)
Loss × age <62	−52.8	−0.101
	(−42.5)	(−0.047)
Loss × log (PEH)	...	...
Loss × first quartile of PEH	111.2	0.098
	(47.7)	(0.054)
Loss × second quartile of PEH	72.8	0.035
	(140.9)	(0.048)
Loss × third quartile of PEH	25.6	0.015
	(41.1)	(0.047)
Loss × low total wealth	−51.2	−0.116
	(−88.8)	(−0.105)
Loss × low wealth × eligible for social security	−3.77	0.045
	(−54.8)	(0.061)

Source: See table 2. Numbers in parentheses are *t*- statistics.

person.[25] The probability depends on the person's age, health status, and financial situation. These predicted probabilities were then used as instrumental variables for the observed retirement status in the consumption equations. Similarly, we used an instrumental variable procedure that also treated the level of wealth as endogenous (see table 9).[26]

The results in table 9 should be compared with columns 2 and 4 of table 6 to which they correspond. Note that the coefficients are not estimated as precisely in table 9 because instrumental variables estimators have been

25. See Diamond and Hausman, "Retirement and Unemployment Behavior"; and Hausman and Wise, "Attrition Bias."

26. This instrumental variable technique is similar to the use of two-stage least squares in more standard simultaneous equation specifications.

used. But for most of the estimated coefficients, the two sets of estimates give similar results. A statistical test for significant differences in the two sets of estimates fails to reject the hypothesis that the estimates are the same.[27] To some extent, however, the result of this test suffers from the imprecise estimates in table 9. If the retirement coefficients and the job loss coefficients in the respective tables are examined, the estimated coefficients change in the expected direction. Both coefficients increase in magnitude in table 9 over those in table 6. Thus we conclude that the instrumental variable and least-squares results lead to similar conclusions about food consumption reductions.

The last set of consumption results that we consider are regression specifications for the level of food consumption and the log of food consumption. That is, rather than examining the change in food consumption, we attempt to determine the amount of money spent on food consumption in a given year. This specification corresponds more closely to the traditional approach to consumption analysis, in which demand for a commodity depends on (permanent) income or wealth as well as relative price and socioeconomic characteristics. The danger in this type of specification is that people with involuntary job losses may have lower levels of consumption than non–job losers because of our inability to control totally for observed variables, such as wealth, and unobserved individual characteristics. Thus the possibility of spurious results is higher when we consider the amount of food consumption to determine the effect of involuntary job loss. The specification has the same variables as the first-difference specification, with additional variables added to control for individual budget levels. These variables are permanent earnings of the husband, permanent earnings of the wife, wealth at the beginning of the survey, and eligibility for a private pension. Tables 10 and 11 present the results analogous to tables 7 and 8, which look at the net effect on consumption of involuntary job loss.[28]

For people under 62, consumption does not fall by as much in table 10 as it did in table 7. The difference is about $60 for low-wealth people. But the difference is considerably more dramatic for high-wealth people. In

27. See Jerry A. Hausman, "Specification Tests in Econometrics," *Econometrica,* vol. 46 (November 1978), pp. 1251–71.

28. The statistical precision of the estimates used in tables 10 and 11 is somewhat less than in tables 7 and 8, but the coefficient estimates remain statistically significant at standard levels of significance. A generalized "random effects" specification rather than the previous "fixed effects" specification is used here. For an explanation of the differences in these econometric specifications, see Hausman and Taylor, "Panel Data."

Table 10. Change in Expenditure on Food Consumption from Involuntary Job Loss, Using Food Consumption Specification
Dollars

Age and wealth	Permanent earnings quartile			
	1	2	3	4
Under 62, no social security				
Low wealth	−134	−169	−186	−196
High wealth	−30	−64	−82	−92
62 and over, social security				
Low wealth	29	−6	−24	−33
High wealth	−13	−48	−66	−75

Source: See table 2.

table 10 consumption for high-wealth people declines about $100 more than for low-wealth people; in table 7 it declines about $50. When we consider people over 62, we find even larger differences. The decrease in consumption is much less; for the lowest income quartile consumption actually increases. In this instance, the consumption of high-wealth men declines by a greater amount than that of low-wealth men.

We now do a similar comparison for percentage change in food consumption using the log of food expenditure equation (table 11). These results should be compared with those in table 8, which also considered percentage changes. The percentage decreases in table 11 are again smaller than the percentage decreases in table 8. But the difference between low-wealth people and high-wealth people under 62 is similar to that in table 8. For people over 62, the pattern is similar to that in table 9. Consumption decreases less for low-wealth people and even increases for the lowest-income group.

Tables 10 and 11 give results for the effect of involuntary job loss

Table 11. Percentage Change in Food Consumption from Involuntary Job Loss, Using Log Food Consumption Specification

Age and wealth	Permanent earnings quartile			
	1	2	3	4
Under 62, no social security				
Low wealth	−16	−21	−25	−26
High wealth	−3	−7	−12	−12
62 and over, social security				
Low wealth	5	1	−3	−4
High wealth	2	−3	−7	−8

Source: See table 2.

similar to those in tables 7 and 8. Involuntary job loss leads to a significant decrease in consumption. But for those people who can receive social security benefits the decrease in consumption is significantly less. Social security thus plays an important role in alleviating the effects of unexpected job loss. People appear to be unable to adjust sufficiently to the loss of their jobs before age 62. And the total effect seems quite large.

Conclusions

In our study of the causes of retirement and variations in food consumption we have found a number of results that may affect accepted views on the social security system. Though labor-force participation of men under age 62 has been declining, many of the retirements that occur follow an involuntary job loss. We found that 75 percent of retirements of men under age 56, 60 percent of retirements of men aged 56–59, and 40 percent of retirements of men aged 60 and 61 are involuntary. It is only at age 62 and over, when men qualify for social security benefits, that we find that the great majority of retirements are voluntary.

When a person retires before age 62, he can finance his consumption either from financial wealth or from other retirement income. Our results indicate that the level of financial wealth is quite low for our sample and exceptionally low for the group of involuntary retirees. Nor do a significant fraction qualify for private pension benefits. For men who retired at age 54 or under only 3 percent received private pensions, and for retirees aged 55–61 only 54 percent qualified to receive private pensions when they retired. Therefore, early retirees do not appear to have the financial resources to finance their previous consumption pattern until they begin to receive social security benefits. Food consumption fell significantly more for involuntary retirees than for voluntary retirees. It fell by approximately 20 percent more for low-wealth involuntary retirees than for voluntary retirees under 62, and it fell by about 10 percent more for high-wealth involuntary retirees than for voluntary retirees under 62. But there was a much smaller difference in food consumption between involuntary retirees and voluntary retirees aged 62 or more.

We conclude that people who involuntarily retire before age 62 are constrained in their consumption patterns. That is, not only does their consumption decline because of their decrease in lifetime wealth, but their immediate consumption falls more than its permanent level, since it rises again after they begin to receive social security benefits.[29] Thus involuntary retirees under 62, especially those with low wealth, have a decrease in their food consumption large enough to indicate the clear possibility of financial distress.

Present government policy allows penalty-free withdrawal of money from certain private pension plans, such as the 401 savings plans, when involuntary job loss or financial distress occurs. Insofar as social security is seen as a forced savings plan, similar penalty-free "withdrawals" of contributions might be in order when involuntary retirement occurs. Reducing the age at which early retirement can be taken seems objectionable to some people on paternalistic grounds. But if involuntary retirement occurs, withdrawals of contributions through a real annuity could lead to increased welfare for people who might otherwise have to wait many years before they are eligible to receive social security or private pension benefits.

Comment by Edward Lazear

In their paper, Jerry Hausman and Lynn Paquette address two questions. First, if an older male worker is forced to retire because of poor health or involuntary layoff, does he suffer a fall in consumption? Such a decline in consumption might occur because of the unanticipated, and presumably involuntary, fall in income. Second, for a worker who suffers involuntary retirement, is there enough wealth for him to maintain a reasonable consumption level? If wealth is too low for a substantial percent of involuntary retirees, there may be justification for reforms in the social security system to help some of them.

The authors conclude that involuntary early retirement does result in a sharp decline in consumption. In particular, they find evidence that food consumption declines by as much as 20 percent. This implies that significant distress could occur in families whose breadwinners are forced to retire early. Hausman and Paquette draw a policy implication from this

29. Using aggregate data, Wilcox also found evidence of constrained consumption patterns. He found that retail sales increased only when social security benefits *actually* increased, not when increases in benefits were announced. Since sales increase only when the benefit check arrives, liquidity-constrained consumption is clearly implied. David W. Wilcox, "Social Security Benefits, Consumption Expenditure, and the Failure of Ricardian Equivalence" (MIT, 1985).

finding. Early retirement benefits from social security should not be limited to retirees who have attained their 62d birthday. Under some circumstances workers under 62 should be permitted to draw benefits to alleviate the hardship of involuntary retirement.

The authors do three things. First, they classify early retirements into voluntary and involuntary. They show how the frequency of involuntary retirement varies with age. Second, they examine the effects of early retirement on food consumption. And finally, they attempt to draw some policy conclusions from their results.

The source of data for the paper is the Retirement History Survey. The data set is familiar because it has been used extensively in studying the elderly. The authors use information from six of the biannual surveys, covering the years 1969 through 1979. Respondents in the survey were aged 58 through 63 during the baseline interview in 1969. The authors combine the information obtained on the surveys with earnings information in the Social Security Administration's earnings history files to obtain estimates of respondents' permanent income. They also compute the financial wealth holdings of survey respondents.

The analysis sample contains slightly more than 4,000 observations. Government employees and the self-employed are excluded from the sample; only wage and salary employees are considered. Retirement is defined as not working and not seeking employment. In some cases, workers who are working short hours are also considered to be retired. People are considered involuntarily retired if they were discharged from work or forced to leave it, either because of an employer layoff or because of bad health.

Food consumption is measured in a straightforward way. The authors consider expenditures on food consumed inside and outside the home. They argue that food consumption provides a good measure of total average consumption, since it is an outlay on a necessity rather than a luxury.

Using their definitions, the authors estimate that 37 percent of retirements in their sample are involuntary. One of their more important findings is that the relative frequency of involuntary retirement is much higher at lower ages, say, below 60. Among people retiring before 60, the probability of an involuntary retirement is high. In fact, 19 percent of all retirements are involuntary and occur before age 62, when early social security benefits are first available.

Hausman and Paquette then examine the potential sources of income of early retirees. They find, perhaps not surprisingly, that a high percent of early retirees must wait one or more years before they are eligible to begin drawing retirement income, such as social security or private pensions. For example, 18 percent of retirees between ages 55 and 61 must wait at least two years for retirement benefits to begin. This delay in retirement income might imply potential hardship for many of these workers. This point is reinforced when the authors consider the retirement wealth of retirees. People who are forced to leave employment involuntarily are disproportionately represented among those with extremely low wealth. This finding suggests that their assets do not provide a comfortable reserve against unanticipated loss of earnings.

The most important findings reported in the first section of the paper are related to food consumption. The authors examine the ratio of food consumption before retirement to consumption after retirement. They find that for men retiring before age 62 the ratio of postretirement to preretirement food consumption is much lower in the case of men forced to leave work involuntarily. Hence there is apparently a larger decline in food consumption among those who involuntarily retire. The evidence suggests that the effect is not quite as important for those who retire after age 62, but even for those men a sizable difference exists between voluntary and involuntary retirees.

The information in the first section is presented in terms of simple distributions—differences in means, quartile rankings, and so forth. This kind of evidence makes the authors' point almost as well as that reported in the second part of the paper, which is based on a more formal statistical model. The advantage of the formal modeling is that it permits Hausman and Paquette to hold other factors constant when they compare voluntary with involuntary retirees. The authors derive two equations to explain food consumption, one measured in terms of changes in the level of expenditure and the other in terms of changes in the log of expenditure. They use these equations to determine whether involuntary retirement has an effect on the consumption level. The key to the approach, of course, is that by looking at *changes* in consumption the analysts have implicitly controlled for all the individual effects that remain constant over time. A critic cannot argue that there are unobserved differences causing some individuals to be low consumers of food in the first place.

The equations are estimated by using seemingly unrelated regressions. The basic results do not seem to depend critically on the functional form specification. The findings are as follows. Involuntary job loss leads to a decline in per person consumption of a little over 10 percent. The percentage fall depends on permanent income level. For workers in the *lowest* wealth quartile, involuntary job loss is associated with a 19 percent fall in food consumption. When social security benefits commence, food consumption rises again, but by less than the 19 percent decline. For those who retire when social security benefits are available, the reduction in food expenditures is much smaller. Involuntary retirement really does appear to affect food consumption. The results do not seem to be sensitive to the statistical endogeneity of wealth accumulation or the retirement age.

From the evidence in their paper, Hausman and Paquette conclude that a reexamination of social security early retirement benefits is in order. They suggest that the government should consider permitting people to withdraw money from social security before age 62. Such permission should be granted to workers who suffer involuntary job loss and who would otherwise face sharp drops in consumption.

I have a few comments on the paper and its policy suggestions. This is really a simple paper—not simple-minded, but simple. Because it is so straightforward, it is easy to believe the reported findings. While reading it, I frequently thought of things that I would do were I writing the paper, but then I found that the authors did them. The point of the paper is made in several different ways: in simple tabulations and in sophisticated regression analysis. But the basic conclusion—that food consumption falls substantially after involuntary early retirement—is strong and holds up no matter how simple or sophisticated the analysis.

The finding is important because it has implications for the design of social security. When thinking about the social security system, one is likely to focus first on the age of normal and early retirement benefits. The normal retirement age has recently been raised for people retiring in the next century. Many critics have pointed out that this change is regressive, since people who are likely to be hurt by it are the ones who can least afford to suffer reductions in benefits. Workers who retire early comprise a large group of individuals who suffer job loss because of poor health. These are not the kind of workers the nation wants to penalize. Hausman and Paquette confirm that a significant part of the retirement population that will be harmed by the reform consists of people suffering involuntary job loss.

I have a number of suggestions for improving or extending the research reported here. Some suggestions are general; others specific. I begin with some general points.

Before considering the policy implications of the paper, it is worth stepping back and asking a more fundamental question. What is an "appropriate" reduction in food consumption upon retirement? At first blush, any decline at all might seem to be a bad thing. But this is not obviously true. Should social security benefits always be high enough so that retirees *never* suffer a drop in consumption? If not, what should the standard be?

This issue seems especially troublesome when one looks at one of the components of food consumption examined in the paper, consumption outside the home. Consider two families, both with the same income. One family has two earners; the second only one. The two-earner family will probably eat a larger proportion of its meals outside the home and thus have higher food expenditures. But which family is richer? Clearly the family earning the same income with fewer earners is better off, because it has more leisure available. So one cannot necessarily conclude that the richer family is the one with the higher reported food consumption.

That objection to using food expenditures as a reliable index of the family's consumption well-being may be less important for this paper than it would be elsewhere. For one thing, food consumption in this elderly sample may not be very sensitive to that particular issue. Especially for poorer families, the food consumed should represent a necessity. For another, most of the conclusions drawn in the paper are based on a comparison between involuntarily retired men and voluntary retirees. It is not clear that the leisure versus food consumption issue should affect one of these groups more than the other.

A second general comment involves the distinction between involuntary and unanticipated retirement. When the authors use the phrase "involuntary retirement," I think they mean "involuntary *and* unanticipated retirement." There is a difference between "involuntary and anticipated" and "involuntary and unanticipated." For example, a mandatory retirement is involuntary by the definition in this paper. But one should not worry as much about an "involuntary" retiree forced to leave work by mandatory retirement as one does about the person forced to retire because of a sudden heart attack. I think there is an important distinction here that is ignored in the paper.

As a practical matter, the issue may be relatively unimportant for men forced to retire before age 60. Few workers subject to mandatory retirement provisions face a mandatory retirement age of less than 60. And most of the interesting results in the paper seem to focus on men retiring before age 60.

There remains a fundamental question about the difference between a voluntary and an involuntary retirement. Consider a 57-year-old employee who is getting somewhat slow on his job. His employer might sweeten his pension to encourage him to leave. If the employee accepts the offer, Hausman and Paquette would treat the retirement as "voluntary," even though its voluntary nature is not clear. As a general point, when one considers a voluntary versus involuntary separation, the issue is, who initiated the separation? One can change who initiates the separation by changing the price of a separation. That is a common criticism of attempts to distinguish between quits and layoffs.

Within the context of this paper, the criticism does not seem especially severe. It is clear from reported food expenditures that the authors' distinction between voluntary and involuntary has some meaning. But it would still be useful to vary the definition of involuntary retirees to exclude those facing mandatory retirement rules, if for no other reason.

My third general comment concerns the issue of who is hurt by early retirement. Are early retirees lucky or unlucky? If a worker retires early it is because some alternative use of time has jumped in value in comparison with his wage rate at his current firm. There are two ways that can happen: if his wage rate suddenly falls, or if the value of an alternative use of his time rises. These two explanations have different implications. If the value of an alternative use of time has gone up, the early retiree may be lucky. If the wage rate has fallen, the early retiree is unfortunate. The usual idea is that the early retiree is unlucky rather than lucky, which is why some of us worry about the consequences of raising the retirement age.

I think it is useful to have additional information on this issue. The material presented in the first part of the paper sheds some light on the problem. The authors find that involuntary retirement is relatively more common among younger retirees than older ones. This finding suggests that a typical early retiree has a high probability of being "unlucky." But other types of evidence are also relevant. For example, the authors could simply examine income levels and consumption levels by age of retirement. This type of comparison is implicitly made within the regressions reported in the paper, but it would be useful to see the results explicitly displayed in a table. Such a table would give the reader a clearer sense of the relative well-being of early versus late retirees.

I also have a minor criticism of the paper. When the authors define involuntary retirees, they include a group of part-time workers who work less than thirty-five hours a week. But these workers should probably be excluded. Their income situation is most likely different from that of men forced to discontinue work altogether.

In closing, I would like to comment on the authors' policy proposal. They suggest offering very early social security benefits to workers who involuntarily retire before age 62. I am bothered by this proposal for several reasons. Most important, the definition of involuntary retirement could be easily manipulated. The firm and the worker could collude against the government to ensure that all early leaves are recorded as involuntary terminations. The standard problem exists of simultaneously creating efficient incentives for separation and efficient insurance. Hence I think the authors might be a little too quick to draw their policy conclusion.

Robert A. Moffitt

Life-Cycle Labor Supply and Social Security: A Time-Series Analysis

Between the end of World War II and the present, there have been marked reductions in the employment rates, hours of work, and other measures of labor supply for men in the United States. These reductions have occurred at all ages but have been particularly strong at older ages. The reductions for older men are widely believed to be a result of the increasing generosity of the social security system, the benefits and coverage of which have grown over this period. The system was created in 1935, and benefits began to be paid in 1940, but benefit levels and recipiency rates were low for the first decade or so of the system. In the 1950s, however, coverage rates, recipiency rates, and benefit levels began to grow, and in the late 1960s and early 1970s large increases in real benefits were legislated by Congress. The labor supply of older men dropped sharply in the 1970s as well, lending further specific support to the hypothesis that the social security system has caused the decline in labor supply.

The resolution of the empirical question of the magnitude of the contribution of social security to these declines in labor supply is important for social security policy. A specific example of its importance lies in the cost implications of advancing or lowering the retirement ages of the elderly. If the growth rate of real social security benefits declines in the future, as it must, it is possible that retirement ages of the aged will eventually creep upward. This advancement of the retirement age in turn will have a significant effect on the cost consequences of planned increases in "normal" retirement ages under social security in the next century. The magnitude of

I thank Joseph Quinn, the participants of the Brookings Conference on Retirement and Aging, and the participants in a workshop at McMaster University for comments. The able assistance of Ralph Buckley, Suk-Jae Noh, and Anuradha Rangarajan is also gratefully acknowledged.

such consequences will clearly depend critically on the responsiveness of retirement decisions to the level of social security benefits.

Nevertheless, the hypothesis that the social security system has induced the time-series decline in the labor supply of the aged is based primarily on studies of individuals' behavior in the late 1960s and 1970s, both cross-sectional studies of individuals and panel-data studies following individuals over time. Evidence from the 1950s and early 1960s is sparse, other than aggregate time-series evidence, and the time-series data have rarely been used in the economic literature. A good example of the type of study that has been done is the early study of Boskin, who estimated what was essentially a cross-sectional model with data on individuals from 1968–72 and then used the results to "backcast" time-series trends in labor supply.[1] Boskin's results indicated that social security was the most important explanatory factor for the reductions in time-series labor supply. Other studies have used panel data sets on individuals from the Retirement History Survey or the National Longitudinal Survey, but these again cover only the late 1960s or the 1970s.[2] Such data are appropriately used for a direct study of the effects of the benefit increases in the late 1960s and early 1970s, but they are not sufficient for an examination of the effect of social security in the earlier years of the postwar period.

This study provides a direct examination of the postwar time-series aggregate data. Annual data on labor supply of men in the United States are used in conjunction with measures of the social security system to obtain estimates of the effect of the system on work effort. The study can thus provide, at minimum, an estimate of the extent to which the individual-data studies just mentioned provide accurate indicators of the entire postwar experience, and of the extent to which time-series trends of the 1950s and early 1960s are consistent with those studies.

---

1. Michael J. Boskin, "Social Security and Retirement Decisions," *Economic Inquiry,* vol. 15 (January 1977), pp. 1–25.

2. A few examples are two studies by Gary Burtless and Robert A. Moffitt, "The Effect of Social Security Benefits on the Labor Supply of the Aged," in Henry J. Aaron and Gary Burtless, eds., *Retirement and Economic Behavior* (Brookings, 1984), pp. 135–74, and "The Joint Choice of Retirement Age and Postretirement Hours of Work," *Journal of Labor Economics,* vol. 3 (April 1985), pp. 209–36; Peter A. Diamond and Jerry A Hausman, "The Retirement and Unemployment Behavior of Older Men," in Aaron and Burtless, *Retirement and Economic Behavior,* pp. 97–134; and Michael D. Hurd and Michael J. Boskin, "The Effect of Social Security on Retirement in the Early 1970s," *Quarterly Journal of Economics,* vol. 99 (November 1984), pp. 767–90. A literature review is provided in Henry J. Aaron, *Economic Effects of Social Security* (Brookings, 1982).

Because the primary motivation for the paper rests in the argument that the time-series data are worthy of examination—if they may not be preferable in some ways to cross-sectional data and short panels—a brief review of the relative advantages and disadvantages of cross-sectional and panel data is necessary.

Cross-sectional individual data currently tend to be favored over time-series, aggregate data because of the large number of degrees of freedom in cross-sectional data. But use of cross-sectional data requires making statistical inferences solely from comparisons of individuals, a difficulty particularly important for the analysis of social security. For social security, the law is the same for all people at any given time; consequently, all cross-sectional variation in social security benefits or any other measure of the system must arise from cross-sectional variation in earnings received over the lifetime, in family size and the number of dependents, in marital status, and in other such variables. That is, there is no variation in the law itself. The potential difficulty of course is that the variables for which variation is available may have independent effects on labor supply; hence there is a fundamental identification problem in cross-sectional data, a problem that can only be overcome by making restrictions in functional form of one kind or another. This identification problem is only partially overcome by existing micropanels, for most of these are too short to capture many of the important changes in the law.[3]

Time-series data do not have this problem but do have problems associated with low degrees of freedom. Because of the small number of observations and because many variables trend together and hence are highly correlated, inferences made from time-series data are inherently weaker than those made from cross-sectional data. As a consequence, only simple tests have much statistical power; it is virtually impossible to discriminate

3. The microdata panels can capture the major changes in the law in 1972 and the late 1960s. Indeed, at least two studies (Hurd and Boskin, "Effect of Social Security on Retirement," and Gary Burtless, "Social Security, Unanticipated Benefit Increases, and the Timing of Retirement," *Review of Economic Studies,* forthcoming) have treated these law changes as unexpected shocks, just as in this study, and have directly examined the labor supply response to the shock. Relative to those studies, the present study considers a longer time span and a greater number of law changes. There is some question, however, whether the 1972 law did constitute a "shock" (see below). The time-series evidence has been used previously to examine the effects of the social security system on saving. See Martin Feldstein, "Social Security, Induced Retirement, and Aggregate Capital Accumulation," *Journal of Political Economy,* vol. 82 (September–October 1974), pp. 905–26; and Dean R. Leimer and Selig D. Lesnoy, "Social Security and Private Saving: New Time-Series Evidence," *Journal of Political Economy,* vol. 90 (June 1982), pp. 606–29.

between competing hypotheses of great sophistication and subtlety. There-fore, only a simple model of the effect of social security on life-cycle labor supply will be examined here—social security will be assumed simply to set off wealth effects that may decrease labor supply over the lifetime. Even in this simple model, however, the high correlation between trends in real income and in social security wealth makes it quite difficult, if not impossible, to estimate the separate effects of these two variables on labor supply. Indeed, an alternative hypothesis for the observed reductions in time-series measures of labor supply is that they have been a result of rising private income levels, not social security.

This identification problem in the time-series data provides a point of focus for the paper. Solution of the problem is found here by estimating the wealth elasticity of labor supply only from variations in *unexpected changes* in net social security wealth (that is, net of taxes) over the life cycle. Neither the value of private wealth nor the value of net social security wealth at the beginning of a cohort's life cycle is used to identify the elasticity; these variables are not even included in the estimating equa-tions.

In the next section a brief overview of the time-series trends in labor supply and social security is provided. That first provides the background for the rest of the paper and documents the trend discussed here in the introduction. The second section contains a discussion of the life-cycle model of labor supply, on which the estimating equations in the study are based, as well as further discussion of the identification problem just described. The third section presents the existing time-series data and shows how limiting those data are. That section provides an illustration of the general point made about the inability of time-series data to discrimi-nate between subtle hypotheses. Although the data are sufficiently weak to sustain legitimate doubt that an analysis can be undertaken, it is argued that the estimating equations can be reformulated in such a way as to provide a sound and potentially fruitful test of the effect of social security on labor supply. The equations represent little more than simple correla-tional analysis but capture correctly the intuition of how social security affects labor supply. The fourth section discusses how unexpected changes, or "shocks," in social security wealth are calculated and presents several alternative methods of calculation. There are major surprises in this section, for the results do not correspond to expectations. The fifth section, which presents the estimating results, confirms these unexpected findings. The final section offers a summary and conclusions.

Trends in Labor Supply and Social Security since World War II

Figures 1 and 2 show the trends in the labor-force participation and in annual hours of work of men over the postwar period separately by age group. Both participation rates and hours of work show declines after the late 1960s. For younger men there were increases in the measures in the 1950s, but for older men there is a continuous decline over the entire period. Note that the trends for the two older male categories are not the same. For the oldest age category, males 65 years old and older, participation rates seem to have declined the most in the 1950s and 1960s, less so in the 1970s. The hours worked by these men show a fairly steady decline, although somewhat larger in the early 1950s and 1970s than in the 1960s. For men aged 45–64, however, there is an accelerating rate of reduction in participation rates starting in the early 1960s.

An unpublished appendix to this paper, available from the author on request, shows trends for employment rates (that is, employment-to-population ratios) and for weeks worked over the year, as well as the trends in all four measures for women. The trends in employment rates and weeks worked for men follow those in figures 1 and 2, as should be expected. For women, increases in labor supply have been the rule over the postwar period; of interest, however, is that the rates of increase have declined for women over time. The labor supply levels of older women have actually declined, in marked contrast to those of other women.

There is a prima facie case that these declines in labor supply are a result of the social security system. Real benefit levels have increased, and coverage of the system has been broadened over time. Regressions of participation rates and hours of work for older age groups, performed on the real benefit, yield coefficients that are strongly negative and significant, reflecting their obvious negative correlation over time. At the same time, real wage rates have risen as the result of normal economic growth. Regressions of the same labor supply measures on real wage rates again yield significantly negative coefficients, a result in general interpreted as evidence of backward-bending labor supply. Separating the effects of benefits and wages is difficult in the presence of the high correlation between them.

Fortunately for the purposes of analysis, the rising benefit levels have not occurred steadily. Although coverage rates and recipiency rates have trended upward gradually, and although social security tax rates were steady until the 1970s, benefit levels underwent dramatic changes. After

Figure 1. Labor-Force Participation Rate of Men, by Age Group, 1947–82

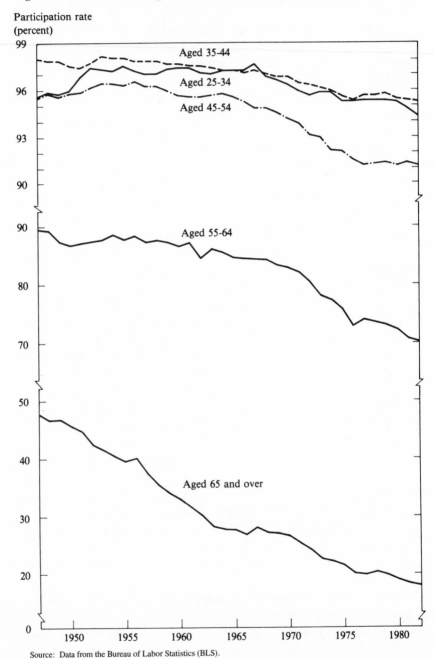

Participation rate
(percent)

Source: Data from the Bureau of Labor Statistics (BLS).

Figure 2. Annual Hours of Work for Men, by Age Group, 1950–81[a]

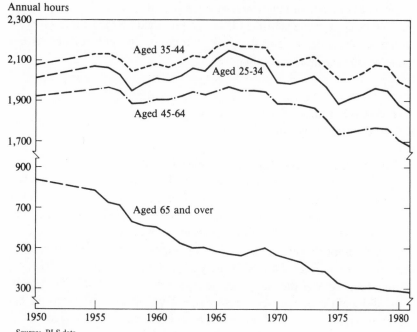

Annual hours

Source: BLS data.
a. Annual hours are defined as workers' hours per week times weeks worked per year.

being initially set in 1937, benefits were held constant in nominal terms until 1949, with the result that real benefits were reduced over that period. Then in 1950 benefits were increased by up to 60 percent in a single year. Subsequently, benefits rose steadily but without dramatic change until the late 1960s and early 1970s, when benefits were increased frequently. That series of increases culminated in 1972 legislation that not only increased benefits by about 20 percent in a single year but also indexed benefits for the first time. Since then benefits have again risen only steadily.

The trends in figures 1 and 2 correspond partially, but not fully, to the expectations generated by the timing of these shocks. Although as a general rule the figures show that labor supply declined more in the late 1960s and 1970s than it did previously, this is not the case for every group (for example, not for males 65 years and older). Furthermore, although the 1950 benefit increase was equal to or larger in percentage terms than the 1972 increase, there is no indication of any significant post-1950 decline in participation rates (except possibly for the group over age 65) or in any of the participation rates or hours worked for groups of younger men.

Clearly there may be other time-varying explanatory factors for the differences in labor supply trends over the period, thus leading to multivariate analysis. But the statistical leverage provided by the sudden changes in the structure of the social security program will still be used as the primary identifying causal influence.

Life-Cycle Labor Supply, Social Security, and the Identification Problem

In this section I shall discuss a simple life-cycle model theory of labor supply and shall present some basic results showing how unexpected changes in the value of lifetime wealth affect the life-cycle profile of labor supply. The model will then be made concrete by specifying a particular form (Stone-Geary) for the utility function and by introducing social security as a simple wealth transfer that undergoes unexpected alterations. Equations are derived for labor supply at each age that are a function of, among other things, the entire past sequence of wealth shocks. The problem of identification arises because the level of private assets is not observed and because the trend in this level is correlated with that of social security wealth. The identification problem can be solved by simple first-differencing of the equation, by the introduction of cohort dummies, or by both. In all cases, the coefficient measuring the wealth elasticity of labor supply—which also measures the effect of social security—is identified in these equations solely by the values of the social security shocks.

The Theory of Wealth Shocks

Here it will be shown that unexpected changes in wealth have a greater negative effect on labor supply than do expected changes in wealth, and that such shocks have larger effects as the age at which the shock occurs increases. The reader who wishes to do so may skip this section because the subsequent subsection, on a specific model, does not depend for understanding on the material presented here.

In the life-cycle theory of labor supply, a person chooses labor supply in each period of life in response to values of wages and prices over a lifetime and to the value of exogenous wealth. As a first approximation in this framework, the social security system can be modeled as providing an increment to the value of exogenous wealth. This treatment is only an approximation because the system also alters the relative price of leisure over the lifetime, but it can be safely assumed that the wealth effects of social security dominate its substitution effects in time series.[4] Increases in the value of exogenous wealth decrease labor supply in all periods of the lifetime, if it is assumed that leisure is a normal good in all.

Unanticipated wealth increments have the same direction of effect but differ in their magnitude and pattern over the life cycle. Such increments in wealth decrease labor supply more than do expected increments because past labor supply was chosen on the basis of an expectation of lower lifetime wealth. When a wealth shock occurs, a person must replan his labor supply profile and make up for lost time.

In formal terms, suppose that the lifetime utility function is of the general nonseparable form:

(1) $U(H_1, H_2, \ldots, H_T, C_1, C_2, \ldots, C_T),$

where H_a is a labor supply at age a, C_a is consumption at age a, and T is the length of adult life. For convenience, hours of work are used in the utility function instead of hours of leisure. The lifetime budget constraint at $a = 1$ is

(2) $$A + \sum_{a=1}^{T} r_a W_a H_a = \sum_{a=1}^{T} r_a C_a,$$

where A is exogenous wealth at the start of the lifetime; r_a is the market discount rate, defined as one, divided by one plus the interest rate raised to

4. Although the social security system sets off both substitution and income effects (see Gary Burtless and Robert A. Moffitt, "Social Security, Earnings Tests, and Age at Retirement," *Public Finance Quarterly*, vol. 14 [January 1986], pp. 3–27, for a simple graphical exposition), econometric estimates of the elasticities of substitution are not large (Burtless and Moffitt, "Effect of Social Security Benefits" and "Choice of Retirement Age"). Moreover, the elasticities of substitution would have to be extraordinarily high to outweigh the large wealth effects set off by social security transfers, especially in time series, since the shocks in the 1950s, late 1960s, and early 1970s were predominantly due to changes in benefit levels rather than in tax rates. The one time-series study of relative price effects is that of Richard V. Burkhauser and John A. Turner, "A Time-Series Analysis on Social Security and Its Effect on the Market Work of Men at Younger Ages," *Journal of Political Economy*, vol. 86 (August 1978), pp. 701–15, which offered the interesting hypothesis that the retirement test induces younger men to work longer hours than older men. Burkhauser and Turner's empirical evidence, however, was based on trends in hours of work for all men, whereas the evidence given above indicates that men aged 45–64 (most of whom do not receive benefits) reduced their labor supply.

the ath power; and W_a is the hourly wage rate at age a. The price of consumption goods is normalized to unity. The utility-maximizing labor supply functions can then be written in general form as[5]

$$(3) \qquad H_a = f_a(W_1, W_2, \ldots, W_T, A), \qquad a = 1, 2, \ldots, T.$$

It is expected that an increase in A will decrease all H_a.

Now suppose that there is an unanticipated increment to wealth in the amount ΔA at age q. If $q = 1$, and thus if the individual is aware of the increment from the start, then labor supply in all future periods is

$$(4) \qquad H_a^* = f_a(W_1, W_2, \ldots, W_T, A + \Delta A), \qquad a = 1, 2, \ldots, T.$$

But if $q > 1$, then the individual must remaximize the utility function:

$$(5) \quad U(\bar{H}_1, \ldots, \bar{H}_{q-1}, H_q, \ldots, H_T, \bar{C}_1, \ldots, \bar{C}_{q-1}, C_q, \ldots, C_T),$$

where an overbar denotes a quantity that is given. The values of H_a and C_a for all $q \geq a$ must be chosen subject to the constraint

$$(6) \quad \left[(A + \Delta A) + \sum_{a=1}^{q-1} r_a(W_a\bar{H}_a - \bar{C}_a) \right] + \sum_{a=q}^{T} r_a W_a H_a = \sum_{a=q}^{T} r_a C_a.$$

Here the term in brackets is the value of "exogenous" wealth (discounted back to $a = 1$) at period q, given that $\bar{H}_a$ and $\bar{C}_a$ have been chosen up to q. The solution to the maximization will not give functions of the form f_a used above, so it is a bit awkward to compare labor supply before and after the shock. But one may consult the literature on rationing to use the function f_a after all, by defining the "virtual wages," $W'_1, W'_2, \ldots, W'_{q-1}$, as the wage rates that would have generated $\bar{H}_1, \bar{H}_2, \ldots, \bar{H}_{q-1}$ as utility-maximizing choices had wealth been equal to $A + \Delta A$ at the start of the life cycle.[6] These wages are obtainable by solving the $q - 1$ equations for

5. The discount rates r_a are suppressed in all subsequent functions in the interest of notational simplicity.

6. See Angus Deaton and John Muellbauer, *Economics and Consumer Behavior* (New York: Cambridge University Press, 1980), for a textbook treatment of the theory of rationing.

$\bar{H}_a$ as a function of the wages and of $A + \Delta A$. In this formulation one may write labor supply after $a = q$ with the functions f_a:

(7) $\qquad H_a^{**} = f_a(W_1', W_2', \ldots, W_{q-1}', W_q, \ldots, W_T, A + \Delta A),$

$\qquad a = q, \ldots, T.$

Thus expressions have been formulated for labor supply in the absence of the wealth shock—H_a in equation 3; labor supply in the presence of the wealth shock if it had been known at the beginning of the lifetime—H_a^* in equation 4; and actual labor supply given that the shock occurred in year q—H_a^{**} in equation 7. The following propositions can then be demonstrated (proofs have been omitted), with ΔA assumed to be greater than zero:

—Proposition 1:

(8) $\qquad\qquad\qquad\qquad H_a^* \le H_a;$

—Proposition 2:

(9) $\qquad\qquad\qquad\qquad H_a^{**} \le H_a^*;$

—Proposition 3:

(10) $\qquad \partial D/\partial q < 0, \qquad$ where $D = H_a^{**} - H_a^*, \qquad a \ge q.$

Proposition 1 simply states that wealth effects on labor supply are negative. Proposition 2 states that labor supply will be reduced more by an unanticipated wealth shock than by one that is anticipated at the beginning of the life cycle. Because it was not known at the beginning that the wealth increment would later occur, labor supply and consumption prior to q were "misplanned." The reductions in labor supply generated by the wealth increment would have been spread over the entire lifetime if all had been known at the beginning. Proposition 3 is suggested by proposition 2, for proposition 3 states that this "excess reduction" caused by the early misplanning is greater, the later the shock occurs in the lifetime. All these propositions, including the third, are in principle testable. If a social security shock at a given time increases the wealth of all cohorts by the same increment, and if the cohorts are alike in all other respects, then the reduction in labor supply induced by the shock will be greater for those who are older. Note that this effect is implied even if a cohort has not yet received any benefits at the time of the shock.

A Specific Model

The specific functional form used will be the Stone-Geary utility function, which generates the linear expenditure system.[7] The utility function is assumed to be

$$(11) \qquad U = \sum_{a=1}^{T} p_a[\beta \ln (\alpha - H_a) + \gamma \ln (C_a - \delta)],$$

where $p_a = s_a/(1 + \rho)^a$, the probability of survival to age a (s_a) divided by one plus the subjective rate of discount (ρ) raised to the ath power. The lifetime budget constraint at $a = 1$ is

$$(12) \qquad A = \sum_{a=1}^{T} r_a(C_a - W_a H_a),$$

where $r_a = s_a/(1 + i)^a$, the survival rate divided by one plus the interest rate raised to the ath power. The labor supply functions expressed in the form of earnings are[8]

$$(13) \qquad W_a H_a = \alpha W_a - \beta \eta^a Y,$$

where

$$(14) \qquad \eta = [(1 + i)/(1 + \rho)]$$

and

$$(15) \qquad Y = A + \sum_{a=1}^{T} r_a (W_a \alpha - \delta).$$

Substituting equation 15 into equation 13 gives

$$(16) \qquad W_a H_a = \alpha W_a - \beta \eta^a A - \beta \eta^a \alpha \sum_{\tau=1}^{T} r_\tau W_\tau + \beta \eta^a \delta \sum_{\tau=1}^{T} r_\tau.$$

7. See Orley Ashenfelter, "Macroeconomic and Microeconomic Analyses of Labor Supply" (Princeton University, 1984), for a discussion of the Stone-Geary model in a life-cycle context.

8. The normalization imposed is $\sum_{a=1}^{T} Pa(\beta + \gamma) = 1$.

Thus earnings at age a are a linear function of the wage at age a and of the variable Y—or, in equation 16, a linear function of the current wage, the initial level of assets, and the (discounted) sum of wage rates over the lifetime. The intertemporal wage elasticity for this function is $(\alpha/H_a) - 1$. This function has never been estimated in this form because the initial level of assets A (say, at age 20 or 25) is never available in time-series or individual data sets. But if A is left out of the equation, the wealth effect β cannot be identified.

This difficulty leads to the identification problem if social security is added to the model. If someone has a fixed stock of social security wealth known at the beginning of the life cycle, equal to the discounted sum of the difference between benefits and taxes and denoted S, then the variable $A + S$ would appear in place of A in the equation. If S were unobserved, one would again be unable to identify β. If a value of S were calculable (as it will be below), then one would be able to identify β. But if A is unobserved, then the effects of A and S cannot be disentangled; omission of A from the equation would bias the estimate of β. Note that it is the unobservability of assets, not of wages, that creates these difficulties.

To identify β instead from a social security shock, consider an unexpected net wealth increment from the social security system in the amount Q at age q. Then the solution to the replanning problem yields the earnings function:

$$(17) \qquad W_a H_a = \alpha W_a - \beta \eta^a (Y + k_q Q),$$

where

$$(18) \qquad k_q = \sum_{\tau=1}^{T} p_\tau / \sum_{\tau=q}^{T} p_\tau,$$

and where Y now includes $A + S$. The wealth increment Q appears with a coefficient that is greater than unity and that increases with q, as discussed earlier. If there are continual unexpected net wealth increments of Q_q at each q, the earnings function becomes

$$(19) \qquad W_a H_a = \alpha W_a - \beta \eta^a \left(Y + \sum_{\tau=2}^{a} k_\tau Q_\tau \right).$$

Here there is a "weighted" supernumerary income, in parentheses, that is equal not to the straight sum of wealth over the lifetime but rather to the sum of such increments weighted by the age at which they occur.[9] For empirical purposes, the two parameters η^a and k_q will be approximated by their first-order Taylor-series expansions:

$$(20) \qquad\qquad \eta^a \simeq 1 + a \ln \eta = 1 + a\eta'$$

$$(21) \qquad\qquad k_q \simeq T/(T - q + 1) = k_q',$$

thus giving the earnings function:

$$(22) \quad W_a H_a = \alpha W_a - \beta\left(Y + \sum_{\tau=2}^{a} k_\tau' Q_\tau\right) - \beta\eta' a\left(Y + \sum_{\tau=2}^{a} k_\tau' Q_\tau\right).$$

If Y is unobserved, then equation 22 cannot be estimated in this form. But if $\eta' = 0$ (that is, $i = \rho$), then a first-differenced equation would give

$$(23) \qquad W_{a+1} H_{a+1} - W_a H_a = \alpha(W_{a+1} - W_a) - \beta(k_{a+1}' Q_{a+1}).$$

Regressing the change in earnings on the change in the wage rate and the $(a + 1)^{st}$ weighted net wealth increment thus allows both α and β to be identified.[10] In particular, the wealth effect can be identified solely from the response to social security wealth shocks, not from the values of either

9. Certainty equivalence is assumed here; having to specify the effect of the variance of uncertain social security wealth is thus avoided. Note also that uncertainty in variables other than social security wealth is ignored. The first-differencing techniques used below are, in some circumstances, approximately equivalent to those that would be used in the case of uncertainty.

10. Ashenfelter and Ham also treated supernumerary income in a Stone-Geary model as a fixed effect. Orley Ashenfelter and John Ham, "Education, Unemployment, and Earnings," *Journal of Political Economy*, vol. 87 (October 1979), pp. S99–S116. Note that this treatment is quite different from first-differencing the Frisch demands. See Thomas E. MaCurdy, "An Empirical Model of Labor Supply in a Life-Cycle Setting," *Journal of Political Economy*, vol. 89 (December 1981), pp. 1059–85; and Martin Browning, Angus Deaton, and Margaret Irish, "A Profitable Approach to Labor Supply and Commodity Demands over the Life-Cycle," *Econometrica*, vol. 53 (May 1985), pp. 503–43. In that case, no wealth measures appear in the first-differenced equation, since the marginal utility of wealth is held constant. That formulation is not convenient for the application here because it is the uncertainty in wealth that is of direct interest; in Frisch models the uncertainty in wealth is instead subsumed in the (time-varying) function for the marginal utility of wealth.

private wealth or the level of social security wealth at any previous period. The problem of collinearity between unobserved private wealth and observed social security wealth is therefore eliminated.

If $i \neq \rho$, the first-differenced equation is

$$(24) \quad W_{a+1}H_{a+1} - W_aH_a = \alpha(W_{a+1} - W_a) - \beta(k'_{a+1}Q_{a+1})$$

$$- \beta\eta'(ak'_{a+1}Q_{a+1})$$

$$- \beta\eta'Y - \beta\eta'\left(\sum_{\tau=2}^{a+1} k'_\tau Q_\tau\right).$$

Here the parameter η' is identified from the coefficient on the interaction between age and the weighted wealth shock, but the unobservable Y also appears. To estimate Y, one can assume formally that Y is a fixed effect— that is, a fixed value for each cohort—and replace Y by a set of dummy variables for the cohorts in the sample.[11] This procedure allows the consistency of the other coefficients to be retained but does not alter the sources of parameter identification. But if Y is replaced by dummy variables here, it may also be replaced in the level equation 22, regardless of the value of η', with the same consequences. Hence equations 22–24 can all be estimated, and in each the wealth effect is identified solely by the presence of unexpected increments in social security net wealth.

Data and Empirical Implementation

The estimating equations for the paper are equations 22–24 above, which contain a dependent variable for earnings (hours of work times the wage rate) and independent variables for the hourly wage rate, age, and the weighted social security wealth (the weight is merely a function of age; see equation 21). The variable Y is to be proxied by dummy variables for cohort (that is, birth year). By the nature of the model, the variables for hours of work, wage, and social security must be broken down by age.[12]

11. Browning and others, "A Profitable Approach," followed this same strategy.
12. Note here that the dependent variable in the model is hours of work, not the retirement date. No data on retirement dates are available in time series; in any case, the retirement date is not unambiguously defined even in microdata. If individuals work a fixed number of hours both before and after retirement, and if the only life-cycle decision is when to retire and move from one level of work hours to another, the model used here would yield lower elasticities than it would if hours were flexible. Because the hours variable used is a

Labor Supply and Wage Data

Information on hours of work by age is available for the postwar period only from the *Current Population Survey* (CPS). The March survey has always collected data not only on hours of work but also on weeks worked in the preceding year. To construct the variable for annual hours needed here, the average number of hours worked over each calendar year was multiplied by the number of average weeks worked in the same year.[13]

Calculating hourly wage rates in the time series is more difficult. In what must rank among the most frustrating discoveries this researcher has experienced, I found that the published and unpublished CPS data do not include any summary information on earnings by age. Information on individual income is widely available, but the difference between income and earnings is quite significant for the aged—and probably for younger segments of the population as well. As a substitute, earnings data by age were taken from the published reports of the Social Security Administration. The disadvantages of such data are that they are based only on workers covered and that the published reports were forced to rely on an imputation procedure to obtain earnings above the taxable maximum.[14] In any case, these are the only data with which to work. Divided by annual hours, the requisite hourly wage is obtained.

The data impose another important limitation on implementation of the model because they are not available by single years of age, but rather by age categories. Unfortunately, hours of work are not available by age at all for years before 1955 (except from the decennial censuses) and exist only in four broad age categories for years after 1955: 25–34, 35–44, 45–64, and 65+. Thus one can study only the young, the youthful (for lack of a better term), the middle-aged, and the elderly. The more serious implica-

---

mean and would include both retirees and nonretirees, the trend in the dependent variable in the equations would reflect only the changing percentage of retirees in each age group. There is nothing particularly disadvantageous, however, in the use of time-series data in this case; microdata equations of the same type could be estimated and would also capture trends in retirement, even though with microdata one is more likely to model directly the probability of retirement for each individual.

13. Although some data on hours worked and weeks worked are available from published *Current Population Survey* (CPS) reports, better age detail is available from unpublished data from the Bureau of Labor Statistics. The data used here were obtained from these unpublished files.

14. The social security earnings data were obtained from various issues of the *Social Security Bulletin, Annual Statistical Supplement,* which contains data on earnings by age and by sex for all years from 1937 to the present.

tion of this age grouping is that exact cohorts cannot be identified and, hence, the first-differencing procedure described in the preceding section cannot be implemented. Instead, the best that can be done is take first differences of a particular age grouping for adjacent years, a procedure that will leave some cohort effects in the equation.[15] Unfortunately, an additional problem created by the presence of cohort effects in all the equations is that the approach of using cohort dummy variables becomes impractical. For the ages 25–84 (using 84 as the upper age limit) over the years in the sample (1955–81), there are 91 birth cohorts. But there are only 108 observations in the entire sample because of the age grouping, not enough to estimate these cohort dummy variables.

To address these problems, the estimating equations 22–24 must be modified in two ways. First, those equations need to be modified to reflect the grouping over different ages, with the effect that average values of the variables must be used. Second, the variable Y must be proxied not by a set of cohort dummy variables but by some simple form of trend in Y that permits estimation. The reader interested only in the results of these modifications can directly inspect equations 28 and 29 below.

To solve the second problem, the unobservable cohort effect Y will be assumed to grow at a constant proportional rate over time. With this assumption, a variable denoting the year of the cohort will appear in the equations instead of the cohort dummy variables. Let Y_c be the value of Y for cohort c. Let c denote the year at which the cohort becomes 25, the earliest age in the data, and let $c = 0$ correspond to 1935, the year in which social security was put into effect. Then, the assumption is that Y_c follows the path

$$(25) \qquad Y_c = (1 + g_1 + g_2 D)^c Y_0,$$

where D is a dummy variable equal to unity if c is greater than or equal to zero. Thus Y_c is assumed to grow at different rates depending on whether the cohort began its adult life before or after the introduction of social security. A different rate must be assumed because Y_c includes initial social security wealth as well as initial private assets.

Grouping equation 22 (the basic earnings function) over the ages in each age interval gives the approximate result

15. An alternative is to match up each ten-year age category across ten-year intervals, and the twenty-year age category across twenty-year intervals. Unfortunately, this would reduce the sample to about fifteen observations.

$$(26) \qquad W_{\bar{a}}H_{\bar{a}} = \alpha W_{\bar{a}} - \beta Y_{\bar{c}} - \beta \sum_{\tau=2}^{\bar{a}} k_{\tau}'Q_{\tau\bar{c}} - \beta\eta'\bar{a} \sum_{\tau=2}^{\bar{a}} k_{\tau}'Q_{\tau\bar{c}},$$

where an overbar denotes the average value in the age interval. Note that a cohort subscript is now added to the social security wealth variable to represent explicitly differences in the wealth variable across cohorts. If the first-order Taylor-series approximation,

$$(27) \qquad Y_{\bar{c}} = (1 + g_1\bar{c} + g_2\overline{cD})Y_0,$$

is used, equation 26 becomes

$$(28) \qquad W_{\bar{a}}H_{\bar{a}} = \psi_0 + \psi_1 W_{\bar{a}} + \psi_2 \sum_{\tau=2}^{\bar{a}} k_{\tau}'Q_{\tau\bar{c}} + \psi_3\bar{c}$$

$$+ \psi_4\overline{cD} + \psi_5\bar{a} \sum_{\tau=2}^{\bar{a}} k_{\tau}'Q_{\tau\bar{c}} + \psi_6\bar{a}$$

$$+ \psi_7\bar{c}\bar{a} + \psi_8\overline{cD}\bar{a},$$

where

$$
\begin{array}{lll}
\psi_0 = -\beta Y_0 & \psi_3 = -\beta Y_0 g_1 & \psi_6 = -\beta Y_0\eta' \\
\psi_1 = \alpha & \psi_4 = -\beta Y_0 g_2 & \psi_7 = -\beta Y_0\eta'g_1 \\
\psi_2 = -\beta & \psi_5 = -\beta\eta' & \psi_8 = -\beta Y_0\eta'g_2.
\end{array}
$$

Thus the function contains the usual variables for wage rate and wealth shocks as well as the mean cohort value (essentially a time trend) and the fraction of those in the age grouping who reached age 25 after 1937. All variables also interact with age.

The first-difference version becomes

$$(29) \qquad \Delta W_{\bar{a}}H_{\bar{a}} = \phi_1 + \phi_2\Delta W_{\bar{a}} + \phi_2\Delta\left(\sum_{\tau=2}^{\bar{a}} k_{\tau}'Q_{\tau\bar{c}}\right)$$

$$+ \phi_3\Delta(\overline{cD}) + \phi_4\Delta\left(\bar{a} \sum_{\tau=2}^{\bar{a}} k_{\tau}'Q_{\tau\bar{c}}\right)$$

$$+ \phi_5\bar{a} + \phi_6\bar{a}\,\Delta(\overline{cD}),$$

where

$$\phi_0 = -\beta Y_0 g_1 \qquad \phi_3 = -\beta Y_0 g_2 \qquad \phi_6 = -\beta Y_0 \eta' g_2,$$
$$\phi_1 = \alpha \qquad\qquad \phi_4 = -\beta \eta'$$
$$\phi_2 = -\beta \qquad\quad \phi_5 = -\beta Y_0 \eta' g_1$$

where it is understood that the differencing takes place across adjacent years for the same age grouping.

New equations 28 and 29 represent the model in the form in which it will be estimated and illustrate both the limitations and the value of the analysis. In the equations earnings of an age group are assumed to be a function of the wage rate, age, a cohort trend (essentially a time trend), a variable for the alteration in the time trend of earnings after 1937, and a social security shock variable. By the standards of microdata analyses, the specification is thus extremely parsimonious. Because only 108 observations are in the sample (twenty-seven years for four age groups), any more elaborate specification would not be warranted. The model is indeed so simple that the estimate of the effect of social security on labor supply is not much more than a trend-adjusted simple correlation coefficient between the age-specific labor supply and social security variables, with an extra control variable for the wage rate trend.[16]

Nevertheless, the conventional wisdom that reductions in labor supply in time-series data have been largely a result of social security is not based so much on the cross-sectional elasticities and their backcasts, all of which have problems of their own. Rather, this conventional view rests on the strong prima facie evidence provided by the graphical evidence discussed in the second section and on knowledge of the trend in real social security benefits—in particular, that the two are in general negatively correlated and that in the 1970s the growth rate of real social security benefits accelerated at the same time that labor supply declines did. Equations 28–29 capture that two-variable correlation plus a little more and, hence, are adequate tests of what has been a very simple but also very persuasive hypothesis. The interesting aspect of equations 28–29 is that their estimation does not simply confirm the graphical intuition. As the next section ("Results") will indicate, equations 28–29 are not so parsimonious as to preclude unexpected findings.

16. Some regressions were run that included the annual age-specific unemployment rate. The coefficients were weak in significance and did not alter the values of the other coefficients.

Calculation of Social Security Wealth

To implement the models that have been discussed, it is of course necessary that some assumption about expectations of future social security wealth be made so that deviations from those expectations may be calculated. This problem has been discussed at times in the literature on social security, although not in as formal a fashion as here.[17] To estimate expected social security wealth here, I shall simply specify a separate equation for the wealth-generating process and assume that people use that equation to forecast their own wealth values. Deviations in those forecasts from year to year will then constitute the values of the Q_t. An alternative procedure would be to use the information in the legislation concerning future tax rates, benefit schedules, and so on, and to forecast what individuals would actually receive when they retire under the law in effect in each year. In addition to being a very large and complex undertaking, such a procedure assumes that individuals expect the law to remain fixed. Such an assumption is implausible, for the social security law is periodically changed by Congress. This potential for change was particularly evident in the period since the 1960s, during which the law was changed every year or two on average.

It is well known that the assumptions of economists about the forecasting equations for individuals are often inadequate descriptors of real-world forecasts, and that quite restrictive and simple forms of forecasting equations may be in serious error. This problem is addressed here in part by the use of several different forecasting equations, each constituting a slight deviation from a general form. The extent to which the estimates of the model are sensitive to different but equally defensible forecasting assumptions will be an indication of the stability of the results.

To specify a forecasting equation, the values of net social security wealth for all cohorts retiring to date must be calculated. Net social security wealth at each age is equal to the difference between the present value of benefits received by that age and the present value of taxes paid. The method of calculation is a modification of that used earlier by Moffitt.[18]

---

17. See Burtless, "Social Security, Unanticipated Benefit Increases"; Hurd and Boskin, "Effect of Social Security on Retirement"; and Kathryn H. Anderson, Richard V. Burkhauser, and Joseph F. Quinn, "Do Retirement Dreams Come True? The Effect of Unanticipated Events on Retirement Plans," *Industrial and Labor Relations Review*, vol 39 (July 1986), pp. 518–26.

18. Robert Moffitt, "Trends in Social Security Wealth by Cohort," in Marilyn Moon, ed., *Economic Transfers in the United States* (University of Chicago Press, 1984), pp. 327–53.

Data on benefits, taxes paid, coverage, and recipiency rates by age were obtained for each cohort alive since 1937 and are used to calculate SB_{ca}, the present value of benefits received by cohort c by age $a;$ ST_{ca}, the present value of taxes paid by cohort c at age $a;$ and $S_{ca} = SB_{ca} - ST_{ca}$, net social security wealth of cohort c by age a. The details of the computation are reported in the appendix.

An important characteristic of this concept of social security wealth is that such wealth will rise over time not only if real benefits rise, but also if coverage rates and recipiency rates rise (or even if life expectancy rises—this possibility is included in the calculation). The calculation simply involves dividing total benefits paid to a cohort minus total taxes paid by that cohort by the number of individuals in the cohort at age 20. It thus gives the average increment of net wealth per cohort member. Because this wealth value will be the measure of the generosity of the system used here, an implicit assumption in the analysis is that the effects of changes in benefits, tax rates, coverage rates, and recipiency rates have the same effects on labor supply if they also have the same effects on average social security wealth per cohort member.[19]

ACTUAL VALUES OF WEALTH RECEIVED TO DATE. Figure 3 shows the calculated values of S at various ages for selected cohorts. The early cohorts reached the end of their lifetimes having obtained little wealth (for example, the cohort that was 20 years old in 1897 and was already 60 years old by 1937)—in part because benefits were low in the beginning and in part because these cohorts had accumulated little coverage; hence their recipiency rate was extremely low (less than 10 percent). More recent cohorts had higher coverage and recipiency rates as well as higher benefits. The figures show, as also found by Moffitt, that the absolute size of the intergenerational transfer (although not the rate of return) by the end of life has grown monotonically for each successive retiring cohort since the system began.[20] The increased tax burden is also clearly shown in the figures for the more recent cohorts, particularly at young ages.

The more important figures are figures 4 and 5, which illustrate how the present values of benefits, taxes, and benefits minus taxes at the end of life

19. Although there certainly may be some cases in which this equivalence of effects will be incorrect, such instances are likely to be of second-order importance. Moreover, the assumption has been maintained just as strongly in most of the microdata studies, in which measures of social security benefits or wealth, for example, are set equal to zero for those not covered. The equations estimated here are, aside from differences in functional form, linear aggregates of those microdata equations; these aggregates yield social security values that are weighted values in the microdata equations for covered and uncovered workers.

20. Moffitt, "Trends in Social Security Wealth."

Figure 3. Net Social Security Wealth, by Age and Cohort[a]

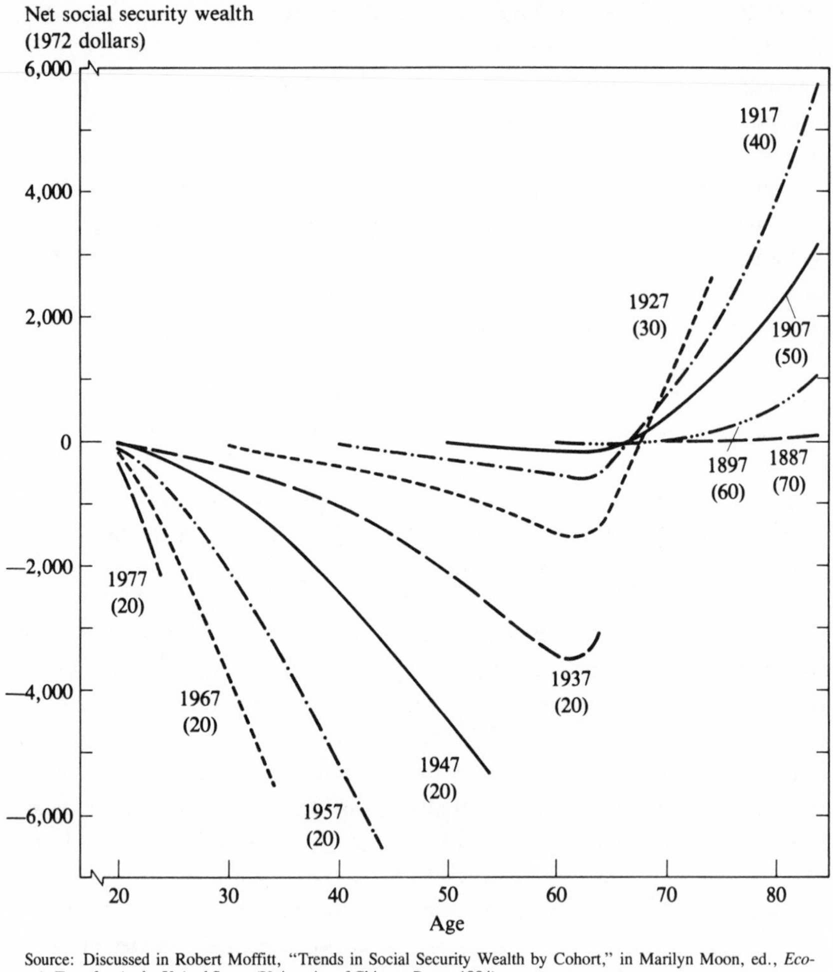

Net social security wealth
(1972 dollars)

Source: Discussed in Robert Moffitt, "Trends in Social Security Wealth by Cohort," in Marilyn Moon, ed., *Economic Transfers in the United States* (University of Chicago Press, 1984).

a. Year denotes point at which cohort reached age 20; age in parentheses is that of cohort at entry into the system.

(taken to be 80 years) have changed over time. Figure 4 shows that the present value of benefits for cohorts reaching age 80 in each successive year has grown monotonically over time. Despite the sizable increases in benefits in 1950 and in the late 1960s and the 1970s, however, there is no dramatic change in the present value of benefits at those times. There is a slight increase in the rate of growth of the present value of benefits in the

Figure 4. Present Value of Social Security Benefits, Taxes, and Differences between Them, 1937–81[a]

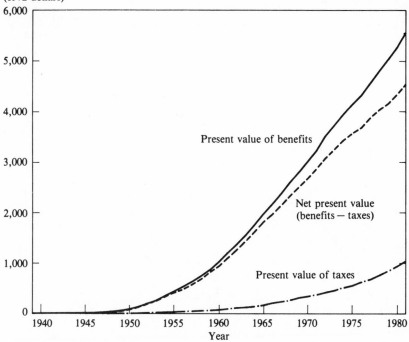

Present value
(1972 dollars)

Present value of benefits

Net present value
(benefits – taxes)

Present value of taxes

Year

Source: See figure 3.
a. Values in each year are those for the cohort that had reached 80 years of age in that year.

late 1960s and early 1970s, but this alteration in the trend is only barely perceptible visually.

The strong growth in the 1950s and early 1960s is simply a result of the maturation of the social security system. Each successive cohort had spent more years in the system and, hence, had higher covered earnings; the total value of benefits received would therefore have risen even if the benefit schedule had not been altered. In addition, as coverage was legislatively expanded in the 1950s, recipiency rates increased even more. There consequently was tremendous growth in the present value of benefits in the 1950s, at rates only barely below those in the late 1960s and early 1970s.

Tax payments were of course also increasing, as shown in figure 4; indeed, they have increased exponentially. The net value of social security wealth is also shown. The general shape of the net wealth curve is the

**Figure 5. Logarithms of Net Present Value of Social Security Benefits
Minus Taxes, 1941–81**
1972 dollars

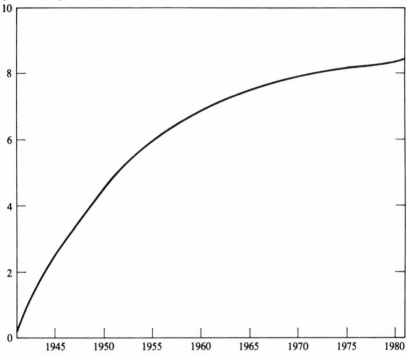

Log of present value
(1972 dollars)

Source: Author's calculations based on data in figure 4.

same as that of benefits, despite the increase in taxes: steady growth
throughout the 1950s and early 1960s, followed by a slight increase in the
growth rate in the late 1960s and early 1970s.

The importance of these findings of steady growth over the entire
period lies in the realization that such growth rates would appear, at first
glance, to be rather easy to forecast. It appears as though a simple linear
trend forecast would be fairly accurate, for example, and that there would
be little or no social security shock in the late 1960s and early 1970s as a
result.

Figure 5, which shows the profile of the logarithm of social security
wealth, is even more striking. The growth rate of social security wealth
has fallen monotonically over time, and visually it is almost impossible to
discern any interruption in the late 1960s and early 1970s. As documented

elsewhere,[21] the absolute value of the net wealth increment has grown monotonically for all successive retiring cohorts, but the rate of growth has monotonically fallen, and the internal rate of return has monotonically fallen as well. Again, these trends are natural results of a maturing pay-as-you-go system; as the system ages, tax rates must be increased, and individuals have spent more time in the system and therefore have paid more taxes. Cohorts retiring in the late 1960s and early 1970s were actually getting less out of the system in this sense than had earlier retirees. The benefit increases in the late 1960s and early 1970s merely kept the rate of return from falling faster.

FORECASTS AND CONSTRUCTION OF SHOCKS. To generate forecasts of expected wealth at the end of the lifetime, a separate regression is run at each year t using the data on social security wealth at age 80 in periods $\tau \leq t$. Simple moving-average representations of the process are assumed. At each t the resultant coefficients are used to forecast the expected end-of-lifetime wealth for each age group a at time t, by forecasting the equation $(80 - a)$ years into the future. Values of the social security shock are then calculated as the deviations of these forecasts for the same cohort in successive t's.

Let S_t be the value of social security wealth for the cohort of age 80 in year t (shown in figure 4). Let l be the length of the moving-average process, and let $t_0 = t - l$ be the beginning year of the process. Then, for each t the following two different functional forms, a linear and a logarithmic equation, are estimated:

$$(30) \qquad S_\tau = b_t + c_t\tau, \qquad \tau = t_0, \ldots, t$$

$$(31) \qquad \log(S_\tau) = d_t + e_t \log(\tau - t_0 - 1), \qquad \tau = t_0, \ldots, t.$$

In the linear form, equation 30, wealth is fit to a simple linear trend. In the logarithmic form, equation 31, the logarithm of wealth is fit to a logarithmic trend starting at the beginning of the moving-average process. Most work was performed with equation 30, which was estimated using five-, ten-, and fifteen-year moving-average frames. The logarithmic equation was then estimated with a ten-year frame as well.[22] At each t the coeffi-

---

21. Ibid.

22. Five-year and fifteen-year moving-average logarithmic equations were later estimated as well, with similar results. Tables of the results are available from the author on request.

Figure 6. Size of Forecast Shock in Net Social Security Wealth, by Age, Year, and Type of Forecast, 1950–81

Net social security wealth
(1972 dollars)

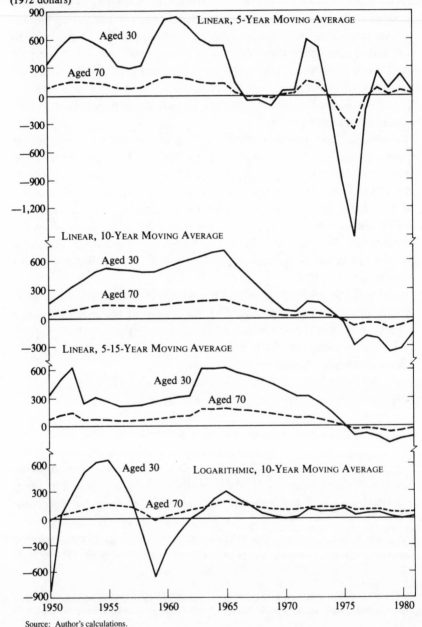

Source: Author's calculations.

cients (b_t, c_t) or (d_t, e_t) are used to forecast end-of-lifetime wealth for each age group a, equal to $\hat{S}_{t+80-a}$. The previous year's forecast for the same cohort, $\hat{S}_{(t-1)+80-(a-1)}$, are based on the coefficients (b_{t-1}, c_{t-1}) or (d_{t-1}, e_{t-1}). The value of the shock is then computed as the difference.[23]

Figure 6 shows the estimated values of shock at each t for two of the age groups, a young group (30 years old) and an aged group (70 years old). The figure shows the estimated shocks from the linear five-year moving-average forecast. The curves indicate positive shocks throughout the 1950s and early 1960s, a second positive shock in 1972, but negative shocks throughout the rest of the 1970s. The negative shocks are a result of the rate of growth of wealth in the later 1970s, which did not keep up with the relatively rapid growth in the late 1960s and early 1970s. The shocks are smaller in absolute size for the aged group simply because its members are much closer to age 80; hence a change in the time profile of wealth has less aggregate effect.

The shock values for the ten-year moving averages show considerably larger values in the 1950s but a smaller shock in 1972. The ten-year moving averages clearly indicate falling shocks after about 1965. The fifteen-year moving average goes further in this direction: 1972 shows up only as a brief slowdown in the rate of decline of the shocks. As longer moving-averages are used, the 1972 blip has less of an effect on the forecasted wealth values. The logarithmic forecast goes even further in this direction. There are positive shocks around the mid-1950s and mid-1960s, but the shocks quiet down in the 1970s (the profile settles down to a smooth logarithm), and the 1972 episode does not show up at all, as presaged by figure 5.

Thus, the implication of virtually all the forecasts is that the shocks were larger in the 1950s and early 1960s than later. This result should not be surprising given the discussion of figures 4 and 5, for those illustrations also showed graphically that the benefit increases of the late 1960s and early 1970s had slight discernible effect on the rate of growth of social

23. More sophisticated forecasting equations were also estimated, such as equations including lagged values of S_t as regressors. The fits from those equations invariably produced implausible results, either predicting stationary values of S_t four to five years in the future or predicting exploding values of S_t. Recall that the difficulty here, relative to some other economic models, arises because the S_t values must be projected as much as sixty years into the future. Because more complex equations than equations 30 and 31 were unable to forecast plausibly this far in time, only the simpler equations were used.

security wealth. Nor is this result at all implausible. In the 1940s there was little reason to expect that the social security system would increase in generosity at the rate that it did in the 1950s, when coverage rates grew dramatically, when benefits were increased dramatically in 1950 and at slower rates thereafter, and when recipiency rates grew rapidly among the elderly. In essence, the growth of the system in the 1950s represents the change from virtually no system at all (that is, one trivial in magnitude) to one with sizable aggregate wealth transfers. Retirees in the 1950s no doubt were much better off than they had expected they would be.

The lack of growth in the late 1960s and early 1970s is also not implausible once the principles of a pay-as-you-go system are realized, as noted earlier.[24] The cohorts retiring in that period were among the first to have paid taxes into the system for their entire lives, and the aggregate tax bite was increasing exponentially for each successive retiring cohort. For this reason the growth rate of wealth in a maturing pay-as-you-go system *must* fall unless benefits are increased by extraordinary amounts. What the results here indicate is that the benefit increases in the late 1960s and early 1970s, although large by some standards, were not sufficiently great to offset the forces of system maturation. Indeed, the implication of the results here is that, had those benefit increases not been legislated, retirees would have felt negative shocks when they retired. They did "expect" the benefit increases to occur; hence those increases were not shocks. This outcome seems implausible only if one believes that people expect current law to remain constant—an expectation that does not seem likely and one that the analysis here obviously does not assume. If people instead are thought to make only extremely simple linear or logarithmic projections of the trends they see in the past five to fifteen years, the wealth values in the late 1960s and early 1970s were easily forecastable.

Results

Tables 1 and 2 show the results of estimating equations 28 and 29 in level and difference form, respectively, by ordinary least-squares meth-

---

24. In the 1950s the social security system was not pay-as-you-go, for a large trust fund was accumulated. The trust fund was gradually dissipated and reached a stationary minimum amount only in 1965, from which time the system has been pay-as-you-go.

ods.[25] To recapitulate, recall that equation 28 requires regressing earnings on the wage rate, a cohort trend, a deviation in the cohort trend after 1937, age, and a weighted social security wealth variable (see also footnote b in table 1 for the definition of this last term). The age variable may or may not be made to interact with all other variables on the right-hand side of equation 28 except the wage rate. Equation 29 is equation 28 in first-difference form.

A set of weighted wealth variables is constructed for each of forecast equations 30–31. For each type of forecast equation, the estimated coefficients from each year's equation plus those of the previous year's equation are used to compute a shock value for individuals at all single years of age at that year. As described above, the shock value is equal to the change in the predicted value of end-of-lifetime social security wealth from one year to the next. Each of these shocks (one for each single year of age in each year) is then weighted by k_q (see equation 21), which is merely a weight for age. Finally, a weighted wealth value is calculated for each of the 108 observations in the sample (twenty-seven years, four age groups) by summing the weighted shock values over all ages of the lifetime for an individual of the mean age $\bar{a}$ in each age group in each year. This weighted wealth value (see equation 28 or footnote b in table 1) is then used directly in the level equations in table 1. In the first-difference equations is entered the change in the variable, which is, aside from the adjustment for the change in cohort composition of adjacent age intervals, roughly equal to the weighted wealth shock for an individual of each mean age.

The coefficient on the wage rate is always the estimate of α, which is only of secondary interest here. The coefficient on the noninteracting

25. Two econometric issues are worth mentioning here. First, there is a question about the correctness of the standard errors on the social security variable, since that variable is a predicted value from an auxiliary equation. As Pagan has shown, if the predicted values are constructed from first-stage residuals, as those here are, an ordinary least-squares package gives correct standard errors. Adrian Pagan, "Econometric Issues in the Analysis of Regressions with Generated Regressors," *International Economic Review*, vol. 25 (February 1984), pp. 221–47. The second issue relates to an error-in-variables problem pointed out by Angus Deaton, "Panel Data from Time Series of Cross-Sections," *Journal of Econometrics*, vol. 30 (October–November 1985), pp. 109–26. The model here treats the aggregate means as true means in the population, whereas they are actually drawn only from samples. Hence the implicit treatment of data for groups of individuals—in successive years at successive ages—as being measures of means from identical cohort populations is incorrect because (more-or-less) independent samples are drawn from the CPS each year. The only solution to this problem requires an estimate of the covariance matrix of the regressors in the sample, which was not undertaken here because microdata from the CPS are not available for years before 1968.

Table 1. Earning Regressions by Type of Shock Forecast, Equation 28
Levels; moving averages[a]

Variable	Without social security variables (1)	Linear, five-year (2)	Linear, five-year (3)	Linear, ten-year (4)	Linear, ten-year (5)	Linear, fifteen-year (6)	Linear, fifteen-year (7)	Logarithmic, ten-year (8)	Logarithmic, ten-year (9)
W	2,319.9*	2,446.8*	2,556.3*	2,612.2*	2,402.1*	2,834.8*	2,112.8*	2,121.9*	2,650.2*
	(124.2)	(121.5)	(75.1)	(115.5)	(75.4)	(93.0)	(83.5)	(77.4)	(212.2)
$\bar{c}$	59.5*	79.6*	−104.5*	76.7*	−76.1*	66.6*	−58.4*	74.3*	−133.3*
	(14.1)	(14.3)	(39.7)	(12.3)	(38.1)	(9.3)	(33.0)	(8.8)	(35.9)
$\bar{c}D$	−43.3*	−105.6*	72.8*	−111.6*	59.1	−111.7*	47.1	−115.1*	67.0*
	(17.3)	(27.0)	(40.7)	(18.2)	(38.3)	(12.8)	(33.2)	(11.9)	(36.9)
$\hat{Q}$ [b]	...	−158.6*	130.1*	−215.9*	204.8*	−315.3*	299.1*	−458.7*	−31.0
		(41.6)	(34.1)	(34.1)	(32.7)	(27.0)	(37.9)	(34.5)	(58.6)
$\bar{a}$ [c]	...	...	−48.1*	...	−20.2	...	−2.8	...	−101.6*
			(16.4)		(15.2)		(3.5)		(24.3)
$\hat{Q}\bar{a}$	...	...	−6.1*	...	−9.1*	...	−12.4*	...	0.6
			(1.8)		(1.5)		(1.4)		(3.0)
$\overline{ca}$	...	...	1.8*	...	1.8*	...	2.1*	...	1.6*
			(0.7)		(0.7)		(0.6)		(0.9)
$\overline{cDa}$	...	...	−3.3*	...	−3.5*	...	−3.3*	...	−1.9*
			(0.8)		(0.8)		(0.7)		(0.8)
Constant	−1,646.4	−766.6	−670.3	−909.5	−788.6	−1,186.6	−226.7	759.1	171.7
$R^2 \times 100$	93.9	96.5	99.3	95.6	99.4	97.4	99.6	97.7	99.2

Source: Author's calculations.
*Significant at 10 percent level.
a. Standard errors appear in parentheses; $n = 108$; R^2 is the coefficient of determination.
b. $\hat{Q} = \sum_{\tau=2}^{\kappa'} {}_{\kappa'} Q_{\kappa'}$ divided by 1,000.
c. $\bar{a}$ is average age minus 25.

social security wealth variable is the estimate of the negative of β, which is of direct interest here because it measures the wealth elasticity of labor supply and, hence, the effect of social security on labor supply. The parameter β is hypothesized to be positive, so the wealth coefficient is expected to be negative. When social security is made to interact with age, some of the social security effect enters through the interaction variable. In the level equation, equation 28, some of the other parameters (Y_0, g_1, and so on) can be identified from the other coefficients, but these parameters are of no direct interest.

Column 1 of table 1 shows the estimates of the level equation without any social security variables. This form is somewhat similar to some of the equations estimated by Browning (and others) and by MaCurdy.[26] The results indicate a positive and significant wage effect. At the mean hours of work of 1,900, the estimate of α implies an intertemporal substitution elasticity of 0.22. This wage elasticity is reasonably robust across all columns in tables 1 and 2, varying from 0.11 to 0.39 across the equations. Thus, positive but small intertemporal elasticities are present in the time-series data.

Columns 2 and 3 in table 1, whose shock variables employ the linear five-year moving-average specification, show estimates of equation 28 with and without age interactions (the model without age interactions assumes that $i = \rho$). The first equation shows a negative and significant coefficient on the wealth variable and implies that β is about equal to 0.16. This simple level equation thus gives some indication of the expected social security effects. These effects disappear, however, when age is made to interact with the wealth variable, as shown in column 3, for the coefficient on the noninteracting wealth variable has the "wrong" (that is, unexpected) sign and is also significant. The interaction coefficient between age and the social security shock is negative and significant, however, and implies that social security has a negative effect on labor supply for individuals over the age of 40. This result is not implausible, for it may be that only after age 40 do individuals begin to make decisions influenced by retirement expectations. The magnitudes of the coefficients imply, for example, that at age 65 a dollar increase in $\hat{Q}$ reduces earnings by about 0.11. The implication is, in turn, that the negative coefficient in equation 2 was due primarily to effects at the older age points.

---

26. See Browning and others, "A Profitable Approach," and MaCurdy, "An Empirical Model."

Table 2. Earning Regressions by Type of Shock Forecast, Equation 29
First differences; moving averages[a]

Variable	Linear, five-year			Linear, ten-year		Linear, fifteen-year		Logarithmic, ten-year	
	(1)	(2)	(3)	(4)	(5)	(6)	(7)	(8)	(9)
ΔW	2,125.3*	2,116.3*	2,097.2*	2,049.4*	2,046.8*	1,993.5*	1,958.2*	2,128.7*	2,100.2*
	(173.9)	(176.1)	(182.0)	(177.0)	(182.5)	(183.2)	(189.5)	(177.2)	(185.1)
$\Delta(c\overline{D})$	...	12.3	-9.9	29.6	20.9	30.9	4.0	4.1	-44.1
		(27.8)	(109.7)	(29.2)	(111.3)	(29.3)	(107.1)	(27.1)	(110.6)
$\Delta\hat{Q}$	...	30.7	-9.0	-78.1*	72.5	104.5*	133.4	20.6	51.6
		(24.0)	(41.2)	(36.6)	(73.5)	(47.5)	(87.9)	(34.5)	(60.8)
$\Delta[\overline{Q}a]$	...	...	2.9	...	0.7	...	-0.4	...	-1.5
			(2.5)		(3.8)		(3.9)		(3.3)
$\bar{a}$	...	...	-1.7	...	-1.3	...	-1.9	...	-1.7
			(2.3)		(2.3)		(2.3)		(2.5)
$\Delta(c\overline{D}a)$	...	...	-0.0[b]	...	-1.1	...	-1.0	...	-0.1
			(2.9)		(2.9)		(2.9)		(2.0)
Constant	-46.9	-55.0	-6.6	-66.6	-21.8	-69.0	3.8	-50.6	28.4
$R^2 \times 100$	59.4	60.1	61.2	61.2	62.1	61.3	62.6	59.6	60.5

Source: Author's calculations.
*Significant at 10 percent level.
a. Standard errors in parentheses; $n = 104$.
b. Less than 0.05 in absolute value.

Columns 4–9 in table 1 show the corresponding estimates obtained when the three other forecast equations are used to construct the wealth variables. The equations utilizing the other two linear forecasting equations yield results quite similar to those utilizing the five-year linear forecast. In both cases, the coefficients on the wealth variables are negative when no age interactions are included but positive when they are included. In both cases the interaction coefficients are again negative and significant and imply that negative effects begin among people in their 40s. At age 65 the ten-year and fifteen-year equations imply that an extra dollar of $\hat{Q}$ reduces earnings by 0.16 and 0.20, respectively.

The logarithmic equation in column 9 of table 1 gives quite different results. Whereas the wealth coefficient in column 8 is again negative and significant, in column 9 the noninteracting wealth coefficient is negative, but the interacting coefficient is positive; both are insignificant. These results therefore indicate a very weak negative response to social security that is spread over all ages more or less uniformly. Exactly why the results should differ in this way from the linear forecast equations is not clear. The logarithmic forecasts did imply, as noted previously, much smaller shocks than the linear forms, shocks that virtually disappear in the later years of the data set. These shocks are apparently much more weakly correlated with labor supply in general and with the labor supply values of older age groups in particular. Although there is no a priori basis for rejecting logarithmic expectations and accepting linear ones, the results based on the latter appear more plausible.

Table 2 shows the first-difference results, estimates of equation 29. As noted earlier, the wage coefficients are quite robust across all specifications. The estimates of the effects of social security, however, virtually disappear entirely in these sets of regressions. Among the four equations with no age interactions (columns 2, 4, 6, and 8), the shock coefficient is unexpectedly positive in three of four cases. In the one case in which it is negative (the ten-year moving-average equation), its value is about -0.08, smaller than, for example, the results for age 65 implied by the level equations. In one case, the fifteen-year moving average, the shock coefficient is not only positive but significant. When age is made to interact with the variables, the effects are further weakened. In only one case (the five-year moving-average equation) is the noninteracting coefficient of the expected negative sign, but there it has a standard error over four times its size. The interaction coefficients in the four specifications are negative only half the time and are insignificant in all cases. Even if the standard errors in the equations are ignored, the point estimate of the effects of an extra dollar of $\hat{Q}$ is negative at age 65 only in the logarithmic specification, in which case it is only -0.008.

Thus, the pattern of effects in the first-difference equations in table 2 is quite sensitive to the forecast equation used to generate the shock values and shows, in general, a virtually undetectable social security response. The null hypothesis that social security has no effect on labor supply could obviously not be rejected by the results in table 2. The reason for the difference in the results of tables 1 and 2 is relatively simple. In the level equations, the wealth coefficients reflect the adjusted correlation between the summed wealth shocks over an individual's lifetime and labor supply. Despite the finding that the pattern of wealth shocks differed from expectations between the 1950s and the 1970s, the summed wealth shocks show a rising profile over time. The negative coefficients on the wealth coefficients in the level equations thus arise naturally from the falling trend in labor supply and reflect the secular, negative correlation that has been discussed throughout this paper. In the first-difference equations, in contrast, only the adjusted correlation between the change in wealth values over time (that is, the shocks) and changes in labor supply influence the coefficient signs. As discussed in the last section, because of the pattern of shocks in the 1950s and 1970s the raw correlation between the shocks and labor supply is positive, not negative. Thus, although the hypothesis of a nonzero effect of social security on labor supply is consistent with the overall trends in total social security wealth over the postwar period, it is not consistent with the relative growth rates of wealth and labor supply in the 1950s and 1970s. This is the major finding of this study. It implies that, loosely speaking, the lower-bound estimate of the effect of social security implied by the time-series data is in essence zero.

Treating the estimates in table 1 loosely as upper-bound estimates allows the corresponding effects of social security on labor supply to be calculated. Consider a man 65 years old in 1955 and assume that a dollar of $\hat{Q}$ decreases earnings by 0.13. Then the effect of social security can be calculated from the *total* social security wealth for the individual at this age, which is equal to the sum of his initially forecast wealth level (not in the regressions) plus the sum of the weighted shocks $\hat{Q}$. For the man aged 65, the value of this total wealth in 1955 implies a reduction in annual hours of work of 3–5 percent across the four forecast specifications, each of which implies a slightly different value for the shocks. If he had known at age 25 that his social security wealth would be what it came to be in

1955, his hours would have been 2–3 percent lower at all ages of his life. As emphasized in the second section of the paper, the unexpected nature of the actual pattern of shocks causes a larger decrease. The lower labor supply effects are also those that would apply in a steady state in which social security wealth stabilized in value. For a man 65 years old in 1975, however, reductions in hours are 13–19 percent, and 9–14 percent had social security wealth been known in the beginning. The absolute value of social security wealth is, of course, larger for the cohort aged 65 in 1975 than for the cohort aged 65 in 1955.

A separate question is whether these upper-bound estimates can explain the acceleration in the decline in hours of work during the 1970s. The answer is not quite as obvious as it may appear. On the one hand, none of the four forecasting equations predicts larger shocks in the 1970s than earlier—in general, the opposite is true. But the cohorts approaching retirement age in the 1970s had begun their adult lives after the start of the social security system and, hence, I had higher expected wealth values all along. If these values were sufficiently high, their magnitude could out-weigh the smaller size of the shocks they faced over their lifetimes.

Table 3 indicates that this is not the case. Under the linear ten-year moving-average forecast, men 55 years old in 1975 had a quite small initial expected wealth ($329), given that in 1945 the system was small and that a linear forecast kept it so. Thus, a $5,336 (= $7,446 − $2,110) increase in the value of wealth expected by the cohorts aged 55 in 1955 and 1965 was still larger than the $2,507 increase for the cohorts aged 55

Table 3. Values of Social Security Wealth of Men at Ages 55 and 75 in 1955, 1965, and 1975
Moving averages

Age and year	Linear, ten-year			Logarithmic, ten-year		
	Total wealth	Wealth at age 25	Weighted shocks	Total wealth	Wealth at age 25	Weighted shocks
55						
1955	2,110	0	2,110	2,453	0	2,453
1965	7,446	0	7,446	3,927	0	3,927
1975	9,953	329	9,624	5,433	2,348	3,085
75						
1955	1,263	0	1,263	1,129	0	1,129
1965	4,975	0	4,975	3,746	0	3,746
1975	7,637	0	7,637	6,351	0	6,351

Source: Authors' calculations.

in 1965 and 1975. (The latter figure can explain about 20 percent of the reduction in hours over 1965–75.) Under the logarithmic forecast, in contrast, a man 55 years old in 1975 would have begun with an expected wealth of \$2,348. As a consequence, expected wealth at age 55 increased by about the same amount in the two intervals under this forecast. Nevertheless, this finding still cannot explain the large declines in hours worked in the 1970s. The panel in table 3 for men aged 75 gives the same results.

Summary

This paper has been a time-series examination of the effect of social security on labor supply. The existing time-series data for the United States, although quite scanty and weak in nature, allow one to estimate adjusted correlations between labor supply and measures of the generosity of the social security system. The evidence adduced here is intended to complement the cross-sectional and panel-data studies of the labor supply effects of social security, which have covered only the experience in the late 1960s and 1970s, and to determine whether the results of those micro-data studies are consistent with trends in the earlier postwar years.

The major finding of the study is that there is an important inconsistency between the microdata studies in the later periods and the time-series data for the entire postwar period. The microdata studies in general show nonzero effects of social security on labor supply, although the effects vary in magnitude from one study to another, and also in general support the hypothesis that the sharp acceleration in the decline of labor supply of men in the 1970s was in part a result of the benefit increases in those years. The time-series data are inconsistent with this pattern because they show that social security wealth grew faster in the 1950s than it did in the later periods. Furthermore, by any of the assumptions about expectation formation tested in this paper, the wealth increments in the 1950s were more unexpected than were those in the late 1960s and early 1970s. The 1950s was a period in which the social security system grew from one trivial in magnitude to one with sizable aggregate wealth transfers, the growth arising from both increased benefit levels and increases in coverage rates. Cohorts maturing in the late 1960s and early 1970s, in contrast, had paid taxes into the system for most of their working lives, and growth rates of coverage had stabilized by that time. As a result, the benefit increases of the late 1960s and early 1970s only served to keep social security wealth more or less equal to what could have been easily forecast from earlier growth rates. This finding is in retrospect obvious. By the basic principles of a pay-as-you-go system, the internal rate of return of contributions must fall over time, as must the growth rate of the net wealth increment.

The results of the paper also suggest, however, that the overall negative correlation in the levels of social security wealth and labor supply in time-series data is preserved when only the unexpected wealth increments are used to identify the social security (that is, wealth) elasticity. In other words, even when a model is formulated that excludes the initial level of private assets and social security wealth that an individual faces at the beginning of his working life—thus removing some of the time-series correlation between the growth rates of private wealth and social security wealth—there is still an estimated disincentive effect of social security on labor supply. The results obtained using this method imply labor supply reductions of 3–5 percent for the aged in the 1950s and of 13–19 percent for the aged in the 1970s. As just noted, however, the results cannot explain much of the acceleration in the decline of labor supply in the 1970s: the maximum percentage of the 1965–75 labor supply decline that can be explained by social security in the estimates is 20 percent, smaller than the previous estimates of Diamond and Hausman or of Hurd and Boskin.[27]

Appendix: Algorithm for Computation of Social Security Wealth

The algorithm for the present value of social security benefits received by an individual in cohort c by age a' is

$$(32) \qquad SB_{ca'} = \frac{1}{N} \sum_{a=a_m}^{a'} \frac{R_{ca}(B_{ca}^m + 0.5B_{ca}^f)}{(1 + r)^{a-24}},$$

where
N = size of cohort at age 20
R_{ca} = number of social security recipients of cohort c at age a
B_{ca}^m = mean real social security benefit for retired men of cohort c at age a

---

27. Diamond and Hausman, "Retirement and Unemployment Behavior," and Hurd and Boskin, "Effect of Social Security on Retirement."

B^f_{ca} = mean real social security benefit for wives of cohort c at age a

a_m = 65 before 1961, 62 after 1961.

It is assumed that half of the men are married during receipt of benefits and have wives who are collecting under the men's earning records. The implicit recipiency ratio in the calculation is R_{ca}/N. The value of this ratio is affected by the survival probabilities of the cohort, probabilities of employment and coverage during the working life, and probabilities of actually receiving benefits during retirement. SB is thus the wealth value for the average member of the cohort. The benefits are discounted to age 24 because the labor supply data used subsequently begin at age 25.

The algorithm for the present value of social security tax payments made by the average member of cohort c by age a' is

$$(33) \qquad ST_{ca'} = \frac{1}{N} \sum_{a=20}^{a'} \frac{C_{ca}T_{ca}}{(1 + r)^{a-24}},$$

where C_{ca} is the number of workers of cohort c at age a in covered employment, and T_{ca} is the mean real tax payment of a covered worker of cohort c at age a. The mean tax payment is obtained by applying the tax rates for employers and employees to the earning level of the group.[28] The implicit coverage ratio C_{ca}/N will change over time as coverage expands, as survival probabilities change, and as employment probabilities change.

The calculated value of net social security wealth at age a' is

$$(34) \qquad S_{ca'} = SB_{ca'} - ST_{ca'}.$$

A real interest rate of 3 percent is used in the calculations.

Comment by Joseph F. Quinn

This paper by Robert Moffitt is a time-series analysis of the effect of social security on life-cycle labor supply. As are many of the papers in this volume, it really is two papers. The author first describes a common problem that exists in the time-series analysis of the effect of social security on labor supply. In the theoretical section of the paper, he sketches out a highly creative solution to this problem. He then describes the data construction needed to test the impact of social security on labor supply.

28. See Moffitt, "Trends in Social Security Wealth."

The second part of the paper presents the estimation and discusses the results.

The two parts of the paper are well integrated. The empirical work follows as closely as can be hoped from the theory. The first part is quite successful and interesting; the second, as I read it, is less so.

Below I will describe the problem at hand, and the nature of the solution that Moffitt has proposed, and discuss why I would have predicted trouble in the empirical section. In addition, I would like to use this opportunity to pose a more general question. What, if anything, can aggregate time-series analyses of this sort tell us about the nature of the labor supply decision, and about the effect of social security on retirement?

As we all know, the world is divided into two types of people—not "big-enders" and "little-enders," as Swift would have us believe, but people who like microeconomic cross-sectional data and people who like aggregate time-series data. There are good reasons for being in either camp.

Moffitt begins his paper with a discussion of just these issues. Why cross-sectional data? Most current microdata sets have huge sample sizes that allow precise estimation of parameters and interesting disaggregation into subgroups. The microdata sets have extensive demographic and economic information on each person in the sample, in some cases including each person's entire social security record. Another advantage of this micro-cross-sectional approach is that there is extreme variation in the values of the demographic variables. There are people with no pension wealth and people with pension wealth in the hundreds of thousands of dollars. There are people who do not work at all and people who work 4,000 hours a year. There are people in good, poor, and mediocre health. They are all there in the microdata files.

Unfortunately, they are all there at the same time—the year of the cross section. This fact creates at least two problems with the cross-sectional approach. It is difficult to discern how a person will react to changes in his circumstances in the future on the basis of the responses of other people to different circumstances at a point in time. How I will react if you change my X_1 to X_2 may not be the difference between my current response to X_1 and someone else's current response to X_2. Because it is the reaction to possible policy changes that is of primary interest, this problem can be a serious shortcoming of cross-sectional data.

The other problem is that, despite all the variation in the variables in the survey, there is no variation in certain common circumstances. At any time, all Americans have the same president. We all have the same federal budget deficit. We all pay taxes or receive benefits under the same social security law. One cannot estimate the effect of factors that are the same for everybody in the cross section. With respect to social security, the subject of this paper, it is true that people under the same law have different benefits because they have different inputs (wage histories) to the common formula. The question then becomes how to differentiate between the direct effects of those inputs on labor supply and the effects of the output (benefits) that emerge from the common social security law.

An obvious solution to this problem is to examine time-series data, in which the institutional parameters do change. When one does so, another whole set of problems emerges, as Moffitt has discussed. First, one has samples of very small size, numbering now in the dozens rather than the thousands. For example, in Moffitt's research, hours of work for different age categories are available only since 1955. Second, one has data on many fewer explanatory variables. Many of these simply do not exist by age category, as Moffitt's research requires. Finally, many of the time-series variables that do exist are highly collinear with one other. This last problem with the time-series data is really the focus of Moffitt's paper.

Moffitt describes this as an identification problem. How can the analyst tease out, or identify, the individual effects of highly collinear explanatory variables? More specifically, Moffitt's hypóthesis is that the decrease in the labor-force participation rates of men over recent decades has been at least in part a result of the increased generosity of the social security system. I am confident that he is correct. The problem, as he points out, is that at the same time that real social security benefits (or wealth) have risen, so have real incomes. An alternative hypothesis is that the rising real incomes are responsible for what we have observed, and that declines in labor supply might have occurred even if we had not had a social security system. Because social security wealth and incomes are highly correlated over time (as are many other macroeconomic variables), it is difficult to tell "who dunnit." If thunder and lightning always come together, which is scaring the dog? This is what Moffitt's paper is about.

The solution comes from a central feature of the life-cycle model that Moffitt describes. In a world of perfect certainty, a person makes a whole lifetime of decisions at the beginning, on the basis of initial conditions and what he knows is going to happen over the life cycle. An implication of this model is that an anticipated change in a variable way out in period q has a very small influence on contemporaneous decisions during period q, since the effects of the change are spread over all the time periods.

If someone expects to win the John Bates Clark medal, for example—
and many people do—and if that award were to come with a substantial
cash prize, the recipient's consumption in all the time periods would be
affected, not just consumption in the 40th year. An analogy is piles of ice
cubes in a row, with each column representing an annual income. A year's
consumption does not depend on that year's column of ice, but rather on
the common level of water once all the ice cubes have melted. An additional cube in year q has only a small effect on the water level, and
therefore on each year's consumption.

Now, here is the good news with respect to the problem at hand.
Unanticipated changes in the state of the world can affect behavior only
after the change. The later a given surprise or "shock" occurs, the larger
the yearly effect of that change because there are fewer years left over in
which to adjust.

Although social security wealth (from the growth in benefits) is highly
correlated with many macroeconomic variables (such as real income),
unanticipated changes in social security wealth are not highly correlated
with these other variables. According to Moffitt, these unanticipated
changes in social security wealth actually occurred in two big blips—one
in 1950 and one in the late 1960s and early 1970s. The identification of the
labor supply effect of social security comes from these unanticipated
changes in social security wealth over the life cycle. This is a nice idea,
and it is the primary contribution of the paper.

Let us look a little more closely at what the paper does. Moffitt begins
with a description of labor force participation rates over time. There are
declines since the 1960s for all age categories of men. The decline has
been very modest for those under age 55 but dramatic for those aged 55
and older. For those 65 years old and over, the decline began earlier,
before 1950. There is a similar story for annual hours of work, although it
is not clear whether these hours of work are for all people or for only the
people who are still working. The story is about the same in either case.
There is not much new here; this decline is a well-documented and well-
known phenomenon.

Moffitt then moves to a standard life-cycle consumption model. Utility
depends on leisure and consumption in each year, subject to the lifetime
budget constraint that initial wealth plus discounted earnings must equal
discounted consumption.

Then comes the question. What happens if wealth A is augmented by
ΔA? All subsequent leisure and consumption demands rise. Moffitt demonstrates that the effect on leisure demand (or labor supply) is larger, the

larger is the increase in wealth and the later the increase comes in the life cycle. The intuition here is straightforward. The unanticipated ΔA means that one misplanned in the beginning. The later it occurs, the shorter is the time horizon over which one can adjust. In the extreme, if the ΔA comes in the last period, one has to consume it all at once.

Moffitt utilizes a Stone-Geary—Sir Stone–Geary now, I suppose—utility function, which is a good idea for at least two reasons. First, such a model yields a nice linear earnings function, and all Moffitt's empirical work is done with earnings rather than with hours of labor supply. Second, Sir Richard Stone himself is an appropriate test case for this theory because he has recently won the Nobel Prize in economics and has been awarded a huge ΔA.

In any case, the level of exogenous wealth in this model includes the traditionally defined assets, A, and a component called S. S is the net wealth that an individual (or a cohort, since aggregate data are used) will receive from the social security system; it is the difference between discounted benefits and discounted contributions. This social security component includes both an initial value and the unanticipated changes. Such changes are not simply added in but are weighted by a variable that depends on when the changes occurred. The later these surprises have occurred, the model predicts, the larger are the effects on behavior.

At this point Moffitt has produced a tractable linear earnings equation with initial wealth A and social security wealth S in it. Unfortunately, A is unobserved, so the equation as it stands cannot be estimated. Even if it could, only imprecise estimates of the two effects of A and S could be obtained because these variables are highly collinear in the aggregate.

Now here is the trick. The equation is first-differenced. In the first-differencing, traditional wealth and the initial level of social security wealth disappear from the equation. What remains is an equation in which the change in earnings from year to year is a function of the change in the wage rate and of the unanticipated social security shocks. The unobserved A and the potential collinearity disappear. The social security wealth effect is then identified by the unanticipated shocks that are left in the equation. This solution is very elegant and creative work.

Now the reader is prepared for the empirical work, and here is where one feels somewhat disappointed—like shopping in Poland, one cannot find any of the things one wants.

For example, hours of work are not available by age. Before 1955 there were no disaggregated age data available from the CPS. After 1955 such data were available, but only for four broad age categories. The result is that, because of the data, one cannot follow a specific age cohort over time. If this is the case, then one cannot first-difference as one had hoped—one cannot first-difference the 51-year-olds in 1981 and the 50-year-olds in 1980. These would have been exactly the same people, which is what the theory was about.

What one can do is first-difference cohorts of those aged 45–64 in 1981 and 1980. But these are not exactly the same people. By 1981, the people 64 years old in 1980 have moved on to the next cohort and have been replaced by a new batch of 45-year-olds. So cohort effects began to sneak into the empirical work, after having washed out nicely in the theory. One cannot use dummy variables for each of the cohort-year combinations because there are too many of them, and these dummy variables would use up too many precious degrees of freedom. The solution is the introduction of an unobserved cohort factor that is assumed to grow steadily over time.

The second problem is that the CPS reports do not contain earnings by age—income, yes, but earnings, no. Moffitt therefore turns to published reports from the Social Security Administration. Unfortunately, these data include only the covered population, and the coverage changed dramatically over this time period. They also include earnings only up to the maximum taxable amount, necessitating imputation beyond that. These earnings estimates are then divided by estimates of hours of work to yield the wage rates that show up as an explanatory variable in the empirical work.

Moffitt next considers the social security wealth shocks, the key to the estimation procedure. One approach would have been to include dummy variables for when each of the big surprises occurred—around 1950 and again in the late 1960s and early 1970s. But this procedure would have implied that the size of the shock is the same for all cohorts, which it is not. The same change in the rule has different effects on different cohorts, both because it changes their wealth in different ways and because a given change in wealth has a larger effect on the behavior of older cohorts, who have fewer years left to adjust to the change. It is unlikely that a dummy variable would pick up these subtleties, so Moffitt has estimated the magnitude of the social security shocks for each of the cohorts.

The shock equals the change, from one year to the next, in the net aggregate social security wealth that a cohort expects to enjoy at age 80. Net social security wealth for a given cohort is defined as the difference between the present discounted value of past and future benefits, on the one hand, and past and future tax contributions, on the other. In principle this difference will remain constant as long as a cohort's expectations about taxes and benefits remain unchanged.

The shock depends on what the cohort expected to receive at age 80. Rather than utilize the often changing legislation that regulates future benefits and taxes, Moffitt forecasts on the basis of what other cohorts of men 80 years old have enjoyed. He uses five-, ten-, and fifteen-year moving averages, in linear and logarithmic scale, and assumes that cohorts expect recent trends to continue.

A surprising finding emerges from these calculations. The net social security wealth of cohorts of 80-year-olds rose steadily between 1950 and 1980. (See figure 4 in the paper.) There are no jumps. *Natura* (nor social security) *non facit saltum*. The growth in the 1950s and early 1960s was primarily a result of expansions in coverage, and the maturation of a pay-as-you-go system. In the late 1960s and early 1970s the growth continued, but for a very different reason—the huge legislated increases in real benefits, and the subsequent indexing of benefits to inflation. From the perspective of an entire cohort (rather than simply those covered by the system), net social security wealth has been growing smoothly (although at a decreasing rate—see figure 5) for three decades. Moffitt's specifications implicitly assume that the labor supply effects of these two very different sources of increase in cohort wealth are the same—an assumption that may or may not make sense at the microeconomic level.

Figure 6 shows the shocks, calculated from this procedure, for a young and an old cohort. The most distinctive feature is the huge negative shock in the late 1970s, when the system failed to continue the real benefit increases of the early 1970s. The size of the disappointment, of course, is larger the shorter is the moving average, but the shock is still negative even with the fifteen-year window. Obviously, these negative shocks will make it difficult to explain the continuing decreases in the labor-force participation rate.

The results in the first-differenced earnings equations in table 2 of the paper bear this difficulty out. The shock coefficients are in general insignificant and often of the wrong sign. There is no evidence of a social security shock effect. (In the linear, *non*-first-differenced equations in table 1, a negative social security effect is found for men over age 40, but this, Moffitt explains, is probably due to the data collinearities discussed above.) The overall insight of the paper is this: the social security explanation of recent retirement patterns, now much in vogue, is less obvious than it appears. The largest unexpected social security shocks occurred in the 1950s, when retirement changes were far less dramatic. Moreover, the shocks may have been negative during much of the 1970s, when the declines in labor-force participation rates accelerated.

What does a microdata fan (a little-ender) make of all this? I have two somewhat contradictory reactions. Moffitt's paper is a very useful addition to the retirement literature because it is one of the few papers to throw sand in the path of the "social security" bandwagon. Perhaps social security changes are not the sole answer to the question of recent retirement patterns. Perhaps such changes are not even the primary answer. Maybe, as Moffitt's results imply, these changes are not an answer at all.

But I doubt it. I doubt it because of the inherent limitations of the macroeconomic time-series data. They are too aggregate; none of the variables available is what one really wants. One is constrained to the aggregations and categorizations of others. I do not question Moffitt's use of these data. His is a competent and extremely creative paper. But that creativity itself reflects the problem—one has to be extremely innovative to work with the published macrodata. Every variable derived has a huge element of measurement error, which tends to bias coefficient estimates toward zero. Can a single aggregate social security variable possibly capture all the subtle effects of social security legislation on the lifetime budget constraint—the changes in wealth, the kinks at various levels of labor supply, and the intertemporal changes in the wage rate? It is too much to ask. When one adds to this the limitation of relatively small numbers of time-series observations, precise estimation of these behavioral effects becomes nearly impossible.

None of this is news to Moffitt. He acknowledges these shortcomings at the beginning of the paper. Time-series analyses "have problems associated with low degrees of freedom." Because of the small number of observations, and because many variables are highly correlated, "inferences made from time-series data are inherently weaker than those made from cross-sectional data. As a consequence, only simple tests have much statistical power; it is virtually impossible to discriminate between competing hypotheses of great sophistication and subtlety."

I agree. Moreover, for these reasons I tend to trust the cross-sectional, microeconomic results. These findings suggest that the wealth increments and the implicit wage cuts that the social security system imposes on older workers do affect individual behavior and have contributed to the dramatic changes in retirement patterns documented here. Admittedly, no method—micro or macro—has been able to explain all, or even most, of the changes that have occurred, and in this respect Moffitt's results are consistent with the literature. There is more here than meets the eye, and plenty of room for new and inventive research.

Alan J. Auerbach and Laurence J. Kotlikoff

Life Insurance of the Elderly:
Adequacy and Determinants

The general economic status of the elderly has improved significantly in the past several decades. In contrast to 1960, when over a third of elderly households had incomes below the official poverty level, the current figure is below 15 percent. Despite the general reduction in poverty among the aged, the poverty rate among elderly nonmarried women, including widows, remains high. Today roughly one-third (31 percent) of elderly nonmarried women, compared with only 8 percent of elderly married women, are poor.[1]

That fact suggests a significant economic risk to women from the dissolution of marriage through divorce or a husband's death. Divorce insurance may not exist, but life insurance is readily available. Many households, however, may fail to buy enough life insurance. Concern about insufficient life insurance presumably underlies the provision of survivor and death benefits by the social security system. This paper examines the adequacy of the life insurance protection conferred by the combination of private and public insurance. It also investigates the determinants of private life insurance purchases.

Three central questions are addressed in the study:

—How large are private life insurance holdings relative to the amounts needed to maintain the previous standard of living of surviving spouses?

—Do social security survivor benefits significantly increase the amount of life insurance protection?

—Is the pattern of private insurance purchases in general accord with the predictions of economic theory, particularly the proposition that social

We thank Peter A. Diamond, Jagadeesh Gokhale, and Jerry A. Hausman for many useful comments and suggestions. Jagadeesh Gokhale provided excellent research assistance.

1. U.S. Department of Health and Human Services, Federal Council on the Aging, *The Need for Long-Term Care* (Government Printing Office, 1981).

security survivor insurance should substitute (under assumptions specified below) dollar for dollar for private life insurance?

The answers to these questions clearly are important for understanding the cause of poverty among widows, the extent of government intervention in the life insurance market, and the effectiveness of that intervention in increasing the sum of private and public life insurance. Despite the importance of these issues, there has been relatively little research to date on the adequacy of insurance. Two articles by Holden, Burkhauser, and Myers appear to be the only other analyses related to the problem of inadequate life insurance purchase.[2] These articles suggest that the probability for women of being below the poverty level is increased significantly by the death of their husbands.

The data set chosen for this study, the Retirement History Survey (RHS), is attractive because it focuses on the elderly and because it permits the observation of household economic status before and after the death of a spouse.[3] These data, however, are deficient in several respects for the study of life insurance. First, they include the face value, but not the cash value, of life insurance policies. Second, although various questions about retirement plans and expected future income were posed to RHS participants, a considerable number of respondents did not answer many of these questions. Understanding the magnitude of expected future income, particularly labor earnings, is obviously important in assessing the adequacy of life insurance holdings. Given these data problems, our results should be viewed cautiously. In some important respects, however, correcting biases that arise from missing data would likely strengthen our conclusions.

The principal inferences we draw from this study are the following:

—Combined private and public life insurance is inadequate for a significant minority of elderly households.

2. Karen C. Holden, Richard V. Burkhauser, and Daniel A. Myers, "Pensioners' Annuity Choice: Is the Well-Being of Widows Considered?" Discussion Paper 802-86 (University of Wisconsin—Madison, Institute for Research on Poverty, 1986); and Daniel A. Myers, Richard V. Burkhauser, and Karen C. Holden, "The Transition from Wife to Widow: The Importance of Survivor Benefits to the Well-Being of Widows," Discussion Paper 806-86 (University of Wisconsin—Madison, Institute for Research on Poverty, 1986).

3. The RHS data are available on tapes. The data are described in Lola M. Irelan and others, *Almost 65: Baseline Data for the Retirement History Study*, U.S. Department of Health, Education, and Welfare, Social Security Administration, Office of Research and Statistics, Research Report 49 (GPO, 1976).

—Almost one-half of households at risk (those for whom a significant portion of household resources take the form of earnings and benefits that cease with the death of the husband or wife) are inadequately insured.

—Empirical estimation of the demand for life insurance produces many results that are greatly at odds with theoretical predictions.

—Households do not appear to offset significantly the provision of social security survivor insurance by reducing their private purchase of life insurance.

There are five remaining sections in the paper. The first presents general descriptive information about the extent and adequacy of life insurance. Adequacy of life insurance is assessed in terms of the ability of surviving spouses to maintain their previous standard of living. Comparisons of previous and current standards of living are made for households in which a spouse died between 1969 and 1971. In addition, similar comparisons for hypothetical surviving spouses are made for all married households in 1969. After presenting these comparisons of standards of living before and after the death of a spouse, we discuss six potential biases in the comparisons. These six sources of bias taken together lead us to believe that our calculations have understated the inadequacy of life insurance holdings.

The second section examines the optimal choice of life insurance holdings within a simple two-period model. The substitutability of private and public insurance is considered, as well as the proper valuation of future income streams under the assumption of an incomplete (or imperfect) market in life insurance and annuities.

The two-period model illustrates the interdependence of choices of life insurance made by husbands and wives. As stressed in the section, the insurance demand of one spouse depends on whether the other spouse has positive or no life insurance. The model assumes that private annuities are unavailable. As Yaari has pointed out, purchasing private annuities is in effect equivalent to having negative holdings of life insurance.[4] Negative holdings of life insurance are ruled out because annuities appear on the private market only at actuarially unfair rates.[5] None of the households in the RHS sample used here reported holding private annuities.

4. Menahem E. Yaari, "Uncertain Lifetime, Life Insurance, and the Theory of the Consumer," *Review of Economic Studies*, vol. 32 (April 1965), pp. 137–50.

5. Benjamin M. Friedman and Mark Warshawsky, "Annuity Prices and Saving Behavior in the United States," National Bureau of Economic Research Working Paper 1683 (Cambridge, Mass.: NBER, 1985).

The theoretical model of the second section motivates the econometric specification of a two-indicator, switching-regressions model in the third section. The fourth section discusses the empirical findings and uses the results to evaluate the effect of social security on the purchase of private insurance. The last section summarizes the paper's findings and suggests directions for further research.

The Adequacy of Life Insurance: A Conceptual Framework

This section considers the adequacy of life insurance by comparing standards of living before and after either the actual or hypothetical death of a spouse. The definition of standard of living is obviously arbitrary; by the term we mean the sustained level of consumption of goods and services that can be afforded on the basis of a household's current assets and current and future income. Calculating affordable consumption annuities both before and after the death of a spouse requires information on the net worth, future labor earnings, private pensions, and social security benefits available to the couple when both spouses are alive as well as those resources available to the actual or hypothetical surviving spouse. Life insurance obviously increases the resources available to surviving spouses, and its purchase can protect surviving spouses from a reduction in their affordable standards of living.

The size of consumption streams that can be financed from a given amount of resources depends on actuarial factors such as the interest rate, the extent to which annuities are implicitly if not explicitly available, and household economies of scale in joint consumption. Economies of scale refers here to the proposition that "two can live cheaper than one." Many goods—such as heating, lighting, and other housing services—are jointly consumed by married couples. Other goods, such as food and clothing, do not have this feature of being public goods.

To see the importance of economies of scale, consider at one extreme that all goods consumed by couples are local public goods such as heating. For surviving spouses to maintain a previously affordable standard of living, they need to be able to purchase the same commodities when single that they and their spouses would have purchased when married. To do so obviously requires the same economic resources. With full insurance of the survival-contingent income stream of each spouse, the standard of living of the surviving spouse will be fully insured.

Fully insuring the survival-contingent income stream maintains the standard of living of survivors when all household consumption is joint, but this relationship fails in the absence of significant economies of scale. Consider the case of no joint consumption by married couples. The surviving spouse will then suffer a drop in the affordable standard of living only if the uninsured decedent's survival-contingent income stream would have financed more than the decedent's own stream of consumption. In other words, fully insuring the surviving spouse requires buying insurance equal to the difference between the value of the decedent's future income stream and the value of the decedent's future consumption. If this difference is negative—that is, if the value of the future income stream the decedent would have earned is less than the potential future value of the decedent's consumption—the surviving spouse's standard of living will be higher than it would have been had the decedent lived.

Because we do not know the precise extent of the economies of scale, we present calculations of the adequacy of life insurance under the assumption that economies of scale do not exist. We then discuss the likely bias arising from that assumption. Standard of living is measured in the calculations as the level annuity that could be financed with available resources. We calculate the combined resources of the couple before the actual or hypothetical death of a spouse and compute the level annuity, A_m, that could be purchased for each spouse under the assumption that each spouse receives an equal annuity. Next we determine the annuity that could be afforded by the surviving spouse, A_s. The ratio of the second annuity to the first annuity (A_s/A_m) is the measure used for the adequacy of insurance. Ratios below 0.75 are described as inadequate.

In more formal terms, let PVR_m be the present value of resources of the couple when they are both alive and let PVR_s be the present value of resources of the surviving spouse. We calculate A_s/A_m, where A_m (the annuity of the surviving spouse when married) and A_s (the annuity of the surviving spouse after the partner's death) are determined by

(1m) $$PVR_m = (D_h + D_w)A_m$$

(1s) $$PVR_s = D_s A_s, \qquad s = h, w.$$

In equations 1, D_h and D_w are discount factors for the husband and wife; D_h equals the present value of a dollar received annually by the husband until his death, and D_w is correspondingly defined for the wife; D_s represents the discount factor for the surviving spouse, where s equals h or w. (Throughout the equations, the subscripts $m, s, d, h,$ and w denote respectively "married," "surviving spouse," "deceased spouse," "husband," and "wife." For clarity, these same symbols have been suffixed to equation numbers—where they appear in roman type—to differentiate among the equations.)

As discussed in the literature and as indicated in the examination of potential biases later in this section, the proper valuation of future income streams in the presence of life-span uncertainty depends critically on the nature of explicit and implicit insurance arrangements.[6] At one extreme one could assume perfect markets in annuities and life insurance in which insurance premiums are actuarially fair. PVR_m and PVR_s would then correspond to the present expected values of the resources of married couples and surviving spouses, where the expectation is taken over survival probabilities. Similarly, $D_h, D_w,$ and D_s would be the discount factors of those expected values.

Even if there were no public market in annuities, Kotlikoff and Spivak have indicated that risk sharing among family members (that is, parents and children) can closely approximate perfect annuity insurance even when the number of family members is as small as four.[7] Although families are not as effective in hedging the loss of future income streams (that is, in providing life insurance) as they are in hedging the duration of future consumption streams (that is, in providing annuity insurance), life insurance that is close to actuarially fair combined with family annuity insurance arrangements may approximate the situation of perfect life and annuity insurance. In this case, using actuarially fair discounting in forming $PVR_m, PVR_s, D_h,$ and D_w would be roughly appropriate.

If public insurance markets are far from perfect, so that market insurance is in effect unavailable, and if family insurance arrangements do not arise, then simple discounting by only the interest rate is appropriate if it is assumed that borrowing and lending are unconstrained. Between the case of perfect insurance and no insurance is a range of partial insurance environments in which future income streams are priced (discounted) by using survival probabilities that depend to some extent on the availability and

6. See Yaari, "Uncertain Lifetime"; Laurence J. Kotlikoff and Avia Spivak, "The Family as an Incomplete Annuities Market," *Journal of Political Economy,* vol. 89 (April 1981), pp. 372–91; and Douglas Bernheim, "Social Security and Private Insurance Arrangements" (Stanford University, Department of Economics, 1985).

7. "Family as Incomplete Annuities Market."

pricing of particular insurance policies. The next subsection examines such cases.

Because assessing the precise degree to which the insurance market is complete is difficult if not impossible, we examine the A_s/A_m ratios under alternative assumptions—at one extreme, perfect insurance and, at the other, no insurance. In our view the assumption of perfect insurance is an approximation closer to the experience of the RHS sample than is the assumption of no insurance; 65 percent of the 1969 RHS sample of elderly couples reported positive life insurance for both spouses, and another 22 percent of couples had positive life insurance for at least one spouse. At least some of this life insurance surely was in the form of term insurance; as Yaari has demonstrated, buying additional life insurance is equivalent to selling an annuity.[8] For at least those couples in which both spouses have term life insurance, one can therefore argue that annuities were available at the margin: had these couples purchased less in term insurance, they would have had more in annuities. In addition, the ability of parents to insure implicitly longevity risk for their children leads us to view the benchmark of perfect insurance as more appropriate than the benchmark of no insurance.

In the following subsection we describe the detailed data definitions that permit us to measure the adequacy of insurance for respondents in the RHS.

Description of Variables, Data, and Sample Selection

The terms for family resources, PVR_m and PVR_s, are defined as

$$(2m) \quad PVR_m = NW_m + PVE_h + PVE_w + PVP_h + PVP_w + PVB_h$$
$$+ PVB_w + PVS_h + PVS_w$$

$$(2s) \quad PVR_s = NW_s + PVE_s + PVP_s + PVB_s + PVS_s + F_d,$$

where NW stands for net worth, PVE is the present expected value of labor earnings, PVP denotes the present expected value of non-social-security pension benefits, PVB is the present expected value of social security retirement benefits, PVS stands for the present expected value of social security survivor benefits, and F represents the insurance on the decedent's

8. "Uncertain Lifetime," p. 140.

life. The subscripts m, h, w, s, and d are as defined earlier. When s equals h, d equals w; when s equals w, d equals h.

As indicated in equation 2s, in calculations of hypothetical annuities for surviving spouses in 1969, PVR_s includes the insurance on the life of the hypothetical deceased spouse, F_d. In comparisons of the 1971 value of A_s with the 1969 value of A_m, reported values of NW_s presumably include unspent proceeds from the deceased spouses' life insurance; hence F_d is not included in forming PVR_s. This formulation of equations 2 treats reported life insurance as if it were only term insurance. We indicate below how the distribution of the A_s/A_m ratios would be affected by making the opposite assumption—that is, that the unreported cash value of life insurance equals the reported face value.

Net worth equals the sum of the reported values of assets less the reported values of liabilities. Observations were deleted if the market value of real estate was not reported, if the value of mortgages was not reported, or if more than two kinds of financial assets had missing values.

PRESENT VALUES OF EARNINGS AND PRIVATE PENSIONS. The present value of earnings was calculated by assuming that current real earnings continue to the reported expected age of retirement. Respondents who indicated that they would never retire were assigned an expected retirement age, calculated in the following manner. Using the RHS records of social security earnings and other RHS data, we determined the actual retirement ages for those nongovernmental workers who stated in 1969 that they would never retire but did stop working before 1975. With these data we were able to calculate age-specific probabilities of retiring at each age between ages 58 and 67. We assumed that those who did not retire by age 67 retired, on average, at age 70. From this information we calculated the expected age of retirement for respondents who stated in 1969 that they never intended to retire because of age.

Similar calculations were made for respondents with positive 1969 labor earnings who indicated that they were partially retired but did not give an expected age of full retirement. Also included in this group were 1969 respondents who reported positive labor earnings but stated that they were fully retired. Because spouses of respondents were not asked in 1969 when they expected to retire, the same technique was used to estimate the expected retirement ages for those spouses with positive labor earnings in 1969. In this case we calculated age-specific probabilities of retiring between ages 51 and 67 and again assumed an average retirement age of 70 for spouses not retiring before age 67.

For employed respondents and spouses, current earnings equal 1968 social security reported earnings (obtained from the RHS records of social security earnings) valued in 1969 dollars, if these earnings were below the 1968 ceiling for such earnings, but above the 1968 earnings reported by the respondent and spouse. If 1968 social security reported earnings were above the ceiling or below 1968 self-reported earnings, 1968 self-reported earnings valued in 1969 dollars were used.

The stream of non-social-security pension benefits equals currently reported pension benefits before the expected retirement age and current pension benefits or reported expected retirement benefits, whichever is larger, after the expected retirement age. Because there is no information on whether these pensions provide joint survivor benefits, we have assumed that such benefits accrue solely to the husbands. It is our understanding that before the passage of the Employee Retirement Income Security Act (ERISA) in 1974, joint survivor annuities were relatively rare. Because pension benefits of the wife were not reported in the 1969 survey, we have included only those of the husband in the analysis. This omission biases our calculation of A_w/A_m downward and biases our calculation of A_h/A_m upward.

PRESENT VALUE OF SOCIAL SECURITY BENEFITS. The stream of future social security benefits was calculated by first determining the primary insurance amount (PIA) at age 62 for each respondent and spouse. Earnings before 1969 that were used in calculating the PIA were obtained from the RHS social security earnings records. Earnings between 1969 and the year in which the respondent or spouse would reach age 62 are projected as just described. The wife's social security benefit is her own benefit or the dependent's benefit once the wife is eligible for that benefit (that is, she has exceeded age 62, and her husband is receiving benefits or is dead), whichever is larger. Before eligibility for the dependent's benefit, the wife may be eligible to collect her own benefit. For respondents and spouses who indicated they were already retired, expected to retire before age 62, or were earning less than $1,680 (the social security exempt amount), the actuarially reduced stream of benefits commences at age 62. For respondents and spouses who expected to retire after age 62 or were earning more than $1,680, actuarially reduced benefits commence at the indicated expected retirement age if that age is less than or equal to 65. Between ages 65 and 72, respondents and spouses who had not yet retired (according to stated or imputed expectations) were assigned benefits according to an earnings test. Past age 72 non-earnings-tested benefits were available for all respondents and spouses.

If the husband was the decedent, survivor benefits were available. As

Table 1. Components of Family Wealth, 1969
Mean values; 1969 dollars

Item	Present value of resources (PVR)[a]						
	<10,000 (55)	10–25,000 (179)	25–50,000 (714)	50–100,000 (2,040)	100–250,000 (1,922)	250,000+ (221)	Total (5,131)
Husband							
Earnings	307	1,099	5,316	16,822	33,312	42,431	21,772
Percent of PVR	5	6	13	22	24	9	20
Benefits	2,059	6,959	13,138	17,304	20,025	18,971	17,269
Percent of PVR	36	38	32	23	14	4	16
Pension	0	759	2,561	5,670	13,663	29,357	9,020
Percent of PVR	0	4	6	8	10	6	8
Insurance	1,247	2,057	2,582	5,042	12,057	55,914	9,360
Percent of PVR	22	11	6	7	9	12	9
Wife							
Earnings	67	973	2,044	5,981	12,271	11,864	7,804
Percent of PVR	1	5	5	8	9	3	7
Benefits	922	3,348	6,354	9,506	12,154	11,389	9,824
Percent of PVR	16	18	16	13	9	2	9
Survivor benefits	571	1,531	2,818	3,551	3,505	4,133	3,348
Percent of PVR	10	8	7	5	3	1	3
Insurance	251	487	687	1,018	1,419	1,260	1,103
Percent of PVR	4	3	2	1	1	0	1
Couple							
Net worth	1,825	3,803	8,484	16,329	44,975	352,834	39,849
Percent of PVR	32	21	21	22	32	75	37
PVR	5,751	18,472	40,715	75,163	139,905	470,978	108,886

Source: Authors' calculations from 1969 Retirement History Survey (RHS) data. Data were aggregated by PVR class.
a. The numbers of observations are in parentheses.

described above, these benefits are provided on an actuarially reduced basis and are earnings-tested where appropriate. Although our calculations of total benefits have followed the social security law, we define the stream of social security survivor benefits to be the excess of the surviving wife's benefit over what she would have received had her husband lived.

In the projections of future real social security benefits, households are assumed to expect that current social security law will continue unchanged except for increased future benefits to adjust for inflation.

DATA CHARACTERISTICS. After deletion of observations with missing data, the 1969 RHS sample of married households numbered 5,131. A total of 4,295 husbands and 3,389 wives reported positive life insurance. Table 1 presents mean values of life insurance holdings as well as components of PVR cross-classified by the level of PVR, which is the present value of family resources. In forming present values, all future earnings, social security, and pension streams were actuarially discounted by using probabilities of mortality and assuming a 4 percent real interest rate. The overall average holdings of life insurance on the husband's life is $9,360, which may be compared with the mean value of family resources, PVR, which is $108,886. Life insurance is small relative to family resources, but is it small relative to the amount of the husband's future earnings and social security and other pension benefit streams that could be insured?

The answer is that the mean value of insurance on the husband's life is less than one-fifth the sum of the mean values of his insurable future income streams. Insurance holdings on wives are even smaller relative to their insurable streams; the ratio of these means is less than 6 percent. These figures would be inconsequential were future income streams only a trivial fraction of current family resources, PVR. This is not the case. The future income streams of husbands make up 44 percent of the total PVR of households in the sample; those of wives are 19 percent. The table also indicates that social security survivor benefits represent almost one fourth of the combined private and public insurance on the husband's life. Even if any offsetting from private insurance is ignored, social security survivor benefits make only a very small contribution to reducing the gap between husbands' insurable income streams and private insurance on their lives.

Table 1 suggests that insurance is much more adequate for those with a PVR less than $25,000. For couples with a PVR above $250,000, insurance on the husband's life is also larger relative to PVR; for this group the husband's future income streams are less than one-fifth of PVR. The concern about inadequate insurance is therefore much more of an issue for middle-class households with a *PVR* between $25,000 and $250,000.

Annuity Ratios

Table 2 compares the annuity that actual surviving wives could purchase in 1971 with the corresponding annuity they could have purchased in 1969 when their husbands were alive (with it assumed, as stated earlier,

Table 2. Widows' Annuity Ratios, 1971

Fraction of potential 1969 annuity	PVR class (1969 dollars)[a]						
	< 10,000	10,000– 25,000	25,000– 50,000	50,000– 100,000	100,000– 250,000	250,000+	Total
	(5)	(5)	(19)	(42)	(16)	(2)	(89)
< 0.10							
Number	0	0	0	0	1	0	1
Percent	0	0	0	0	6	0	1
0.10–0.25							
Number	0	0	0	1	0	1	2
Percent	0	0	0	2	0	50	2
0.25–0.50							
Number	1	0	1	4	5	0	11
Percent	20	0	5	10	31	0	12
0.50–0.75							
Number	0	1	5	10	2	1	19
Percent	0	20	26	24	13	50	21
0.75–1.00							
Number	1	1	5	12	3	0	22
Percent	20	20	26	29	19	0	25
1.00–1.25							
Number	0	1	2	7	1	0	11
Percent	0	20	11	17	6	0	12
1.25–1.50							
Number	0	0	3	3	3	0	9
Percent	0	0	16	7	19	0	10
1.50–1.75							
Number	0	0	0	3	0	0	3
Percent	0	0	0	7	0	0	3
1.75–2.00							
Number	1	0	0	2	1	0	4
Percent	20	0	0	5	6	0	4
> 2.00							
Number	2	2	3	0	0	0	7
Percent	40	40	16	0	0	0	8

Source: Authors' calculations from 1969 and 1971 RHS data.
a. The numbers of observations are in parentheses.

that an annuity of equal amount was purchased for their husbands). In tables 2–7 the assumption of perfect insurance is maintained; hence the annuity ratios are based on discounting by both mortality and interest rates. Over one-third of surviving spouses are unable to afford an annuity as large as 75 percent of the annuity that was affordable while the deceased spouse was alive. For 15 percent of the sample, the affordable annuity is less than half of what could have been purchased (under the assumption of perfect insurance) before the death of a spouse. At the other extreme, a sizable fraction of widows appear economically better off after the death of their husbands. For over a quarter of the sample of surviving widows, the annuity affordable in 1971 is over 25 percent larger than the annuity affordable in 1969.

Table 3 presents similar calculations for men who were actually widowed between 1969 and 1971. Although the sample of such men is small, it appears that the percentage of widowers who experienced a large drop in consumable resources after the death of their wives is smaller than the corresponding figure for widows. Only 13 percent of the widowers have annuity ratios less than 0.75, and 30 percent have ratios greater than 1.25.

Table 4 considers the entire 1969 sample of households and compares the annuity that a wife could have purchased at the time of the RHS interview with the annuity that she could have puchased had her husband died immediately after the interview. This distribution of hypothetical widows by their annuity ratios is quite similar to that in table 2. About 25 percent of the sample have an annuity ratio below 0.75; almost 50 percent have a ratio less than 1.00. A sizable fraction, 33 percent, have an annuity ratio above 1.25.

A dramatically different situation obtains for hypothetical widowers (table 5). Only 2 percent have annuity ratios below 0.75; 95 percent of these men have ratios above 1.00, and 73 percent have ratios above 1.50. Clearly there is little reason for concern about inadequate life insurance for wives in this sample.

Another way of examining the adequacy of insurance coverage is to limit the investigation to those couples for whom substantial insurance would be needed to keep a surviving spouse from suffering a large drop in consumable resources. This approach would exclude couples with most of their wealth held in current net worth, since the death of a spouse in such cases would have little effect on the total family resources (excluding insurance) available to the survivor. We therefore repeat in tables 6 and 7 the calculations done for tables 4 and 5, this time for the subsamples of

Table 3. Widowers' Annuity Ratios, 1971

Fraction of potential 1969 annuity	PVR class (1969 dollars)[a]						
	< 10,000	10,000–25,000	25,000–50,000	50,000–100,000	100,000–250,000	250,000+	Total
	(0)	(6)	(7)	(21)	(13)	(0)	(47)
< 0.10							
Number	0	0	0	0	0	0	0
Percent	0	0	0	0	0	0	0
0.10–0.25							
Number	0	0	0	0	1	0	1
Percent	0	0	0	0	8	0	2
0.25–0.50							
Number	0	0	0	0	1	0	1
Percent	0	0	0	0	8	0	2
0.50–0.75							
Number	0	0	0	3	1	0	4
Percent	0	0	0	14	8	0	9
0.75–1.00							
Number	0	1	2	8	2	0	13
Percent	0	17	29	38	15	0	28
1.00–1.25							
Number	0	2	2	6	4	0	14
Percent	0	33	29	29	31	0	30
1.25–1.50							
Number	0	1	0	3	4	0	8
Percent	0	17	0	14	31	0	17
1.50–1.75							
Number	0	1	1	0	0	0	2
Percent	0	17	14	0	0	0	4
1.75–2.00							
Number	0	0	0	0	0	0	0
Percent	0	0	0	0	0	0	0
> 2.00							
Number	0	1	2	1	0	0	4
Percent	0	17	29	5	0	0	9

Source: Authors' calculations from 1969 and 1971 RHS data.
a. The numbers of observations are in parentheses.

husbands and wives who are "at risk," which we define as those for whom the other spouse's survival-contingent resources (labor earnings, pension benefits, and social security benefits) constitute over half of the couple's total resources.

By this measure, over half of the wives in the full sample are at risk. Of this group, over 45 percent have an annuity ratio of less than 0.75 (table 6). For wives and husbands at risk who are in poorer households, the

Table 4. Wives' Annuity Ratios If Husbands Die, 1969

Fraction of potential 1969 annuity	PVR class (1969 dollars)[a]						
	< 10,000	10,000–25,000	25,000–50,000	50,000–100,000	100,000–250,000	250,000+	Total
	(55)	(179)	(714)	(2,040)	(1,922)	(221)	(5,131)
<0.10							
Number	1	0	5	1	0	0	7
Percent	2	0	1	0	0	0	0
0.10–0.25							
Number	0	4	9	10	3	1	27
Percent	0	2	1	0	0	0	1
0.25–0.50							
Number	3	19	75	155	83	1	336
Percent	5	11	11	8	4	0	7
0.50–0.75							
Number	13	42	156	391	280	4	886
Percent	24	23	22	19	15	2	17
0.75–1.00							
Number	7	35	183	514	418	9	1,166
Percent	13	20	26	25	22	4	23
1.00–1.25							
Number	3	8	131	458	478	16	1,094
Percent	5	4	18	22	25	7	21
1.25–1.50							
Number	6	18	56	306	329	29	744
Percent	11	10	8	15	17	13	15
1.50–1.75							
Number	4	15	37	114	213	56	439
Percent	7	8	5	6	11	25	9
1.75–2.00							
Number	8	11	23	57	83	70	252
Percent	15	6	3	3	4	32	5
>2.00							
Number	10	27	39	34	35	35	180
Percent	18	15	5	2	2	16	4

Source: Authors' calculations from 1969 RHS data.
a. The numbers of observations are in parentheses.

extent of underinsurance is more significant. Consider, for example, wives at risk in households with a *PVR* of $25,000–$50,000 (table 6). Fifty-five percent of this group have an annuity ratio below 0.75, and 20 percent have a ratio below 0.50. Table 7 indicates that 28 percent of husbands at risk have hypothetical annuity ratios below 0.75. The number of husbands at risk, however, is small. These results reinforce the finding that underinsurance, particularly of husbands, is potentially a quite serious problem.

Table 5. Husbands' Annuity Ratios If Wives Die, 1969

Fraction of potential 1969 annuity	PVR class (1969 dollars)[a]						
	< 10,000	10,000– 25,000	25,000– 50,000	50,000– 100,000	100,000– 250,000	250,000+	Total
	(0)	(6)	(7)	(21)	(13)	(0)	(47)
annuity	(55)	(179)	(714)	(2,040)	(1,922)	(221)	(5,131)
< 0.10							
Number	1	2	3	0	0	0	6
Percent	2	1	0	0	0	0	0
0.10–0.25							
Number	1	2	0	3	0	0	6
Percent	2	1	0	0	0	0	0
0.25–0.50							
Number	2	3	12	8	2	1	28
Percent	4	2	2	0	0	0	1
0.50–0.75							
Number	0	6	9	39	8	1	63
Percent	0	3	1	2	0	0	1
0.75–1.00							
Number	0	7	29	76	30	0	142
Percent	0	4	4	4	2	0	3
1.00–1.25							
Number	4	22	58	133	116	1	334
Percent	7	12	8	7	6	0	7
1.25–1.50							
Number	11	37	151	313	256	3	771
Percent	20	21	21	15	13	1	15
1.50–1.75							
Number	16	46	217	596	457	23	1,355
Percent	29	26	30	29	24	10	26
1.75–2.00							
Number	5	30	158	634	621	63	1,511
Percent	9	17	22	31	32	29	29
> 2.00							
Number	15	24	77	238	432	129	915
Percent	27	13	11	12	22	58	18

Source: Authors' calculations from 1969 RHS data.
a. The numbers of observations are in parentheses.

Potential Biases in Calculation of Annuity Ratios

Six sources of potential bias can affect the calculation of the annuity ratios. Each of these sources is examined below in turn.

IGNORING CASH VALUE OF LIFE INSURANCE. To see how excluding the unobserved cash value of life insurance affects the results in tables 4 and 5, consider again equations 1 and 2. For hypothetical surviving wives, PVR_m

Table 6. Wives' Annuity Ratios If Husbands Die, Wives at Risk, 1969

Fraction of potential 1969 annuity	PVR class (1969 dollars)[a]						
	< 10,000	10,000– 25,000	25,000– 50,000	50,000– 100,000	100,000– 250,000	250,000+	Total
	(28)	(99)	(446)	(1,201)	(972)	(30)	(2,776)
< 0.10							
Number	1	0	5	1	0	0	7
Percent	4	0	1	0	0	0	0
0.10–0.25							
Number	0	4	9	10	3	1	27
Percent	0	4	2	1	0	3	1
0.25–0.50							
Number	3	19	75	155	83	1	336
Percent	11	19	17	13	9	3	12
0.50–0.75							
Number	13	42	156	391	280	4	886
Percent	46	42	35	33	29	13	32
0.75–1.00							
Number	7	25	152	454	376	7	1,021
Percent	25	25	34	38	39	23	37
1.00–1.25							
Number	2	3	35	146	171	8	365
Percent	7	3	8	12	18	27	13
1.25–1.50							
Number	0	4	7	36	41	5	93
Percent	0	4	2	3	4	17	3
1.50–1.75							
Number	1	2	5	3	9	1	21
Percent	4	2	1	0	1	3	1
1.75–2.00							
Number	0	0	0	2	6	2	10
Percent	0	0	0	0	1	7	0
> 2.00							
Number	1	0	2	3	3	1	10
Percent	4	0	0	0	0	3	0

Source: Authors' calculations from 1969 RHS data. "At risk" refers to wives for whom the husband's survival-contingent resources constitute over half of the couple's total resources.

a. The numbers of observations are in parentheses.

is too small by an amount equal to the cash value of the husband's and wife's insurance, whereas PVR_s, which includes the face value and thus the cash value of the insurance on the deceased spouse's life (F_d), is too small by an amount equal to only the cash value of the surviving spouse's insurance. Because the average value of insurance on the husband's life is over eight times larger than that on his wife's, one would expect the cash value of the husband's insurance to exceed greatly that of the wife's. As a

Table 7. Husbands' Annuity Ratios If Wives Die, Husbands at Risk, 1969

Fraction of potential 1969 annuity	PVR class (1969 dollars)[a]						
	<10,000	10,000–25,000	25,000–50,000	50,000–100,000	100,000–250,000	250,000+	Total
	(5)	(24)	(62)	(180)	(101)	(2)	(374)
<0.10							
Number	1	2	3	0	0	0	6
Percent	20	8	5	0	0	0	2
0.10–0.25							
Number	1	2	0	3	0	0	6
Percent	20	8	0	2	0	0	2
0.25–0.50							
Number	2	3	12	8	2	1	28
Percent	40	13	19	4	2	50	7
0.50–0.75							
Number	0	6	9	39	8	1	63
Percent	0	25	15	22	4	50	17
0.75–1.00							
Number	0	7	27	74	29	0	137
Percent	0	29	44	41	29	0	37
1.00–1.25							
Number	0	4	10	52	54	0	120
Percent	0	17	16	29	53	0	32
1.25–1.50							
Number	0	0	1	3	8	0	12
Percent	0	0	2	2	8	0	3
1.50–1.75							
Number	1	0	0	1	0	0	2
Percent	20	0	0	1	0	0	1
1.75–2.00							
Number	0	0	0	0	0	0	0
Percent	0	0	0	0	0	0	0
>2.00							
Number	0	0	0	0	0	0	0
Percent	0	0	0	0	0	0	0

Source: Authors' calculations from 1969 RHS data. "At risk" refers to husbands for whom the wife's survival-contingent benefits constitute over half of the couple's total resources.
a. The numbers of observations are in parentheses.

consequence, the omission of cash value implies that the ratio PVR_w/PVR_m is biased upward and that the ratio PVR_h/PVR_m is biased downward. This relation in turn implies an upward bias in the calculation of the hypothetical widows' annuity ratios (A_w/A_m) and a downward bias in the calculated annuity ratios of hypothetical widowers (A_h/A_m).

To consider the possible extent of this bias, we recalculated table 4 under the assumption that the cash value of husbands' and wives' insurance equals the face value; that is, that there is no term insurance. This assumption increases the fraction of hypothetical widows with annuity ratios below 0.75 from 25 percent to 27 percent. The bias with respect to the values of A_h/A_m in table 5 moves in the opposite direction; making the extreme assumption of no term insurance increases the annuity ratio for hypothetical widowers. Again the potential bias is small; the fraction of hypothetical widowers with annuity ratios above 1.50 rises from 73 percent to 74 percent.

ECONOMIES OF SCALE. Ignoring economies of scale in household consumption biases upward both widows' and widowers' annuity ratios, if the annuity is viewed as the level stream of consumption that can be financed. Suppose, for example, that household consumption were a pure public good. In this case the consumption stream that could be financed with A_m would equal twice the value of A_m if both spouses remain alive. For a widow with an annuity ratio of 0.75, according to this reasoning, the death of her spouse has meant a 62.5 percent [(2.0–0.75)/2] decline in consumption and an adjusted annuity ratio of 0.375 (0.75/2). Tables 2–7 may therefore significantly understate the potential welfare decline experienced by surviving spouses.

BEQUESTS TO CHILDREN AND END-OF-LIFE EXPENSES. The hypothetical annuity ratios also ignore possible bequests to children, end-of-life uninsured medical and funeral expenses, and, for those few observed households with considerable wealth, estate taxes. Inclusion of these factors would reduce the hypothetical annuity ratios below the reported values. This point is supported by the finding that the actual annuity ratios of surviving spouses (tables 2 and 3) are smaller than those of hypothetical surviving spouses (tables 4 and 5): 36 percent of actual widows, but only 25 percent of hypothetical widows, have ratios below 0.75; 13 percent of actual widowers, but only 2 percent of hypothetical widowers, have ratios below 0.75.

VALUING FUTURE STREAMS IF INSURANCE IS IMPERFECT. The annuity distributions in tables 2–7 are quite sensitive to the assumption of perfect insurance. For example, if one discounts future streams only by the interest rate, which would be appropriate in the absence of any explicit or implicit insurance arrangement, the fraction of those hypothetical widows at risk and with inadequate insurance protection drops from over 45 percent to only 20 percent. For hypothetical widowers at risk, in contrast, the fraction with inadequate insurance protection rises from 28 percent to 40 percent. The direction of these changes reflects the fact that the discount factor for husbands relative to wives rises when discounting by only the interest rate rather than by both interest and mortality rates. Husbands in the sample are older and have higher age-specific death rates than their wives. Although we mention this alternative assumption to permit the reader to draw his or her own conclusion, in our view the calculations based on the assumption of close-to-perfect insurance arrangements better approximate the insurance environment of the RHS sample.

INCOME TAXES AND CHOICE OF REAL INTEREST RATE. In calculating the annuity ratios we did not attempt to estimate taxes that would be paid on earning and pension streams. Nor did we estimate the marginal effective income tax rate to form an after-tax rate of return for discounting future income streams. We believe that these adjustments taken together would lower the annuity ratios. Present-value calculations of this kind are highly sensitive to the choice of discount rate. Realistic inclusion of tax factors would lead to discounting by an after-tax real rate of return substantially below 4 percent, which would raise considerably the present values of those income streams that would be lost in the event of a spouse's death. Because the ratio of discount factors for husbands and wives, D_h/D_w, is a decreasing function of the discount rate, and if the husband is older than the wife, adjusting for taxes would lower the annuity ratios of widows by more than it would for surviving husbands.

UNCERTAINTY OF EARNINGS. The calculations of annuity ratios assume that future real earnings are certain. The exception is the uncertainty that death poses for earnings. Although we have not closely examined the bias from ignoring other kinds of uncertainty in earnings, we believe that, roughly speaking, uncertain future earnings should be discounted by a risk-adjusted discount rate—a rate that could well be higher than the 4 percent real rate used here. Hence, by ignoring earnings uncertainty, we are probably biasing downward the calculated annuity ratios and, on this score, exaggerating somewhat the need for additional life insurance.

A Model of Life Insurance Demand

This section develops an estimable model of the demand for life insurance by married couples under the assumption of expected utility maximization. The model focuses on the life-cycle consumption of husbands and wives and ignores possible parental bequest motives and longevity risk sharing between parents and children. It also ignores uncertainty in earnings. The purposes of estimating a model of life insurance demand are twofold: first, to determine whether the actual purchase of life insurance is in general accord with the predictions of economic theory; second, to determine the extent to which households reduce their purchase of private life insurance in response to provision of social security survivor insurance. If insurance on the husband's life is assumed to be positive, theory predicts that properly valued income streams of the wife—including her labor earnings, public and private pension benefits, and survivor benefits—should substitute at the margin, dollar for dollar, for the insurance on her husband's life. Similar arbitrage relationships should hold at the margin between the wife's insurance and the properly valued income streams of the husband.

Life insurance transfers income across states of nature and thereby alters the amounts that can be consumed in those different states. The optimal choice of life insurance is thus determined simultaneously with the optimal choice of desired consumption in those states. If insurance markets are complete and actuarially fair, life insurance will be purchased (or sold) up to the point at which the marginal utility of consumption is equalized across each state of nature. Deviation of insurance pricing from actuarially fair values changes the effective prices of consuming in different states of nature and implies differences in the marginal utility of consumption across those different states. These points are illustrated in the equations below.

Our model has two periods. During the first, both the husband and wife are alive. During the second period there are four states of nature, corresponding to only the husband surviving, only the wife surviving, both surviving, and neither surviving. We denote consumption in the first period as C; consumption in the three states in which at least one member of the couple survives is denoted as C_h, C_w, and C_{hw}, respectively. In the first period and in state hw, in which both spouses are alive, *each* spouse separately consumes the amount C and C_{hw}, respectively. If there are no economies of scale, the couple spends $2C$ and $2C_{hw}$ in the first period and in the hw state, respectively. If consumption by a married couple is a pure public good, the couple spends only C and C_{hw} in the two states, although each spouse still consumes C and, if they both survive, C_{hw}. The couple's expected utility maximization problem is therefore

(3) $\quad \max[p_h(1 - p_w)U(C, C_h) + (1 - p_h)p_wU(C, C_w) + p_hp_wU(C, C_{hw})$

$$+ (1 - p_h)(1 - p_w)U(C, 0)],$$

where p_s is the probability that spouse s survives, and s equals h or w.

If both the husband and wife purchase positive amounts of life insurance, then the following equations constrain the choice of consumption in the three states of nature in which at least one member of the couple survives:

(4h) $C_h = E_h + B_h + F_w + (A - \lambda C - \pi_h F_h - \pi_w F_w)(1 + r)$

(4w) $C_w = E_w + B_w + B_w^* + F_h + (A - \lambda C - \pi_h F_h - \pi_w F_w)(1 + r)$

(4hw) $\lambda C_{hw} = E_w + B_w + E_h + B_h + (A - \lambda C - \pi_h F_h - \pi_w F_w)(1 + r)$,

where A is the couple's tangible wealth in the first period, F_s is the face value of insurance purchased for spouse s, π_s is the corresponding premium paid per dollar of face value in the first period, E_s is wages of spouse s in the second period, B_s is the spouse's social security and pension benefits, and B_w^* is the survivor benefits to which the wife is entitled in the event of the husband's death. The terms r and λ are prices: r is the first-period interest rate, and λ is the price of second-period joint consumption. If λ equals 2, there are no economies of scale in consumption; if λ equals 1, household consumption is a pure public good.

These budget constraints are written under the assumptions that husbands will not be entitled to survivor benefits and that all private insurance is term insurance. The former assumption is consistent with observations in the sample. The second is more problematic. To the extent that policies are "whole-life" and not term policies, they will have a cash or asset value corresponding to the insurance policy's previous savings component, or "inside build-up." A whole-life policy may be viewed as a combination of a savings account with liquid assets equal to the policy's cash value and a term insurance policy with a death benefit equal to the difference between the policy's face value and cash value. If we knew how much cash value each policy had, we would subtract this amount from the face value F in equations 4 and add it to A. Unfortunately, no such information is available. We defer further discussion of this data problem until the empirical implementation of the model is considered.

In the case of positive insurance purchases for both spouses, we may use expressions 4h, 4w and 4hw to eliminate F_h and F_w, thus obtaining a single expression in consumption levels that may be interpreted as the household budget constraint:

(5) $\qquad \lambda C + \pi_h C_h + \pi_w C_w + \lambda[1/(1 + r) - \pi_h - \pi_w]C_{hw}$

$$= A + (E_h + B_h)[1/(1 + r) - \pi_h]$$

$$+ (E_w + B_w)[1/(1 + r) - \pi_w] + \pi_h B_w^*,$$

where λ, π_h, π_w and $\lambda[1/(1 + r) - \pi_h - \pi_w]$ are the "prices" of the four consumption levels, and the right-hand side is a weighted sum of the different resource components. We assume that insurance is actuarially fair:

(6) $\qquad \pi_h = (1 - p_w)/(1 + r); \qquad \pi_w = (1 - p_h)/(1+r).$

Combination of expressions 5 and 6 yields a simpler and more intuitive version of the budget constraint:

(7) $\qquad \lambda C + [(1 - p_w)/(1 + r)]C_h + [(1 - p_h)/(1 + r)]C_w$

$$+ \lambda[p_h p_w - (1 - p_h)(1 - p_w)]/(1 + r)]C_{hw}$$

$$= A + [p_h/(1 + r)](E_h + B_h) + [p_w/(1 + r)](E_w + B_w)$$

$$+ [(1 - p_h)/(1 + r)]B_w^*.$$

Note how this result differs from what would obtain in the presence of complete and actuarially fair markets for annuities and life insurance, which would permit state-contingent purchases of consumption. In that case, the present value of resources would equal the sum of the expected values, based on the associated survival probabilities, of each of the components of wealth. The right-hand side of equation 7 differs from the present expected value of resources in that the survivor benefit B_w^* is multiplied only by the husband's death probability rather than by the product of his death probability and the wife's survival probability. This difference is because, without the availability of private annuities, resources that are available when the husband and wife both die are of no value. Put another way, the survivor benefit has the value it would have if it also paid off when both the husband and the wife die.

The implicit prices for second-period, state-contingent consumption also differ from those in the case of complete, actuarially fair insurance markets. The prices for C_h and C_w are higher, representing the fact that, in states in which one spouse dies, the household must commit resources regardless of whether the remaining spouse actually lives. This fact also makes the price of consumption lower in the state in which both spouses survive. The intuition is that, by providing resources for the state in which both live, the household reduces the amount it must waste in the state when both die; that is, increased expenditures for C_{hw} also increase consumption in the states in which one member of the couple survives, so that fewer direct expenditures are necessary.

Expected utility maximization by the household of equation 3 subject to budget constraint 7 leads to an optimal consumption vector that is a function of the implicit prices and the present value of resources given by the right-hand side of budget constraint 7. We label these prices q and the present value of resources PVR. Next, we derive expressions for the demands for life insurance. Subtracting expression 4hw from 4w yields

$$(8h) \qquad F_h = (C_w - \lambda C_{hw}) + (E_h + B_h - B_w^*).$$

From expressions 4h and 4hw we obtain

$$(8w) \qquad F_w = (C_h - \lambda C_{hw}) + (E_w + B_w).$$

Each expression has a clear interpretation, calling for the purchase of insurance for the husband or wife equal to the net loss in resources if that spouse dies plus the additional consumption that must be financed. The latter term may well be negative, depending on the value of λ and the tastes of the household.

Substituting the optimal consumption demands in expressions 8h and 8w yields demand functions for insurance:

$$(9h) \qquad F_h = H(q, PVR) + (E_h + B_h - B_w^*)$$

$$(9w) \qquad F_w = W(q, PVR) + (E_w + B_w),$$

where $H(\ )$ and $W(\ )$ are the consumption demands for C_h and C_w in excess of joint consumption expenditures when both spouses survive (that is, $C_w - \lambda C_{hw}$ and $C_h - \lambda C_{hw}$, respectively).

Equations 9h and 9w are appropriate only when both F_h and F_w are positive, since by assumption neither F_h nor F_w can be negative. We next consider situations in which one or both spouses are constrained at zero in the purchase of life insurance. In such situations the couple faces an optimization problem of reduced dimension, with different implicit prices for consumption and different weights used to calculate PVR. For example, suppose that the value of F_w satisfying equation 9w is negative, requiring that it be constrained to zero. Then, in place of expression 8w we have

(8w') $$0 = (C_h - \lambda C_{hw}) + (E_w + B_w),$$

which implies that the family can no longer independently determine C_h and C_{hw}. Substituting this restriction into expression 7 obtains a new budget constraint that omits C_{hw}:

(7w') $$\lambda C + [p_h/(1 + r)]C_h + [(1 - p_h)/(1 + r)]C_w$$
$$= A + [p_h/(1 + r)](E_h + B_h)$$
$$+ [(1 - p_h)/(1 + r)](E_w + B_w + B_w^*).$$

Note that the implicit price of the husband's consumption is now the probability of his own survival, rather than the probability of his wife's death. Similarly, the wife's wages and benefits are no longer weighted by her survival probability, but by her husband's death probability. Because only the husband may buy insurance, his insurance decision determines the allocation of resources between C_h and C_w, and the cost of this insurance determines the relative prices of these states of consumption. Because the wife cannot transfer resources to her husband through insurance, her survival probability does not enter into the budget constraint.

Letting q_h and PVR_h be the implicit price vector and present value of resources given by the right-hand side of equation 7w', we obtain from equation 8h the husband's demand for life insurance when his wife is constrained at zero life insurance:

(9h') $$F_h = H(q_h, PVR_h) + (E_h + B_h - B_w^*).$$

In an analogous fashion, we may derive prices q_w and the present value of resources PVR_w for the case in which the husband's insurance is constrained to equal zero and obtain the wife's insurance demand function:

(9w') $$F_w = W(q_w, PVR_w) + (E_w + B_w).$$

Four possible demand regimes therefore exist:

—husband and wife unconstrained,

$$F_h = H(q, PVR) + (E_h + B_h - B_w^*)$$
$$F_w = W(q, PVR) + (E_w + B_w);$$

—husband unconstrained but wife constrained,

$$F_h = H(q_h, PVR_h) + (E_h + B_h - B_w^*)$$
$$F_w = 0;$$

—wife unconstrained but husband constrained,

$$F_h = 0$$
$$F_w = W(q_w, PVR_w) + (E_w + B_w);$$

—both spouses constrained,

$$F_h = 0$$
$$F_w = 0.$$

Estimation of the demand for insurance across these regimes involves a switching-regressions model with censored dependent variables. We discuss different estimation strategies in the next section.

A problem involved in estimating the insurance demand functions 9h, 9h′, 9w, and 9w′ is that the RHS data do not report term insurance, which corresponds to F_h and F_w in the equations, but only the face value of insurance. An alternative approach that is robust for this particular problem is to estimate expressions 4h and 4w directly. Rearranging terms in equation 4w and substituting in the demands for consumption, we obtain

(10h) $$F_h + (A - \pi_h F_h - \pi_w F_w)(1 + r)$$
              $$= \hat{H}(q, PVR) - (E_w + B_w + B_w^*),$$

where $\hat{H}(\ )$ is the expenditure on first-period consumption times $1 + r$ plus the wife's second-period consumption when widowed; that is, $\lambda C(1 + r) + C_w$. If we ignore the insurance premiums or assume that assets are measured net of insurance premiums, and assume that interest rates are small, then we have in equation 10h an expression for the sum of insurance on the husband's life plus family assets, which does not require separation of the cash value from the term value of insurance. Equation 4h provides a corresponding expression 10w for F_w:

$$(10w) \quad F_w + (A - \pi_h F_h - \pi_w F_w)(1 + r) = \hat{W}(q, PVR) - (E_h + B_h).$$

As with the previous insurance demand equations, to estimate this model consistently one must allow for different regimes in which the husband's or wife's insurance demand may be constrained to zero. When the wife's insurance is zero but the husband's is positive, $\hat{H}(q, PVR)$ is replaced by $\hat{H}(q_h, PVR_h)$; when the husband's insurance is zero but the wife's is positive, the function $\hat{W}(q, PVR)$ is replaced by $\hat{W}(q_w, PVR_w)$.

Econometric Specification

The model presented in the previous section can be specified as set forth below.

A Two-Indicator, Switching-Regression Model

Let I_h and I_w be zero-one indicators for zero versus positive values of the husband's and wife's insurance, respectively, and expressed as

$$(11) \qquad \qquad \begin{aligned} I_h &= -c_h + \mu_h \\ I_w &= -c_w + \mu_w \end{aligned}$$

where μ_h and μ_w are errors with zero means, and the critical values c_h and c_w are linear combinations of vectors of observable economic and demographic characteristics X_h and X_w:

$$(12) \qquad \qquad \begin{aligned} c_h &= -B_h X_h \\ c_w &= -B_w X_w. \end{aligned}$$

In equations 12, B_h and B_w are coefficient vectors. Referring to discussion of equations 9 and 10, we express the choices of F_h and F_w in the four possible regimes as follows:

—if $I_h > 0$ and $I_w > 0$,

(13)
$$F_h = \gamma_h Z_h + \epsilon_h$$
$$F_w = \gamma_w Z_w + \epsilon_w;$$

—if $I_h > 0$ and $I_w \leq 0$,

(14)
$$F_h = \theta_h Z_h' + \psi_h$$
$$F_w = 0;$$

—if $I_h \leq 0$ and $I_w > 0$,

(15)
$$F_h = 0$$
$$F_w = \theta_w Z_w' + \psi_w;$$

—if $I_h \leq 0$ and $I_w \leq 0$,

(16)
$$F_h = 0$$
$$F_w = 0.$$

In equations 13–15, Z_h, Z_w, Z_h', and Z_w' are vectors of explanatory variables, and γ_h, γ_w, θ_h, and θ_w are coefficient vectors. We assume that the six error terms—μ_h, μ_w, ϵ_h, ϵ_w, ψ_h, and ψ_w—have zero means and are distributed joint-normally. The elements of the covariance matrix of this distribution are denoted by σ_{ij}, where i, j references μ_h, μ_w, ϵ_h, ϵ_w, ψ_h, ψ_w.

Estimation Strategy

We can consistently estimate the econometric model represented by equations 11–16 by first estimating the choice of regimes (equations 11 and 12) with a bivariate probit and then using the results of this probit to correct for sample selection in the regressions for the levels of F_h and F_w in equations 13–15. The appropriate Mills-ratio factors to correct selection bias differ in this case from those suggested by Heckman because the ones used here are based on a bivariate error process.[9] To illustrate the appropriate Mills-ratio formula, consider estimating the regression for F_h in equa-

9. James J. Heckman, "The Common Structure of Statistical Models of Truncation, Sample Selection, and Limited Dependent Variables and a Simple Estimator for such Models," *Annals of Economic and Social Measurement,* vol. 5 (Fall 1976), pp. 475–92.

tion 13. As derived in the appendix to this paper, the expected value of ϵ_h—given that $I_h > 0$ and $I_w > 0$—is

$$E(\epsilon/I_h > 0, I_w > 0) = E(\epsilon_h/\mu_h > c_h, \mu_w > c_w)$$

(17)
$$= \frac{[1 - F(c_h)][1 - F(c_w)]}{1 - \phi(c_h, c_w)}$$

$$\cdot \; [E(\epsilon_h/\mu_h > c_h) + E(\epsilon_h/\mu_w > c_w)].$$

In equation 17, $F(\ )$ is the cumulative normal function, and $\phi(\ )$ is the bivariate cumulative normal function. The last bracketed term on the right-hand side of equation 17 contains the two univariate Mills ratios. If μ_h and μ_w were independent, the term $1 - \phi(c_h, c_w)$ would equal $[1 - F(c_h)][1 - F(c_w)]$, and equation 17 would reduce to the sum of two separate Mills ratios. In this case one could run two separate probits for $I_h > 0$ and $I_w > 0$ to form $E(\epsilon_h/\mu_h > c_h)$ and $E(\epsilon_h/\mu_w > c_w)$. When μ_h and μ_w are not independent, however, the term $\phi(c_h, c_w)$ must be estimated from a bivariate probit.

Empirical Results

In this section we report estimates for husbands' and wives' life insurance demands for the two models described in the previous section. We used Green's LEMDEP routine to estimate the model.[10] LEMDEP correctly calculates standard errors in the selection equations. The results are given in table 8 for husbands and in table 9 for wives.

Of the 5,110 total observations in the sample, there were 3,251 households in which both spouses had insurance, 1,024 households in which only the husband had insurance, 128 households in which only the wife had insurance, and 707 households in which neither family member had positive insurance.

We examined first the results for husbands' life insurance demands. We looked at two samples of households in which the husband's insurance was positive: those in which wives also purchased positive amounts of insurance, and those in which wives purchased no insurance. The first two

---

10. William Green, *LEMDEP* Computer Program, rev. version (New York University, School of Business, 1985).

columns in table 8 present estimates for model 1, based on equation 9h, for the two samples. The last two columns present estimates for model 2, based on equation 10h above. Recall that the second model may be preferred because it does not require distinguishing between the cash and face value of insurance. In all cases, we included PVR, the present value of family resources, PVR^2, PVR^3, the husband's and wife's age, and interaction terms between these ages and PVR to account for the consumption demand functions $H(\ )$ and $\hat{H}(\ )$. The ages are meant to proxy for the survival probabilities that determine the state-contingent prices of consumption. The terms q_w defined by the right-hand side of equation 9h, and q_h, defined by the right-hand side of equation 9h', were used for the regime under which the husband's demand is unconstrained but the wife's demand is constrained.[11]

Consider first the results for model 1 in table 8. To evaluate the performance of the model, note that the components of husbands' receipts should each have a coefficient of 1, the survivor benefits a coefficient of -1. Each of these independent variables is calculated as the present expected value of the relevant income stream. For the sample in which the wife's insurance is positive, the coefficients of the husband's earnings, social security, and pension benefits have the wrong sign, whereas survivor benefits have the right sign but are over seven standard deviations from -1. The results are somewhat better in the sample in which the wife's insurance is zero; these coefficients, albeit positive and significant, are nevertheless significantly below 1. For this sample the wife's survivor benefits have the wrong sign. The two bivariate Mills ratios are highly significant for both samples. Note that the standard errors of the coefficients tend, in general, to be quite small, thus implying a fairly precise rejection of the theoretical model.

The estimates for model 2 in table 8 are not much closer to those predicted by the theoretical model. The model predicts that the wife's social security benefits, survivor benefits, and earnings should all enter with a coefficient of -1; in the two subsamples only four of the eight coefficients have the correct negative sign, and only two are significant. The large -4.39 coefficient in the $F_w = 0$ regression in model 2 for the wife's social security benefits is hard to take seriously in light of the other results. The net worth variable (A) is positive in both samples, although

11. See above, the section entitled "A Model of Life Insurance Demand," the discussion below equation 9w'. See also equation 14.

Table 8. Husband's Insurance Demand
Positive levels only

	Model 1[b]		Model 2[c]	
	Wife's insurance >0	Wife's insurance = 0	Wife's insurance >0	Wife's insurance = 0
Variable[a]	(3,251)	(1,024)	(3,251)	(1,024)
Constant	−16,425	−53,467	−16,030	−427,320
	(−10,130)	(−32,660)	(−13,360)	(−163,300)
Husband earnings	−0.0232	0.656	. . .	. . .
	(−0.0428)	(0.1231)		
Social security benefits	−0.0254	0.327	. . .	. . .
	(−0.05018)	(0.157)		
Pension	−0.02363	0.288	. . .	. . .
	(−0.02266)	(0.075)		
$PVR(h)^2$	−0.00387	0.0043	−0.0039	0.0063
	(−0.00073)	(0.0015)	(−0.00073)	(0.0015)
$PVR(h)^3$	0.0000288	−0.00005	0.000028	−0.000065
	(0.0000062)	(−0.00001)	(0.0000062)	(−0.000011)
Age	−725.16	−99.69	−608.54	3,352.3
	(−194.7)	(−557.3)	(−321.7)	(1,614)
Age × $PVR(w)$	0.66259	−0.70	0.692	0.299
	(0.1040)	(−0.209)	(0.93)	(0.179)
Mills ratio	6.2033	4.07	5.647	−8.477
	(0.65)	(0.86)	(0.97)	(−3.8)
Wife earnings	. . .	. . .	−0.05	−0.35
			(−0.038)	(−0.1611)
Social security benefits	. . .	. . .	−0.0405	−4.39
			(−0.3329)	(−1.624)
Survivor benefits	−0.04199	−0.349	0.0697	−0.434
	(−0.07210)	(−0.205)	(0.0661)	(−0.196)
$PVR(w)$	−0.18159	0.299	−0.1901	−0.212
	(−0.04930)	(0.1214)	(−0.0339)	(−0.97)
Age	397.97	627.7	395.28	1,738.7
	(103.50)	(231.3)	(156.3)	(538.3)
Age × $PVR(h)$	0.4926	−0.26	−0.014	0.022
	(0.7846)	(−0.153)	(−0.0815)	(0.1513)
Mills ratio	2.9189	2.05	1.9127	−15.206
	(0.36)	(0.68)	(1.97)	(−5.8)
Net worth	. . .	. . .	0.0356	0.029
			(0.207)	(0.065)
$\bar{R}^2$	0.28	0.32	0.29	0.31

Source: Authors' calculations. The numbers in parentheses in the body of the table are standard errors.
a. Symbols h and w denote husband and wife.
b. Model 1 is based on equation 9h. The numbers of observations are in parentheses.
c. Model 2 is based on equation 10h. The numbers of observations are in parentheses.

Table 9. Wife's Insurance Demand

Positive levels only

Variable[a]	Model 1[b]		Model 2[c]	
	Husband's insurance >0 (3,251)	Husband's insurance = 0 (128)	Husband's insurance >0 (3,251)	Husband's insurance = 0 (128)
Constant	871.9	−30,244	8,140	12,266
	(3,557)	(−25,900)	(2,420)	(10,810)
Husband earnings	. . .	. . .	−0.47	−0.41
			(−0.019)	(−0.17)
Social security benefits	. . .	. . .	−0.0079	−0.44
			(−0.025)	(−0.19)
Pension	. . .	. . .	−0.0062	−0.32
			(−0.1777)	(−0.107)
$PVR(h)$	0.081	0.43	−0.038	−0.125
	(0.021)	(0.1)	(−0.018)	(−0.070)
Age	−87.3	430	−77.802	−277
	(−81.9)	(447)	(−48.0)	(−194)
Age × $PVR(w)$	−0.116	−0.6	0.093	0.166
	(−0.04)	(−0.18)	(0.020)	(0.082)
Mills ratio	0.901	−0.19	−0.065	−0.127
	(0.228)	(−1.04)	(−0.159)	(−1.168)
Wife earnings	0.122	0.41	. . .	. . .
	(0.019)	(0.093)		
Social security benefits	0.207	−0.27	. . .	. . .
	(0.077)	(−0.45)		
Survivor benefits	. . .	. . .	. . .	. . .
$PVR(w)^2$	−0.0002	−0.00058	−0.2E-03	−0.0026
	(−0.00017)	(−0.0012)	(−0.17E-03)	(−0.0028)
$PVR(w)^3$	0.24E-05	−0.22E-05	−0.22E-05	0.71E-04
	(0.15E-05)	(−0.2E-05)	(−0.15E-05)	(0.62E-04)
Age	−93.7	13.9	−15.8	−176
	(−34.7)	(147)	(−24.5)	(−199)
Age × $PVR(h)$	0.012	−0.07	−0.010	−0.12
	(0.018)	(−0.08)	(−0.019)	(−0.086)
Mills ratio	1.3	−0.38	0.333	−0.581
	(0.46)	(−1.56)	(0.120)	(−0.812)
Net worth	. . .	. . .	0.0075	−0.179
			(0.0179)	(−0.061)
$\bar{R}^2$	0.16	0.58	0.15	0.54

Source: Authors' calculations. The numbers in parentheses in the body of the table are standard errors.
a. Symbols h and w denote husband and wife.
b. Model 1 is based on equation 9w. The numbers of observations are in parentheses.
c. Model 2 is based on equation 10w. The numbers of observations are in parentheses.

quite small in absolute value; recall that its predicted value is -1. The overall goodness of fit for model 2 is quite similar to that for model 1.

Table 9 presents estimates for the analogous two models of wives' life insurance demands. (Models 1 and 2 in table are based on equations 9w and 10w, respectively.) The two samples considered (all for wives who had positive life insurance) were for husbands who had insurance and husbands who had no insurance. The second sample was quite small, as one would expect—only 128 households.

In the two models in table 9 the components of husbands' and wives' earnings and benefits enter with the correct signs in eight of ten cases, and seven of these eight coefficients are significant. None of these coefficients, however, is close to 1 in absolute value. As in table 8, standard errors are typically quite small. The results for model 2 in which the husbands have zero insurance come closest to the theoretical prediction. For this sample each of the husband's streams, as well as net worth, has a negative coefficient as predicted, and each of these coefficients is significant.

Conclusions

A significant minority of elderly households appears to have inadequate life insurance. In addition, estimates of life insurance demand functions are to a great extent at odds with theoretical predictions. There appears to be little systematic response of private life insurance holdings to social security's provision of survivor benefits; hence social security is apparently effective in raising the welfare of widows and widowers through its provision of survivor insurance.

The poor econometric results make us skeptical about the usefulness of the RHS data for estimating sophisticated econometric models that describe the patterns of asset accumulation in households.

Given the significant poverty rates among elderly widows, this paper suggests the need for a reevaluation of the appropriate size of survivor benefits relative to retirement benefits under the social security system. It also suggests that poverty among elderly widows could be reduced by government programs to increase the public's purchase of private life insurance.

Appendix: Derivation of the Bivariate Mills Ratio Sample Selection Correction

Let $x = (\mu_1, \mu_2, \epsilon) \sim \nu(0, \Sigma)$, where the elements of Σ are σ_{ij}. The correction for sample selection is

(A1) $E(\epsilon/\mu_1 > c_1 \text{ and } \mu_2 > c_2) = \dfrac{\int_{c_1}^{\infty} \int_{c_2}^{\infty} \int_{-\infty}^{\infty} \epsilon f(\mu_1, \mu_2, \epsilon)\, d\epsilon d\mu_1 d\mu_2}{\int_{c_1}^{\infty} \int_{c_2}^{\infty} \int_{-\infty}^{\infty} f(\mu_1, \mu_2, \epsilon)\, d\epsilon d\mu_1 d\mu_2}$

$$= \frac{\int_{c_1}^{\infty} \int_{c_2}^{\infty} \int_{-\infty}^{\infty} \epsilon \exp(-\frac{1}{2}x'\Sigma^{-1}x)d\epsilon d\mu_1 d\mu_2}{1 - \phi(c_1, c_2)},$$

where $\theta(c_1, c_2)$ is the bivariate cumulative density function for (μ_1, μ_2).

Consider the numerator of equation A1. Call it Q and write:

(A2) $Q = \displaystyle\int_{c_1}^{\infty}\int_{c_2}^{\infty}\int_{-\infty}^{\infty} \epsilon \exp -\frac{1}{2}(\mu_1^2\sigma^{11} + 2\mu_1\mu_2\sigma^{12} + \mu_2^2\sigma^{22}$

$+ \epsilon^2\sigma^{33} + 2\epsilon\mu_1\sigma^{13} + 2\epsilon\mu_2\sigma^{23})d\epsilon d\mu_2 d\mu_1$

$= \displaystyle\int_{c_1}^{\infty}\int_{c_2}^{\infty} \exp -\frac{1}{2}\Big[\mu_1^2\sigma_z^{11} + 2\mu_1\mu_2\sigma^{12} + \mu_2^2\sigma^{22}$

$- \dfrac{(\mu_1\sigma^{13} + \mu_2\sigma^{23})^2}{\sigma^{33}}\Big]\displaystyle\int_{-\infty}^{\infty} \epsilon \exp$

$-\dfrac{1}{2}\sigma^{33}\Big(\epsilon + \dfrac{\mu_1\sigma^{13} + \mu_2\sigma^{23}}{\sigma^{33}}\Big)^2 d\epsilon d\mu_2 d\mu_1,$

where σ^{ij} is the ijth element of Σ^{-1}.

Let $Z = \epsilon + (\mu_1\sigma^{13} + \mu_2\sigma^{23})/\sigma^{33})$, and let N be the last integral on the right-hand side of equation A2. Then

$$N = \int_{-\infty}^{\infty} Z \exp\left(-\frac{1}{2}\sigma^{33}Z^2\right)dZ$$

$$-\frac{\mu_1\sigma^{13} + \mu_2\sigma^{23}}{\sigma^{33}} \int_{-\infty}^{\infty} \exp\left(-\frac{1}{2}\sigma^{33}Z^2\right)dZ$$

$$= 0 - \frac{\mu_1\sigma^{13} + \mu_2\sigma^{23}}{\sigma^{33}},$$

and

$$(A3) \quad Q = -\int_{c_1}^{\infty}\int_{c_2}^{\infty}\left(\frac{\mu_1\sigma^{13} + \mu_2\sigma^{23}}{\sigma^{33}}\right)\exp -\frac{1}{2}\left[\mu_1^2\left(\sigma^{11} - \frac{\sigma^{13^2}}{\sigma^{33}}\right)\right.$$

$$\left. + \mu_2^2\left(\sigma^{22} - \frac{\sigma^{23^2}}{\sigma^{33}}\right) + 2\mu_1\mu_2\left(\sigma^{12} - \frac{\sigma^{13}\sigma^{23}}{\sigma^{33}}\right)\right]d\mu_1 d\mu_2.$$

Let $\Delta = |\Sigma^{-1}|$. Then

$$\frac{\sigma^{13}}{\sigma^{33}} = \frac{-1/\Delta(\sigma_{13}\sigma_{11} - \sigma_{23}\sigma_{12})}{1/\Delta(\sigma_{11}\sigma_{22} - \sigma_{12}^2)} = -\frac{\sigma_{13} - \sigma_{23}(\sigma_{12}/\sigma_{22})}{\sigma_{11} - \sigma_{12}(\sigma_{12}/\sigma_{22})} = -\frac{\sigma_{31\cdot2}}{\sigma_{11\cdot2}}.$$

Likewise, $\sigma^{23}/\sigma^{33} = -\sigma_{32\cdot1}/\sigma_{22\cdot1}$, and

$$(A4) \quad Q = \int_{c_1}^{\infty}\int_{c_2}^{\infty}\left(\frac{\sigma_{31\cdot2}}{\sigma_{11\cdot2}}\mu_1 + \frac{\sigma_{32\cdot1}}{\sigma_{22\cdot1}}\mu_2\right)\exp -\frac{1}{2}\left[\mu_1^2\left(\sigma^{11} - \frac{\sigma^{13^2}}{\sigma^{33}}\right)\right.$$

$$\left. + \mu_2^2\left(\sigma^{22} - \frac{\sigma^{23^2}}{\sigma^{33}}\right) + 2\mu_1\mu_2\left(\sigma^{12} - \frac{\sigma^{13}\sigma^{23}}{\sigma^{33}}\right)\right]d\mu_2 d\mu_1.$$

Note that

$$\sigma^{11} - \frac{\sigma^{13^2}}{\sigma^{33}} = \frac{1 + \sigma_{12}^2/(\sigma_{11}\sigma_{22} - \sigma_{12}^2)}{\sigma_{11}} = \frac{1}{\sigma_{11} - \sigma_{12}^2/\sigma_{22}} = \frac{1}{\sigma_{11\cdot2}},$$

$$\sigma^{22} - \frac{\sigma^{23^2}}{\sigma^{33}} = \frac{1}{\sigma_{22\cdot1}},$$

$$\sigma^{12} - \frac{\sigma^{13}\sigma^{23}}{\sigma^{33}} = \frac{1}{\sigma_{12} - (\sigma_{11}\sigma_{22}/\sigma_{12})}.$$

These expressions and the last formula for Q imply:

$$(A5) \quad Q = \int_{c_1}^{\infty}\int_{c_2}^{\infty} \left(\frac{\sigma_{31\cdot2}}{\sigma_{11\cdot2}}\mu_1 + \frac{\sigma_{32\cdot1}}{\sigma_{22\cdot1}}\mu_2\right) \exp$$

$$-\frac{1}{2}\left(\frac{\mu_1^2}{\sigma_{11\cdot2}} + \frac{\mu_2^2}{\sigma_{22\cdot1}} + \frac{2\mu_1\mu_2}{\sigma_{12} - [\sigma_{11}\sigma_{22}/\sigma_{12}]}\right)d\mu_2 d\mu_1$$

$$= \frac{\sigma_{31\cdot2}}{\sigma_{11\cdot2}}\int_{c_2}^{\infty}\int_{c_1}^{\infty} \mu_1 b(\mu_1,\mu_2)d\mu_1 d\mu_2 + \frac{\sigma_{32\cdot1}}{\sigma_{22\cdot1}}\int_{c_1}^{\infty}\int_{c_2}^{\infty} \mu_2 b(\mu_1,\mu_2)d\mu_2 d\mu_1,$$

where $b(\ )$ is the bivariate density function. Denote by A the first term on the righthand side of (A5):

$$A = \frac{\sigma_{31\cdot2}}{\sigma_{11\cdot2}}\int_{c_2}^{\infty} \exp\left(-\frac{1}{2}\frac{\mu_2^2}{\sigma_{22\cdot1}}\right)\int_{c_1}^{\infty} \mu_1 \exp$$

$$-\frac{1}{2}\left(\frac{\mu_1^2}{\sigma_{11\cdot2}} + \frac{2\mu_1\mu_2}{\sigma_{12} - (\sigma_{11}\sigma_{22}/\sigma_{12})}\right)d\mu_1 d\mu_2;$$

and define:

$$B = \int_{c_1}^{\infty} \mu_1 \exp -\frac{1}{2}\left(\frac{1}{\sigma_{11\cdot2}}\left(\mu_1^2 + \frac{2\mu_1\mu_2\sigma_{11\cdot2}}{\sigma_{12} - (\sigma_{11}\sigma_{22}/\sigma_{12})}\right)\right)d\mu_1.$$

It can be shown that

$$\frac{\sigma_{11\cdot2}}{\sigma_{12} - \sigma_{11}\sigma_{22}/\sigma_{12}} = \frac{-\sigma_{12}}{\sigma_{22}}$$

and

$$B = \int_{c_1}^{\infty} \mu_1 \exp -\frac{1}{2}\left[\frac{1}{\sigma_{11\cdot2}}\left(\mu_1^2 - 2\mu_1\mu_2\frac{\sigma_{12}}{\sigma_{22}}\right)\right]d\mu_1$$

$$= \exp -\frac{1}{2}\left(-\frac{\sigma_{12}^2\mu_2^2}{\sigma_{22}^2\sigma_{11\cdot2}}\right)\int_{c_1}^{\infty} \mu_1 \exp -\frac{1}{2}\left[\frac{1}{\sigma_{11\cdot2}}\left(\mu_1 - \frac{\sigma_{12}}{\sigma_{22}}\mu_2\right)^2\right]d\mu_1.$$

Thus

$$A = \frac{\sigma_{31 \cdot 2}}{\sigma_{11 \cdot 2}} \int_{c_2}^{\infty} \exp - \frac{1}{2} \Big[\mu_2^2 \Big(\frac{1}{\sigma_{22 \cdot 1}} - \frac{\sigma_{12}^2}{\sigma_{22}^2 \sigma_{11 \cdot 2}} \Big) \Big] \int_{c_1}^{\infty} \mu_1 \exp$$

$$- \frac{1}{2} \Big[\frac{1}{\sigma_{11 \cdot 2}} \Big(\mu_1 - \frac{\sigma_{12}}{\sigma_{22}} \mu_2 \Big)^2 \Big] d\mu_1 d\mu_2.$$

But

$$\frac{1}{\sigma_{22 \cdot 1}} - \frac{\sigma_{12}^2}{\sigma_2^2 \sigma_{11 \cdot 2}} = \frac{1}{\sigma_{22}};$$

hence

$$A = \frac{\sigma_{31 \cdot 2}}{\sigma_{11 \cdot 2}} \int_{c_2}^{\infty} \exp - \frac{1}{2} \frac{\mu_2}{\sigma_{22}} \Big[\int_{c_1}^{\infty} \mu_1 \exp \Big(- \frac{1}{2} \frac{\mu_1 - (\sigma_{12}/\sigma_{22}) \mu_2}{\sigma_{11 \cdot 2}} \Big) d\mu_1 \Big] d\mu_2.$$

Let $Z = \mu_1 - (\sigma_{12}/\sigma_{22}) \mu_2$, and P be the last integral on the right-hand side of the above equation. Then

$$V(Z) = \sigma_{11} - 2 \frac{\sigma_{12}^2}{\sigma_{22}} + \frac{\sigma_{12}^2}{\sigma_{22}} = \sigma_{11} - \frac{\sigma_{12}^2}{\sigma_{22}} = \sigma_{11 \cdot 2}.$$

Thus

$$P = \int_{c_1}^{\infty} \Big(Z + \frac{\sigma_{12}}{\sigma_{22}} \mu_2 \Big) \exp \Big(- \frac{1}{2} \frac{Z^2}{V(Z)} \Big) dZ$$

$$= \int_{c_1}^{\infty} Z f(Z) dZ + \frac{\sigma_{12}}{\sigma_{22}} \mu_2 \int_{c_1}^{\infty} f(Z) dZ$$

$$= E(Z/Z > c_1)[1 - F(c_1)] + \frac{\sigma_{12}}{\sigma_{22}} \mu_2 [1 - F(c_1)]$$

$$= [1 - F(c_1)] \Big(E(Z/Z > c_1) + \frac{\sigma_{12}}{\sigma_{22}} \mu_2 \Big). \qquad \cdot$$

Thus

$$A = \frac{\sigma_{31\cdot2}}{\sigma_{11\cdot2}} \int_{c_2}^{\infty} \left(\exp - \frac{1}{2} \frac{\mu_2^2}{\sigma_{22}} \right) \left[[1 - F(c_1)] \left(E(Z/Z_1 > c_1) + \frac{\sigma_{12}}{\sigma_{22}} \mu_2 \right) \right] d\mu_2$$

$$= \frac{\sigma_{31\cdot2}}{\sigma_{11\cdot2}} [1 - F(c_1)] \Big(E(Z/Z > c_1)[1 - F(c_2)]$$

$$+ \frac{\sigma_{12}}{\sigma_{22}} E(Z/Z > c_2)[1 - F(c_2)] \Big)$$

$$= \frac{\sigma_{31\cdot2}}{\sigma_{11\cdot2}} [1 - F(c_1)][1 - F(c_2)] \Big(E(Z/Z > c_1) + \frac{\sigma_{12}}{\sigma_{22}} E(Z/Z > c_2) \Big).$$

By symmetry, the second piece of Q is

$$\frac{\sigma_{32\cdot1}}{\sigma_{22\cdot1}} [1 - F(c_1)][1 - F(c_2)] \Big(E(Z/Z > c_2) + \frac{\sigma_{12}}{\sigma_{11}} E(Z/Z > c_1) \Big).$$

Thus

$$Q = [1 - F(c_1)][1 - F(c_2)] \Big[E(Z/Z > c_1) \Big(\frac{\sigma_{31\cdot2}}{\sigma_{11\cdot2}} + \frac{\sigma_{32\cdot1}}{\sigma_{22\cdot1}} \times \frac{\sigma_{21}}{\sigma_{11}} \Big)$$

$$+ E(Z/Z > c_2) \Big(\frac{\sigma_{32\cdot1}}{\sigma_{22\cdot1}} + \frac{\sigma_{31\cdot2}}{\sigma_{11\cdot2}} \times \frac{\sigma_{12}}{\sigma_{22}} \Big) \Big].$$

But

$$\frac{\sigma_{31\cdot2}}{\sigma_{11\cdot2}} + \frac{\sigma_{32\cdot1}}{\sigma_{22\cdot1}} \times \frac{\sigma_{21}}{\sigma_{11}}$$

$$= \sigma_{22} \times \frac{\sigma_{31} - \sigma_{32}(\sigma_{12}/\sigma_{22})}{\sigma_{22}\sigma_{11} - \sigma_{12}^2} + \frac{\sigma_{32} - \sigma_{31}(\sigma_{12}/\sigma_{11})}{\sigma_{11}\sigma_{22} - \sigma_{12}^2} \times \sigma_{21} = \frac{\sigma_{31}}{\sigma_{11}},$$

and by symmetry,

$$\frac{\sigma_{32\cdot1}}{\sigma_{22\cdot1}} + \frac{\sigma_{31\cdot2}}{\sigma_{11\cdot2}} \times \frac{\sigma_{12}}{\sigma_{22}} = \frac{\sigma_{32}}{\sigma_{22}}.$$

Hence

$E(\epsilon/\mu_1 > c_1 \text{ and } \mu_2 > c_2)$

$$= \frac{[1 - F(c_1)][1 - F(c_2)]}{1 - \phi(c_1, c_2)}\left(\frac{\sigma_{31}}{\sigma_{11}} E(Z/Z > c_1) + \frac{\sigma_{32}}{\sigma_{22}}E(Z/Z > c_2)\right).$$

Note that the terms in brackets are the two univariate Mills' ratios.

Conference Participants

with their affiliations at the time of the conference

Michele C. Adler *U.S. Department of Health and Human Services*

Martin Neil Baily *Brookings Institution*

Yves M. Balcer *University of Wisconsin*

Neil M. Briskman *U.S. Department of Health and Human Services*

Richard V. Burkhauser *University of Wisconsin*

Gary Burtless *Brookings Institution*

Deidre D. Duzor *U.S. Department of Health and Human Services*

Thomas J. Espenshade *Urban Institute*

Gordon P. Goodfellow *U.S. Department of Health and Human Services*

John C. Hambor *Social Security Administration*

Jerry A. Hausman *Massachusetts Institute of Technology*

Richard A. Kasten *Congressional Budget Office*

Laurence J. Kotlikoff *Boston University*

Edward Lazear *University of Chicago*

Stephen H. Long *Congressional Budget Office*

Carol R. McHale *U.S. Department of Health and Human Services*

Robert A. Moffitt *Brown University*

Alicia H. Munnell *Federal Reserve Bank, Boston*

Joseph Newhouse *Rand Corporation*

Lynn Paquette *Massachusetts Institute of Technology*

Joseph A. Pechman *Brookings Institution*

Anthony J. Pellechio *Price, Waterhouse*

James M. Poterba *Massachusetts Institute of Technology*

Wendell Primus *House Committee on Ways and Means*

Joseph F. Quinn *Boston College*

Alice M. Rivlin *Brookings Institution*

Frank Sammartino *U.S. Department of Health and Human Services*

Robert Schmidt *U.S. Department of Health and Human Services*

Lawrence H. Summers *Harvard University*

Randy L. Teach *U.S. Department of Health and Human Services*

Lawrence H. Thompson *General Accounting Office*

Joshua M. Wiener *Brookings Institution*

Douglas A. Wolf *Urban Institute*

Index